THE NASTY BITS

THE NASTY BITS

Collected Varietal Cuts, Usable Trim, Scraps, and Bones

**ANTHONY
BOURDAIN**

BLOOMSBURY

Most of these essays originally appeared, in somewhat different form, in the following publications: *Best Life*, *BlackBook*, Chow, eGullet.com, *Esquire* (UK), the *Face*, the *Financial Times*, *Food Arts*, *Gourmet*, the *Independent*, *LA Times*, *Limb by Limb*, *Lizard*, and *Town & Country*.

Published by Bloomsbury Publishing, New York and London
Distributed to the trade by Holtzbrinck Publishers

All papers used by Bloomsbury Publishing are natural, recyclable products made from wood grown in well-managed forests. The manufacturing processes conform to the environmental regulations of the country of origin.

Library of Congress Cataloging-in-Publication Data

Bourdain, Anthony.
The nasty bits : collected varietal cuts, usable trim, scraps, and bones / Anthony Bourdain.—1st U.S. ed.
p. cm.
Includes bibliographical references.
ISBN-13: 978-1-58234-451-5 (hardcover)
ISBN-10: 1-58234-451-5 (hardcover)
1. Cookery. I. Title.

TX652.B67 2006
641.5092—dc22
2005033245

Export paperback ISBN 1-59691-284-7
ISBN-13 978-1-59691-284-7

First U.S. Edition 2006

7 9 10 8

Typeset by Hewer Text UK Ltd, Edinburgh
Printed in the United States of America by Quebecor World Fairfield

To Joey, Johnny, and Dee Dee

CONTENTS

CONTENTS

SOUR

BITTER

UMAMI

A TASTE OF FICTION

PREFACE

I WENT SEAL HUNTING yesterday. At eight a.m., swaddled in caribou, I climbed into a canoe and headed out onto the freezing waters of the Hudson Bay with my Inuit guides and a camera crew. By three p.m., I was sitting cross-legged on a plastic-covered kitchen floor listening to Charlie, my host, his family, and a few tribal elders giggling with joy as they sliced and tore into a seal carcass, the raw meat, blubber, and brains of our just-killed catch. Grandma squealed with delight as Charlie cracked open the seal's skull, revealing its brains—quickly digging into the goo with her fingers. Junior sliced dutifully at a kidney. Mom generously slit open one of the eyeballs (the best part) and showed me how to suck out the interior as if working on an oversize Concord grape. From all sides, happy family members were busily dissecting the seal from different angles, each pausing intermittently to gobble a particularly tasty morsel. Soon, everyone's faces and hands were smeared with blood. The room was filled with smiles and good cheer in spite of the *Night of the Living Dead* overtones and the blood (lots of it) running across the plastic. A *Bonanza* rerun played silently on the TV set in the normal-looking family room adjacent as Mom cut off a piece of snout and whisker, instructing me to hold it by the thick, strawlike follicles and then suck and gnaw on the tiny kernel of pink buried in the leatherlike flesh. After a thorough sampling of raw seal brain, liver, kidney, rib section, and blubber, an elder crawled across the floor and retrieved a platter of frozen blackberries. She generously rolled a fistful of them around in the wet interior of the carcass, glazing them with blood and fat, before offering them to me. They were delicious.

Words fail me. Again and again. Or maybe it's me that fails the English language. My depiction of the day's rather extraordinary events is workmanlike enough, I guess . . . but, typically, I fall short. How to describe the feeling of closeness and intimacy in that otherwise ordinary-looking kitchen? The way the fifteen-year-old daughter and her eighty-five-year-old grandmother faced each other, nearly nose to nose, and began "throat singing," first warming up with simultaneous grunts and rapid breathing patterns, then singing, the tones and words coming from somewhere independent of their mouths, from somewhere . . . else? The sheer, unselfconscious glee (and pride) with which they tore apart that seal—how do I make that beautiful? The sight of Charlie, blood spread all across his face, dripping off his chin . . . Grandma, her legs splayed, rocking a crescent-shaped chopper across blubber, peeling off strips of black seal meat . . . How do I make them as sympathetic, as beautiful, in words as they were in reality?

"Without the seal, we would not be here," said Charlie. "We would not be alive." A true enough statement, but not an explanation. You'd have to have felt the cold up there, have seen it, hundreds and hundreds of miles without a single tree. You'd have to have gone out with Charlie, as I had, out onto that freezing bay, a body of water nearly the size of an ocean, watched him walk across a thin, tilting layer of ice to drag the seal back to the canoe. Heard, as we did, the resigned calls from other hunters over Charlie's radio, stuck out in a blizzard for the night, realizing they would have no shelter and no fire. You'd have to have been in that room. A photograph wouldn't do it. I know. I take them in my travels, look at them later—and they're inevitably, woefully flat, a poor substitute for the smell of a place, the feeling of being there. Videotape? It's another language altogether. You've turned what was experienced in Greek into Latin, edited places and people into something else, and however beautiful or dramatic or funny, it's also . . . different. Maybe only music has the power to bring a place or a person back, so close to you that you can smell them in the air. And I can't play guitar.

Fragments. Pieces of the strange ride, the larger, dysfunctional but wondrous thing my life has become. It's been like this for the last five years. Always in motion, nine, then ten, then eleven months out of the twelve. Maybe three or four nights a month spent in my own bed—the rest in planes, cars, trains, dogsleds, sailboats, helicopters, hotels, longhouses, tents, lodges, jungle floors. I've become some kind of traveling salesman or paid wanderer, both blessed and doomed to travel this world until I can't anymore. Funny what happens when your dreams come true.

My pal A. A. Gill once suggested that the older he gets, and the more he travels, the less he knows. And I know what he means now. Seeing the planet as I'm seeing it, you are constantly reminded of what you don't know—how much more there is to see and learn, how damn big and mysterious this world is. It's both frustrating and addicting, which only makes it harder when you visit, say, China for the first time, and realize how much more of it there is—and how little time you have to see it. It's added a frantic quality to my already absurd life, and an element of both desperation and resignation.

Travel changes you. As you move through this life and this world you change things slightly, you leave marks behind, however small. And in return, life—and travel—leaves marks on you. Most of the time, those marks—on your body or on your heart—are beautiful. Often, though, they hurt. When I look back on the last five years since I wrote the obnoxious, over-testosteroned memoir that transported me out of the kitchen and into a never-ending tunnel of pressurized cabins and airport lounges, it's a rush of fragments, all jostling for attention. Some good, some bad, some pleasurable—and some excruciating to remember. Much, I suspect, like the pieces in this collection.

I've done a lot of writing for magazines and newspapers in the last few years, and it's the better morsels (I hope) from that work that follow. A lot of it is hopelessly dated, or obviously written for a British or Australian publication, and I've added some accompanying notes at the end by way of explanation (or apology). I've been writing this stuff for much the same reasons behind my frenetic traveling: Because I can. Because there's so little time. Because there's been so much to see and remember. Because I always think for sure the next book or the next show will tank, and I better make some fucking money while I can.

It's an irritating reality that many places and events defy description. Angkor Wat and Machu Picchu, for instance, seem to demand silence, like a love affair you can never talk about. For a while after, you fumble for words, trying vainly to assemble a private narrative, an explanation, a comfortable way to frame where you've been and what's happened. In the end, you're just happy you were there—with your eyes open— and lived to see it.

SALTY

SYSTEM D

Débrouillard is what every *plongeur* wants to be called. A *débrouillard* is a man who, even when he is told to do the impossible, will *se débrouiller*—get it done somehow.
　　—George Orwell, *Down and Out in Paris and London*

He was a master of the short cut, the easy way out, the System D. D. stands for *de* as in *débrouiller* or *démerder*—to extricate . . . and to a hair (he) knew how to stay out of trouble. He was a very skillful cook, and a very bad one.
　　—Nicolas Freeling, *The Kitchen*

I STUMBLED ACROSS MY first reference to the mysterious and sinister-sounding System D in Nicolas Freeling's wonderful memoir of his years as a Grand Hotel cook in France. I knew the word *débrouillard* already, having enjoyed reading about the concept of *se débrouiller* or *se démerder* in Orwell's earlier account of his dishwashing/prep-cooking at the pseudonymous Hotel "X" in Paris. But what sent chills down my spine and sent me racing back to my weathered copies of both books was a casual remark by my French sous-chef as he watched a busboy repairing a piece of kitchen equipment with a teaspoon.

"Ahh . . . Le System D!" he said with a smirk, and a warm expression of recognition. For a moment, I thought I'd stumbled across a secret society—a coven of warlocks, a subculture within our subculture of chefs and cooks and restaurant lifers. I was

3

annoyed that what I had thought to be an ancient term from kitchens past, a little bit of culinary arcanum, was in fact still in use, and I felt suddenly threatened—as if my kitchen, my crew, my team of talented throat slitters, fire starters, mercenaries, and hooligans was secretly a hotbed of Trilateralists, Illuminati, Snake Handlers, or Satan Worshippers. I felt left out. I asked, "Did you say 'System D'? What is 'System D'?"

"Tu connais . . . you know MacGyver?" replied my sous-chef thoughtfully.

I nodded, flashing onto the idiotic detective series of years back where the hero would regularly bust out of maximum-security prisons and perform emergency neurosurgery using nothing more than a paper clip and a gum wrapper.

"MacGyver!" pronounced my sous-chef, "CA . . . ca c'est System D."

Whether familiar with the term or not, I have always assigned great value to débrouillards, and at various times in my career, particularly when I was a line cook, I have taken great pride in being one. The ability to think fast, to adapt, to improvise when in danger of falling "in the weeds" or dans la merde, even if a little corner-cutting is required, has been a point of pride with me for years. My previous sous-chef, Steven, a very talented cook with a criminal mind, was a Grandmaster Débrouillard, a Sergeant Bilko–like character who, in addition to being a superb saucier, was fully versed in the manly arts of scrounging, refrigeration repair, surreptitious entry, intelligence collection, subornation, and the effortless acquisition of objects which did not rightly belong to him. He was a very useful person to have around. If I ran out of calves' liver or shell steaks in the middle of a busy Saturday night, Steven could be counted on to slip out the kitchen door and return a few moments later with whatever I needed. Where he got the stuff I never knew. I only knew not to ask. System D, to work right, requires a certain level of plausible deniability.

I am always pleased to find historical precedent for my darker urges. And in the restaurant business, where one's moods tend to swing from near euphoria to crushing misery and back again at least ten times a night, it's always useful to remember that my crew and I are part of a vast and well-documented continuum going back centuries. Why did this particular reference hold such magic for me, though? I had to think about that. Why this perverse pride in finding that my lowest, sleaziest moments of mid-rush hackwork were firmly rooted in tradition, going back to the French masters?

It all comes down to the old dichotomy, the razor's edge of volume versus quality. God knows, all chefs want to make perfect food. We'd *like* to make sixty-five to seventy-five absolutely flawless meals per night, every plate a reflection of our best efforts, all our training and experience, only the finest, most expensive, most seasonal ingredients available— and we'd like to make a lot of money for our masters while we do it. But this is the real world. Most restaurants can't charge a hundred fifty bucks a customer for food alone. Sixty-five meals a night (at least in *my* place) means we'll all be out of work— and fast. Two hundred fifty to three hundred meals a night is more like it when you're talking about a successful New York City restaurant and job security for your posse of well-paid culinarians in the same breath. When I was the executive chef, a few years ago, of a stadium-size nightclub/supper club near Times Square, it often meant six and seven hundred meals a night—a logistical challenge that called for skills closer to those of an air-traffic controller or a military ordnance officer than to those of a classically trained chef. When you're cranking out that kind of volume, especially during the pretheater rush, when everybody in the room expects to wolf down three courses and dessert and *still* be out the door in time to make curtain for *Cats*, you'd better be fast. They want that food. They want it hot, cooked the way they asked, and they want it soon. It may feel wonderfully fulfilling, putting one's best foot forward, sweating and fiddling and wiping and sculpting impeccable little spires of à-la-minute food for an adoring dining public, but there is another kind of satisfaction: the grim pride of the journeyman professional, the cook who's got moves, who can kick ass on the line, who can *do serious numbers*, and "get through."

"How many'd we do?" is the question frequently asked at the end of the shift, when the cooks collapse onto flour sacks and milk crates and piles of dirty linen, smoking their cigarettes, drinking their shift cocktails, and contemplating what kind of felonious activity they will soon take part in during their after-work leisure hours. If the number is high (say three hundred fifty dinners), and there have been few returns or customer complaints, if only happy diners waddled satiated out the crowded doorway to the restaurant, squeezing painfully past the incoming mob—well, that's a statistic we can all appreciate and understand. Drinks and congratulations are in order. We made it through! We didn't fall into the weeds! We ran out of nothing! What could be better? We not only served a monstrous number of meals without a glitch, but we served them on time and in good order. We avoided disaster. We brought honor and riches to our clan.

And if it was a particularly brutal night, if the specter of meltdown loomed near, if we just narrowly avoided the kind of horror that occurs when the kitchen "loses it," if we managed to just squeak through without taking major casualties—then all the better. Picture the worst-case scenario: The saucier is getting hit all night long. Everything ordered is coming off his station instead of being spread around between broiler, middle, and appetizer stations. The poor bastard is being pounded, constantly in danger of falling behind, running out of *mise en place*, losing his mind. Nothing is worse in a situation like this than that terrible moment when a line cook looks up at the board, scans the long line of fluttering dinner orders, and sees only incomprehensible cuneiform, Sanskrit-like chicken scratches that to his shriveled, dehydrated, poached, and abused brain mean nothing at all. He's "lost it" . . . he's *dans la merde* now . . . and because kitchen work requires a great deal of coordination and teamwork, he could take the whole line down with him.

But if you're lucky enough to have a well-oiled machine working for you—a bunch of hardcore, ass-kicking, name-taking *débrouillards* on the payroll—the chances of catastrophe are slim in the extreme. Old-school *cholos, assasinos, vato locos,* veterans of many kitchens like my cooks, they know what to do when there's no space left on the stove for *another* sauté pan. They know how to bump closed a broiler or shut a refrigerator door when their hands are full. They know when to step into another cook's station—and, more importantly, *how* to do it—without that station becoming a rugby match of crushed toes and sharp elbows. They know how to sling dirty pots twenty-five feet across the kitchen so that they drop neatly into the pot sink without disfiguring the dishwasher.

It's when the orders are pouring in and the supplies are running low and the tempers are growing thin that one sees System D practiced at its highest level. Hot water heater explodes? No sweat. Just push the rillettes over and start boiling water, *carnale.* Run out of those nice square dinner plates for the lobster spring rolls? No problem. Dummy up a new presentation and serve on the round plates. We know what to do. Meat grinder broken? It's steak tartare cut by hand, *papi.* Few things are more beautiful to me than a bunch of thuggish, heavily-tattooed line cooks moving around each other like ballerinas on a busy Saturday night. Seeing two guys who'd just as soon cut each other's throats in their off hours moving in unison with grace and ease can be as uplifting as any chemical stimulant or organized religion.

At times like these, under fire, in battlefield conditions, the kitchen reverts to what it has always been since Escoffier's time: a *brigade,* a paramilitary unit, in which everyone knows what they have to do, and how to do it. Officers make fast and necessarily irrevocable decisions, and damn the torpedoes if it isn't the best decision. There's no time to dither, to waffle, to ponder, to empathize when there's incoming fire threatening to bring the whole kitchen and dining room crashing down. Move forward! Take that hill! Forced out of expediency to lose that cute herbal garnish on the Saddle of Lamb en Crépinette? It's a shame—but we'll cry about it later, at the after-action reporting, when we're all comfortably sucking down late-night sushi together and drinking iced sake or vodka shots at some chef-friendly joint. Right now it's System D time, bro'—and there's no time for that bouquet of herbs. There's the fish to contend with, and one of the runners just fell down the stairs and broke his ankle, and they need forks on table number seven, and that twelve-top arrived late and is eating up half the dining room while they linger over cognacs, and the customers waiting by the bar and shivering in the street are starting to get that angry, haunted look you see in lynch mobs and Liberian militia who've spent too much time in the jungle. Running out of arugula? Substitute mâche for Chrissakes! Fluff it out with spinach, watercress . . . *anything green!*

At times like these, even one heroic practitioner of System D can save the day, step in and turn the tide. One guy can make the difference between another successful Saturday night and total chaos. We can go home laughing about all we endured, feeling good about ourselves, talking about the bus that *didn't* hit us instead of slinking out the door quietly, mulling over *la puta vida,* muttering half-formed recriminations.

Now, I've heard and seen some very fine chefs sneer at The System. "I would *never* do that," they say, when told of some culinary outrage performed in another kitchen. "Never!" they insist, with all the assurance of an officer on the prewar Maginot Line. But when the Hun starts pouring over the wall, and there's no fire support, and the rear guard is in full retreat—these same chefs are often the first guys to commit food crimes that even the most pragmatic practitioner of System D would never (okay, *almost* never) do.

Fast well-done steak? I've watched French grads of three-star kitchens squeeze the blood out of filet mignons with their full body weight, turning a medium to well in seconds. I've watched in horror as chefs have hurled beautiful chateaubriands into the deep-fat fryer, microwaved veal chops, thinned sauce with the brackish greasy water in the steam table. And when it gets busy? *Everything* that falls on the floor, amazingly, falls "right on the napkin." Let me tell you—that's one mighty big napkin.

System D, arguably, reached its heyday in the Victorian-era railway hotels, where the menus were huge and it was not unusual for an extra two hundred guests to show up wanting, say, the Fricassee of Lobster Thermidor—for which only fifty portions were ever available. Suddenly, Thermidor for fifty was transformed into Thermidor for two hundred. Don't ask how. You don't want to know. It is possible that the system began with the ever-changing requirements of volume cookery, only to be perpetuated by subsequent generations as the golden age of mammoth hotels began to wane and the enormous dining halls and banquet facilities of days past were faced with the necessity of serving grande luxe–style meals and bloated menus with ever-shrinking staffs and more stringent economizing. I suspect that some of the classic dishes of that era reflect System D philosophy, particularly the efforts to get more bang from limited ingredients. Potage Mongole, for instance, allowed a chef to take a little pea soup and a little tomato soup, combine them, and come up with a third menu selection. New York's fabled Delmonico's offered, at one time, a staggering array of soups, numbering over a hundred. One can only assume that not all of those were made individually and from scratch every day. Parsimonious and forward-thinking Frenchmen—already inclined to make the most of humble (read *cheap*) ingredients, utilized every scrap of stock meat, hoof, snout, tongue, organs, creating dishes that are now popular stand-alone and frequently expensive favorites, ordered on their own merits, rather than served as cleverly disguised by-products.

The traditional bistros that grew up around Les Halles, Paris's central marketplace, were fertile ground for hotel-trained cooks and chefs to take System D to even more extreme lengths. They had limited space to work with, most had limited capital, and the markets—whence came their clientele—generated huge amounts of what might have been considered unpalatable foodstuffs. If you're stocking your larder from a place proudly named The Tripe Pavillion, you tend to develop a cuisine heavy on *boudins*, *tête de porc*, confit of ears, stomach lining, shanks, pâtés, and galantines. Don't take my word for it. Read Orwell, or Freeling, or Zola's masterful *Belly of Paris*; nothing I've said here or will ever say approaches the terrifying accounts of mishandled food, criminally misrepresented menu items, marginal sanitation practices, and dubious sources of supply in these classic accounts. Orwell describes working ankle deep in garbage and outgoing dinners in one such establishment—and this was by no means a slophouse. Even today, French veterans of bistro cooking are masters of System D, inured as they are to working in tiny kitchens with dollhouse-size ranges, producing ten or twelve menu items despite access to only minimal storage, refrigeration, and work area, with a *plongeur* bumping them from behind. Work with some of these folks, even in the relatively roomy kitchens of Manhattan, and you're likely to see a number of practices they definitely do *not* teach at culinary school.

Of course, expediency is one thing. Laziness is another. I hate, for instance, to see a cook "sear, slice, and flash," where instead of searing, say, a gigot, then finishing to proper doneness in the oven, he'll sear the outside of the mat, slice it nearly raw, then color the slices under the salamander. I've seen jammed-up cooks searing lamb, beef, and duck simultaneously—all in the same pan. I hate that too. And instead of reducing and mounting sauces to order, in a clean pot each time, some cooks keep a veritable petri dish of reducing sauce festering on a back burner, adding unreduced sauce as needed until the pot is a crusty, horrible abomination of oversalted, scorched, and bitter swill. Not for me, thanks—and not in my kitchen. The microwave was a blessing to full-time System D experts. I've seen veterans of three-star kitchens throw absolutely raw, unseared *côte de boeuf* for two into a microwave oven, presumably to "warm it up" to cut cooking time!

One *can* be a proud practitioner of The System without resorting to food murder. With a fine set of moves, a strong, adaptable mind, and a certain threshold, a level beyond which one will *not* under any circumstances go, one can break all the rules and still make good food. One's customers will get what they wanted, when they wanted it. And no one will be the wiser.

If Vatel, the famous French chef of years past who allegedly killed himself when informed that his fish delivery would be delayed, had been fluent in System D, he might have lived a longer, happier, and more prosperous life. We remember him, after all, only for his passing.

Maybe we don't remember the name of whatever early pioneer of System D first gazed upon a snail in a moment of need and thought to himself, "Gee . . . maybe if I cram enough garlic butter in there, I can *serve* that!" But we're still eating *escargots de Bourgogne*, aren't we?

THE EVILDOERS

I'M ON THE SUBWAY after a long, hard day in the kitchen, my feet swelling up like twin Hindenburgs; my back killing me; fourteen hours of hot, sweaty, uncomfortable toil and two hundred eighty dinners under my belt; and I want to sit down. There are three seats in front of me in the crowded subway car. Unfortunately, one miserable, fat bastard is taking up all three of them. As he sits glumly but defiantly in a center seat, his gigantic butt cheeks and thighs spill out of the molded plastic bucket onto the seats on both sides, and his beady eyes dare me to try and squeeze my bony ass into one of the narrow spaces next to him.

Dream sequence: I'm on a packed commuter flight and we're going down for a forced landing in a Midwestern cornfield. Engine one is on fire, the cabin fills up with smoke, panicky passengers overturn their meal trays as they rush the emergency exits. The pilot manages to plow the plane belly-down onto soft earth, but when the plane—in flames now—comes to a full stop and the emergency doors pop free, the three-hundred-pound ectomorph in the window seat becomes lodged firmly and inexorably in the small doorway. At the head of the aisle, another giant fuck collapses wheezing onto the floor, blocking egress. As my hair catches fire, the last thing I see is jiggly, crenulated back fat.

Whose fault is it? Who made my fellow Americans obese—if not *morbidly* obese? How did the age-old equation that poor equals thin and rich equals fat change so that now our working poor are huge and slow-moving and only the wealthy can afford the personal trainers, liposuction, and extended spa treatments required, it seems, to be thin? In whose evil snail tracks across the globe can we watch thighs expand, bellies pooch out over groins, so that fewer and fewer every year of the flower of our youth can even *see* their own genitals without benefit of a mirror? Who is making each new generation from once normally proportioned countries swell up like grain-fed steer?

We know the answer. America's most dangerous export was never nuclear weapons or Jerry Lewis—or even *Baywatch* reruns. It was, is, and probably always will be our fast-food outlets.

The Evildoers of the major chains live nowhere near their businesses. Like crack dealers, they know what they sell is not good for you, that it makes neighborhoods uglier, contributes nothing but a stifling sameness to society. Recently, with Eric Schlosser, the author of the brilliant and terrifying *Fast Food Nation,* I debated two representatives of the fast-food industry at a "multi-unit foodservice operators'" convention in Texas. Our position, unsurprisingly, was that everybody in the room basically sucked. The opposition countered with tortured recitation of numbers and statistics, mostly to do with what a valuable service their industry provided, employing—for a few months at a time—hundreds of thousands of people who (they implied) might otherwise be sticking up liquor stores, setting fires, and sodomizing pets. They neatly deflected Schlosser's own accurate and sobering numbers, mostly to do with workplace injuries in the meat-cutting industry, average length of employment, bankrupt "nutritional" value, the quantifiable path of balooning thighs following in their businesses' wake across the globe, and so on. But when I asked these folks, one by one, if they would live anywhere near their own overlit, maniacally cheery looking restaurants, I got, more often than not, a stunned look and a "Fuck, no!" When I mischievously suggested (opportunistically taking advantage of the current fervor of flag waving) that their chosen enterprise was basically unpatriotic; that they were deliberately targeting children with their advertising, then knowingly raising them to be no-necked arterially clogged diabetics who'd "never in a million years make it through basic training. God *help* us if we ever have to hit Omaha Beach again, those doughy overfed punks'll drown like rats!"—they looked, actually . . . guilty. They *know,* you see. You think they eat their own gruel anywhere *near* as frequently as the average rube? I don't.

But is fast food inherently evil? Is the convenient nature of the beast bad, in and of itself? Decidedly no. Fast food—which traditionally solves very real problems of working families, families with kids, business people on the go, the casually hungry—*can* be good food. If you walk down a street in Saigon, or visit an open-air market in Mexico, you'll see that a quick, easy meal, often enjoyed standing up, does not have to be part of the hideous, generic sprawl of soul-destroying sameness that stretches from strip malls in San Diego, across the U.S.A., through Europe and Asia and around again, looking the same, tasting the same: paper-wrapped morsels of gray "beef" patties with all-purpose sauce. The unbelievably high-caloric horrors of beef-flavor-sprayed chicken nuggets, of "milkshakes" that contain no milk and have never been shaken, of "barbecue" that has never seen a grill, "cheese" with no cheese, and theme monstrosities for whom food is only a lure to buy a T-shirt, is not the way it *has* to be.

There is delicious, even nutritious, fast food to be had in the world—often faster and cheaper than the clown and the colonel and the king and their ilk produce. In Japan (and increasingly in the West), there are quick affordable sushi joints. In Tokyo, you can purchase *yakitori*, small skewers of grilled poultry and meat, from *yakitori* vendors clustered around business districts to serve executives looking for an easy after-work snack. In Spain, tapas (or *pinchos*) are served standing up; you grab something good at one tapas joint, then move over to another, a moveable series of snacks, inevitably delicious—and again, usually good for you.

In Vietnam, fast food is everywhere, right out in the street: freshly made, brightly colored sandwiches on homemade French bread; steaming bowls of *pho,* noodles served from a portable kitchen carried on a yoke on the proprietor's back; grilled shrimp kebabs skewered on sugarcane; tiny bundles of rice and pork wrapped in banana leaves; spicy calamari; crispy little birds; hunks of jackfruit; caramelized bananas and mango—all of it made and served by *individuals,* lone entrepreneurs for whom pride is not a catchphrase or a slogan but an operating principle. In Mexico, one is likely to find happy swarms of people slurping posole, a sort of soupy stew, or *menudo,* a similarly delicious concoction, around primitive carts right out in the street, electric power provided by a chugging gas generator. A few pesos and a few seconds and you're eating better than at any place run by evil clowns or steroid-overdosed action-movie front men. Turn right and there's an old woman making absolutely fresh quesadillas of zucchini flowers and farmer cheese, turn left and a mom and pop are slicing up a tender head of pork and rolling it into soft tacos with *salsa fresca* so fresh and wonderful you'll think you've died and gone to heaven. Total time elapsed from time ordered to actual chewing? About twelve seconds.

Even in Russia they've got blintzes and piroshkis, served on fire-engine-red plastic trays—in the worst American tradition—but again, made by a *human,* fresh, on site, from real, recognizable ingredients, not shipped in frozen, preportioned vacu-seal bags from some meat-extruding facility near a far-away turnpike. And that cherished idea of the Russian as stocky, Krushchev-like babushkas is way wrong, friends. Most of the Russians I saw recently? The guys all looked like Dolph Lundgren and the women were tall, slim, and hard-looking enough to handle themselves in a street fight.

In Cambodia, a desperately poor cyclo driver, munching on a crispy little bird at a market, engaged me in conversation. "Is it true," he asked, "that all Americans eat only hamburgers and KFC?" He looked truly sorry for me.

I wouldn't really care what they put in those burgers—if they tasted good. And though I *do* care that the rivers of Arkansas are clogging up with chicken shit to satisfy the world's relentless craving for crispy fried chicken fingers, I don't believe that we should legislate these cocksuckers out of business. My position is kind of the Nancy Reagan position on drugs: "Just Say No." Next time you find yourself standing slack-jawed and hungry in front of a fast-food counter—and a clown is anywhere nearby— just turn on your heels and head for the lone-wolf, independent operator down the street: a pie shop, a chippie, a kebab joint, or, in New York, a "dirty-water hot dog," *anywhere* that the proprietor has a name. Even that beloved British institution, the chippie, is preferable to the clown's fare; at least you are encouraging individual, local business, an entrepreneur who can react to neighborhood needs and wants, rather than a dictatorial system in which some focus group in an industrial park in Iowa decides for you what you will or should want. Deep-fried cod or plaice with vinegar, haggis with curry sauce; these may not be the apex of healthy eating, but at least they're indigenous to somewhere—and, washed down with enough beer or Irn-Bru, they're quite tasty. The kebab shop makes food that is at least fresh, and a beef shawarma does not require the addition of beef flavor to make it taste like food.

Whenever possible, try to eat food that comes from some-where, from somebody. And stop eating so fucking *much*. A little portion control would go a long way in slimming down our herds of heavyweights in their tent-like T-shirts, Gap easy-fit pants, and baggy shorts. (Apparently taking body-sculpting cues from some of our more humungous rappers, these guys ignore the fact that many of their heroes probably have to wash themselves with a sponge at the end of a stick.)

You may as well stop snacking on crap while you're at it. You don't *need* that bag of chips between meals, do you? You're probably not even enjoying it. Save your appetite for something good! Take a little more time! All that rage and frustration, that hollow feeling so many of us feel—for so many good reasons—

can be filled up with something better than a soggy disk of ground-up assholes and elbows. Eat for nourishment, yes, but eat for pleasure. Stop settling for less. That way, if we ever *do* have to get in there and "smoke evildoers out of their holes," at the very least, we'll be able to squeeze in after them.

A COMMENCEMENT ADDRESS
NOBODY ASKED FOR

IF YOU CAN CATCH a chef in a quiet, reflective moment over a drink, and ask what the worst aspects of the job are, you will probably get the following answer: "The heat, the pressure, the fast pace, the isolation from normal society, the long hours, the pain, the relentless, never-ending demands of the profession."

If you wait awhile, maybe two more drinks, and ask again—this time inquiring about the *best* parts of being a chef—more often than not, the chef will pause, take another sip of beer, smile . . . and give you exactly the same answer.

This is something you might keep in mind at the very beginning of your cooking career, chained to a sink in a crowded sub-cellar, doing nothing more glamorous, hour after hour after hour, than scraping vegetables or washing shellfish: It doesn't really get any better. In fact, I know a number of accomplished chefs and sauciers who suffer from what we call "dishwasher syndrome," meaning that at every available moment between delicately spooning foamy sauces over pan-seared scallops and foie gras, or bullying waiters, they sneak over to the dish station and spend a few happy, carefree moments washing dishes. This is not as bizarre as one might think. Many of us yearn for those relatively carefree days when it was a simple matter of putting dirty plates into one end of a machine and then watching them emerge clean and perfect from the other side. Similarly, I have seen owners of multiunit restaurant empires blissfully sweeping the kitchen floor, temporarily enjoying a Zen-like state of calm, of focused, quantifiable toil far from the multitasking and responsibility of management hell.

Cooking is, and always has been, a cult of pain. Those of us who've spent any time in the business actually *like it that way.* Unless we've gone Kurtz-like over the edge into madness, and started believing, for instance, that we are no longer cooks but spokespersons for supermarket chains, or forces of nature responsible for elevating the eating habits of a nation, then we know who we are: the same people we have always been. We are the backstairs help. We are in the *service industry,* meaning that when rich people come into our restaurants we cook for them. When our customers play, we work. When our customers sleep, we play. We know (or should know) that we are not like our customers, never will be like our customers, and don't want to be, even if we put down a nice score now and again. The people in our dining rooms are different from us. We are *the other thing*—and we like it like that. We may be glorified servants, catering to the whims of those usually wealthier than us (I mean, who among us could afford to eat in our own restaurants regularly?), but we are tougher, meaner, stronger, more reliable, and well aware of the fact that we can do something with our hands, our senses, the accumulated wisdom of thousands of meals served, that *they* can't. When you're tired after a hard day in the kitchen, and some manicured stockbroker is taking up too much room on the subway, you have no problem telling the stupid prick to shove over. You deserve it! He doesn't.

Does this sound macho? It isn't. Men, women, anyone who works in a professional kitchen should feel the same way. They work harder, under more difficult conditions, in an often fly-by-night industry with uncertain futures, catering to a fickle and capricious clientele in an environment in which you can do everything right and *still* fail. This environment tends to breed a clannishness, a tribal subculture, a tunnel-vision view of the world where "there's *us*—and there's those *like us*" and screw everybody else. We have to cook as best we can for them, but that doesn't mean we have to *be* them.

So all those hours scraping carrots, scrubbing oysters, pulling the bones out of pig trotters, tournéeing turnips, in the end, pay off. In addition to becoming expert, presumably, at those valuable tasks, you are asserting your reliability, your toughness, and your worth as someone whom an overworked chef de partie or sous-chef or chef might want to take under their wing, invest a little time and attention actually teaching, helping you to climb out of the cellar and up to the next level. You are also coming to an under-standing—a *real* understanding—of what the hell it is that we really do in this business, meaning, we transform the raw, the ugly, the tough, and the unlovely into the cooked, the beautiful, the tender, and the tasty. Any cretin can grill a steak after a few tries. It takes a cook to transform a humble pig's foot into something people clamor for. This is the real story of haute cuisine, of course: generations of hungry, servile, and increasingly capable French and Italian and Chinese and others, transforming what was readily at hand, or leftover from their cruel masters, into some-thing people actually *wanted* to eat. And as the story of all great cooking is often the story of poverty, hardship, servitude, and cruelty, so is our history. Like the shank of beef that over time becomes a falling-off-the-bone thing of wonder when slowly braised in red wine and seasonings, so too is the prep cook transformed—into a craftsman, an artisan, a professional, respon-sible to himself, his chef, his owners, his coworkers, his customers.

A stressed, badly rested, overworked three-star chef is not going to take time out of his or her very busy day training some young *commis* to clarify stock properly if there's any doubt whether that *commis* will still be around, still focused, and still motivated in three months. The very real need for dreary, repetitive functions like squid cleaning serves a secondary pur-pose in weeding out the goofballs, the people who thought they wanted to be in The Life—but don't really understand or want that level of commitment. If some of these budding culinarians feel that they are not, for instance, comfortable with being spoken to harshly, or dismissed with an expletive in a moment of extremis, then they usually lack the basic character traits needed for a long, successful run in this greatest of all businesses.

Much is made of the emotional volatility, even the apparent cruelty, of some of our better-known culinary warriors. And to the casual observer, the torrent of profanity likely to come the way of an inadequately prepared *poissonier* can seem terrifying and offensive. And there *is* a line not to be crossed. Bullying for its own sake, for the sheer pleasure of exerting power over other, weaker cooks or employees, is shameful. If I verbally disembowel a waiter during a busy shift for some transgression, real or imagined, I sincerely hope and expect that at the shift's end, we will be friendly and laughing about it at the bar. If a cook goes home feeling like an idiot for trusting me, working hard for me, and investing time and toil in pleasing me, then I have failed in my job. Good kitchens, however hard the work, and good chefs, should breed intense loyalty, camaraderie, and relationships that last lifetimes.

Most reasonably coordinated people with hearts, souls, and any kind of emotional connection to food can be taught to cook, at some level or another. It takes a special breed to love the business. When you pursue excellence *for yourself*—not for dreams of TV stardom or endorsement deals, not for the customer, not for your chef, but for yourself—then you are well on your way to becoming the kind of lifetime adrenaline junkie professional culinarian recognizable in any country or culture.

I can't tell you how many times I've talked about this with chefs and cooks around the world. Whether it's Singapore, Sydney, Saint Louis, Paris, Barcelona, or Duluth, you are not alone. When you finally arrive, when you take your place behind a professional range, start slinging serious food, know what the hell you're doing, you are joining an international subculture in "this thing of ours." You will recognize and be recognized by others of your kind. You will be proud and happy to be part of something old and honorable and difficult to do. You will be different, a thing apart—and you will cherish your apartness.

FOOD AND LOATHING IN LAS VEGAS

"MAYBE YOU SHOULD DRIVE," I said.

I yanked the blood-red Cadillac Eldorado onto the shoulder and stomped on the brakes. Ruhlman, sunning himself in the passenger seat, was thrown forward, mashing his folding sun-reflector into the dash and spilling beer all over his lap.

"You filthy pig, Bourdain," he screeched, "that was the last beer!"

Ruhlman is a big man, six-foot-four like me, but wider, with big corn-fed Midwestern shoulders—and when he gets those thick forearms and meat-hook paws around your neck, it's already too late.

I had good reason to be afraid. He was in an ugly mood. I'd dragged him away from his wife and children, from the relative calm and civility of his beloved Cleveland, all the way across the country to this godforsaken desert, to *Las Vegas* no less—the Ugly Shorts Heart of Darkness—to assist me in the production of a television show (and the writing of this article) on the burgeoning celebrity chef scene. As coauthor of the Bouchon and French Laundry cookbooks, and as a respected writer on the subject of chefs, he was uniquely placed to help me. He'd been to Vegas before. He knew the histories of the personalities and operations I was interested in—and his reputation and deceptively innocent aw-shucks manner and preppy good looks might, I hoped, make me (a vicious interloper if ever there was one) more welcome in town. My plan had been to get him liquored up, then piggyback on the research he'd spent many months if not years assembling. If nothing else, I knew he could get me a good table at Bouchon.

But he'd turned on me. And not without reason.

In the past few days, in the interests of television entertainment, I'd induced him to wear the same loud, electric-blue Hawaiian shirt every day. I'd repeatedly shot (and badly bruised) him during a ferocious game of indoor paintball; fed him beer and liquor from sunup to late night; then, when he was vulnerable, remorselessly interrogated him about Vegas culinary history. I'd watched him lose terrible sums at blackjack—all this while being regularly force-fed gargantuan, two-time-a-day tasting menus as the cameras rolled and I jotted down his every comment.

Now, we'd been driving back and forth for hours in the scorching desert sun—so the television crew could get that perfect *Fear and Loathing in Las Vegas* "homage" shot—and it wasn't going well.

He *had* to drive. I was in much worse shape than he, my head pounding from the previous night's mile-high frozen margaritas, my heart racing with terror in my chest. What *had* I been thinking? *Six* days to research, cover, write, rewrite, edit, and deliver an article for a respectable major publication—while *simultaneously* making an hour-long episode of a show that would (and did) require every variety of bestial, excessive behavior. Even now, there was a Sammy Davis Jr. impersonator waiting for me in the Neon Boneyard, an accordion convention to attend, and more food—always more food, more meals to eat—before I was due, on the last day, to jump out of an airplane at two miles over the desert with the Flying Elvi skydiving team.

"Pull yourself together, Ruhlman," I howled over the blaring radio. "Pouring beer on yourself is good. Helps avoid sunstroke. And having an open receptacle in the car is, I'm pretty sure, illegal—even in this state. Now snap out of it. And drive us to Bouchon!"

*   *   *

Las Vegas: a bright, hopeful land of opportunity for chefs—or the elephant graveyard for cynical cooks-turned-restaurateur/ entrepeneurs? A well-deserved final score for celebrity chefs, after a lifetime of toil; a last cash-out before knees fail entirely and brains cook—or just a soulless extension of The Brand? Was it *possible* to serve truly good food; maintain one's standards, one's integrity; do *good works* in Vegas's mammoth, air-conditioned Xanadus, this neon-lit theme park, these Terrordomes of twenty-four-hour beeping, bleeping, and jangling slots? Were these names of recognizable and respected chefs, these distant outposts of empire, simply far-flung knockoffs, expensive reproductions of what were once the soulful, heartfelt expressions of their strengths and dreams—now only farmed out cookie-cutter versions? Or were they just as good as their flagships, the same, only subsidized by the shattered hopes and dreams of the hapless souls two floors down, feeding their disability checks in increments into the endless banks of blinking, uncaring machines?

These were the serious moral issues I was grappling with as Ruhlman crushed his size-thirteen foot onto the gas pedal and powered the eight-cylinder red beast off gravel and onto asphalt, toward Thomas Keller's Bouchon, the place I hoped would provide an answer.

A few days earlier, we'd visited some usual suspects. Inevitable, really, that we'd hit Bobby Flay's Mesa Grill first. I figured that a purer example of branding could scarcely be found. I was looking for an easy hatchet job. A clear case of reptilian regeneration, a restaurant group expanding unthinkingly, like a chameleon grows back a lost tail. The story arc appeared classic: New York chef becomes fantastically well known on the Food Network, widens operation, opens in Vegas. It's easy, so easy, to dismiss Flay's whole Vegas enterprise with a New York sneer. It certainly does no serious restaurant much help in the gravitas department to locate in the Mega-Coliseum of Über-Kitsch, Caesars Palace, among the Italianate statuary, the staff in togas, the gurgling fountains and Celine Dion gift shop. Flay's mug looks down on diners and punters alike from a giant JumboTron over the slots—in a continuous loop of clips from his television shows. The restaurant itself looks, from the exterior, like an over-designed coffee shop; only a layer of slightly tinted glass separates the light, modern, vaguely Southwestern dining room from the killing floor.

As we took our seats in the dining room, Ruhlman pointed out an old woman in a wheelchair being pulled reluctantly away from a slot machine on the other side of the glass.

"That's not putting me in the mood."

Over an open kitchen, a satellite-size rotisserie twirled chickens in slow rotation.

"First night they opened, that thing was roaring red at like . . . nine hundred degrees," said Ruhlman. "Would have looked cool if it was red. Or if you could see flames now. But the thing was so hot it would have cooked the customers if they'd kept it cranked. They had to turn it way down, or they would have had customers bursting into flames, running across the casino floor with their hair on fire."

"That wouldn't be good for business," I said.

"You think that would stop these people from gambling?"

Perhaps sensing the general mood of skepticism at our table, a wary-looking flack from the casino's food and beverage department quickly—and sensibly—plied us with novelty margaritas.

"Just let the kitchen cook for us," suggested Ruhlman. "Do what you're good at. Nothing that's not on the menu."

Our very competent server began to lay on the food, making frequent mention of the Maximum Leader.

"Bobby Flay's Spicy Tuna Tartare" tasted like everybody else's tuna tartare these days, which is to say, perfectly respectable, in a south-of-the-border kinda way. A "Smoked Chicken and Black Bean Quesadilla" was a gussied-up smoked chicken and black bean quesadilla. Our margaritas were replenished. Our server presented "Bobby Flay's Tiger Shrimp and Roasted Garlic Corn Tamale" as if repeating the name would add something to the experience—and, in fact, it was the best of the offerings: pretty, in its artfully opened pocket of corn husk, and flavorful. A very well-conceived dish which, unlike the quesadilla, compared well to the more rustic Mexican versions. "This is as good as any tamale on earth," I offered. "This is great. You could go looking for the perfect tamale in any mercado in Mexico and not find one as good as this. Unimprovable."

"The kitchen does a good job," said Ruhlman, begrudgingly. "Just don't look out the window."

A "Northeast Lobster Out of the Shell with Red Chile Coconut Sauce" masked a perfectly cooked lobster with a fairly insipid and cloyingly sweet sauce, and the Brussels sprouts (which I liked) made absolutely no sense in its proximity. "Sixteen Spice Rotisserie Chicken" was, again, perfectly cooked, but it would have been fine with about eight spices. "Coffee Spice Rubbed Rotisserie Filet Mignon" was also flawlessly cooked, though decorated with the same squeeze-bottled orange sauce as the chicken. The kitchen crew did everything right, cooked everything perfectly, with dead-on technique, but I found myself carping about the conceptual disconnect: "The same damn squeeze bottle stuff. All these years later—"

"The kitchen is doing a really good job," interrupted Ruhlman correctly (if uncharacteristically).

"Why put your personal 'imprint' on this stuff? It's gilding the lily," I griped, wondering why a nice piece of lovingly cooked filet mignon would be in any way improved by a rubdown with coffee.

"They don't come here for a steak, Bourdain," muttered Ruhlman. "They come here for *Bobby's* steak. Taste the magic, man. You're not buying a meal. You're buying a *personality*."

"But the food is fine. The food is good. Why wrestle it into submission?"

"The food is good. They do a good job here," said Ruhlman, looking nervously around for another margarita.

The desserts at Mesa Grill were outstanding. A "Coconut Custard Brûlée Tart" with fresh fruit struck exactly the right balance between Flay's "signature" style and eating pleasure. A "Warm Chocolate and Dulce de Leche Cake," which could easily have been yet another ubiquitous "fallen chocolate soufflé," was extraordinary, and was served with pecan ice cream. The two desserts (and the margaritas) helped put us both into cheerier moods. You could do a lot worse than to eat at the Mesa Grill. It's a hell of a lot better than it has to be. Looking outside the thin glass partition and around the room, one gets the impression that the customers here would be just as happy with a well-prepared burger, as long as it was "Bobby Flay's Burger," served under Bobby Flay's omnipresent, smiling face. That the kitchen clearly works hard to get it right, and that the chef appears to as well (Flay was in town only a couple of days later), speaks well of the place. Now if all concerned could be less insecure about changing with the times, maybe let the ingredients speak more for themselves, it could be pretty damn impeccable. Though I'd suggest tinting the windows. The view from the tables is a little dismaying.

It took a while to locate Todd English's Olives in the gargantuan Bellagio. If anybody's got a right to phone-it-in, crank-out factory food, it's English. He has restaurants all over the world these days, and a chain of airport pit stops (Figs). But I spend a lot of time in airports, often moved to murderous rage by the usual overpriced, not-even-trying gruel that seems to be the norm, and I'm always happy to see Figs. He's made *my* world a better place already. English does not suffer from the burden of too many stars, or a signature style. No one expects to walk into an Olives and find Joël Robuchon. The exterior of Olives at the Bellagio only reinforces that sensibly lowered expectation. It looks like a one-time Bennigan's, without the faux Tiffany lamps. Once one steps inside, however, things only improve. There's a lovely terrace overlooking a huge, man-made lake which one could easily mistake for European—if there weren't casino hotels in the background. With a little willing suspension of disbelief, one could spend a delightful few hours there. As

Ruhlman was MIA for the afternoon (probably squandering his kids' college funds at the crap tables), I dragooned my assistant producer, Nari, into joining me for lunch. The service at Olives was supremely confident, and casually, enjoyably efficient. When we ordered three appetizers and two entrées, our server asked, "Have you eaten with us before?" When I said no, she warned that, "They're large portions."

It was a completely unneurotic meal. English specializes in big servings of very decent, casual Mediterranean, and that's what was delivered: The bread basket, with freshly baked and well-seasoned focaccia and *carta da musica*, was of way above average quality. A flatbread pizza of white clams and broccoli rabe pesto was terrific. Sweet pea ravioli with pea shoots was just right, and a gnocchi with sausage was a bit tougher than it could have been but tasty. Halibut with mascarpone polenta was fresh and correctly cooked and tasted of what it should: halibut and mascarpone polenta. The "Crispy Yellowfin Tuna" was a clunker, deep-fried to rare yet unpleasantly dry and deposited on a perfunctory salad; and the desserts were of hospital quality; but Olives manages to exceed expectations rather than bloat them. It's a welcome counterpoint to the excesses of the casino, a casual, fun, and filling respite from the madness outside.

"This is what's great about Vegas," babbled a momentarily ebullient Ruhlman, well into his fourth sake. He was talking about Okada at the new Wynn Las Vegas, a "combining [of] the French and Japanese worlds" from chef Takashi Yagihashi.

"I mean . . . look at this," he spluttered, "the guy [Yagihashi] goes from a sixty-five-seat restaurant in the suburbs of Detroit to . . . *this*! It's amazing."

And Okada is amazing. The spanking new, two-hundred-thirty-seat restaurant opens onto an artificial, yet stunningly beautiful, bamboo- and tree-lined lagoon. Water falls over rock shelves through what appears to be a dense, Asian jungle just outside. Marginally familiar with the chef's previous venue, the well-reviewed Tribute, I had to admit it was quite a transition. This was what Vegas has to offer: a new life for talented chefs like Yagihashi. Private dining rooms; a sleek, new, stylish, multimillion-dollar main dining room; a large sushi bar manned by "traditional *Edomae* sushi master Miyazawa." An open kitchen serving *robata yaki* (marinated skewers grilled over Japanese charcoal). An open kitchen serving "caviar tastings," braised short ribs, and bento boxes, among other fusion offerings, along with tempura and teriyaki—a scattershot potpourri of mix and match, and a vast selection of sakes.

All right, so the sushi wasn't so hot: The rice was cold and gluey, the *uni* (sea urchin) not the freshest I've had. Perfectly good *otoro* was cut too thick, and across connective tissue. But it's impossible not to be swept along by the enthusiasm of the place. Okada exudes high energy, pride, optimism—and the American dream of a successful future. It celebrates the different and the "exotic" in admirably bold fashion. Our server cheerily explained to Ruhlman and me (two jaded and grizzled food writers if ever there were any) what an *omakase* was (tasting menu), and we felt compelled to feign ignorance and wonder. What followed was a hilariously frenetic, yet intermittently delicious, trainwreck as food cranked continuously from the various stations without coordination. Our serious yet beleaguered sommelier struggled mightily to match always excellent sakes to a double-time procession of courses, arriving with a perfectly matched unfiltered sake, for instance, only to find another course had been plunked down in the few moments it had taken her to fetch it. Plated offerings and family-style tastings seemed stacked in holding patterns around the table like planes over JFK at rush hour.

The always dangerously manic-depressive Ruhlman's mood began to swing.

"I've got The Fear," he murmured, picking unhappily at the "lobster trio," an inexplicably smoked lobster tail which tasted of, well . . . smoke; a lobster croquette that could just as well have been "sea leg," and a "lobster gelée" served in the inevitable shot glass. "Maybe there's a downside to this. If Yagihashi had opened in New York first, before coming here

. . . he would have been *killed* by the critics. He would have learned."

Okada's offerings veered between the truly excellent and the sophomoric, but never without enthusiasm and pride. A sampling of skewered *robata yaki* arrived, a perfect grilled prawn, flawless "BBQ short rib," an unctuous grilled spear of *otoro*, and a bizarrely incongruous grilled lamb chop slathered with black olive tapenade—a discordant note which thankfully didn't take away from the excellence of the rest.

But the "Baked Sweet Sake-Kasu Black Cod" was just fine; the sakes were wonderful; and looking around the beautiful dining room, spying a mulleted, shorts-wearing couple in T-shirts, the man in a trucker hat and sandals, the woman in sneakers, both happily picking over their food with chopsticks at a nearby table, I felt decidedly more sunny about things.

"You miserable, misanthropic, elitist swine, Ruhlman," I barked. "This restaurant is good for the world! Look at this place. Look at this food. Feel it! It's enlightenment! Where do you want these people to go after they've won a few bucks at the tables, in their few moments of hopeful optimism before it all goes down the tubes tomorrow? TGI McFunsters? A steakhouse? The midnight buffet at the Riviera? Look at what they're exposed to here—in the middle of this terrible desert, among the mile-high sno-cone daiquiris and mai tais, the dollar-ninety-nine shrimp cocktails, the cynical crap-fest up and down this strip! A taste of the new, Ruhlman. A taste of Asia! New sensations! New ingredients! They'll get drunk on this fine sake and look out at that lagoon and think, 'Maybe Asia would be cool. I *like* this stuff!' Look around the dining room, Ruhlman. Those are your countrymen—and they're eating *well*. They're eating *new*. Now God bless America and order more sake."

The next morning, Ruhlman disappeared again, leaving an indecipherably scrawled note with the desk at the Wynn. He'd lost tragic amounts of money at the tables, which he'd no doubt have a very hard time explaining to his wife. Though I'd miss his encyclopaedic knowledge of Vegas culinary history, it was none too soon. He needed to hole up somewhere and rest his sushi-bloated body before the final push at Bouchon. Examining the bill he'd left behind, I saw I'd have my own problems explaining to my editor how a man could run up five hundred dollars in "in-room movies." And what had Ruhlman wanted with "1 case of grapefruits," "6 orders of kung pao chicken," "2 cases of Neutrogena soap," not to mention the power tools and lubricants he'd ordered from the gift shop?

It was a relief from Ruhlman's surly disposition and unlovely personal habits to eat lunch with Tracey, one of the camera persons from the production team. She, at least, would be happy to get a good meal—and was unlikely to abuse the waiter.

Unlike Flay and English, Daniel Boulud does have multi-stars to protect—four of them at his eponymous fine dining restaurant in New York. And his other New York store, the more casual DB Bistro Moderne, is nearly as well thought of. But he does everything right in Vegas and generously lets executive chef Philippe Rispoli take the credit (or the blame). In this case, he should be very proud. Everything about the new Daniel Boulud Brasserie in the Wynn Las Vegas is as good as it could be. Canapés of duck confit and foie gras were what you would expect of a hotshot like Boulud (and somewhat daring in Vegas's 110-degree heat). Sevruga caviar with still-warm blinis was classic, fresh, and paired—in this case—with a very respectable house champagne. In the shadow of a monster-size waterfall/movie screen and reflecting pool, the food and service stand up effortlessly to what could have been intimidating, even ludicrous, surroundings. Lobster bisque tasted like lobster—a welcome relief from the two lobsters I'd previously seen victimized in the name of the chef's larger Vision. "Vitello tonnato" actually added something to the moribund tuna tartare idea, pairing it with veal sweetbreads. Cod and clam basquaise was robustly flavored, amazingly fresh, and unpretentious, and a lobster salad only reinforced the notion that it takes a great chef to let the ingredients do the talking. Desserts were appropriately demure, the service exactly the right balance of friendly, good-humored, casual, and bloodlessly efficient. They should send Boulud and Rispoli next door to Okada to show them how the big boys do it.

You have to love a town where you can both smoke and gamble in a pharmacy. That night, temporarily burned out on fine dining and casino hotels, I wheeled the red Caddy into the parking lot of Tiffany's Cafe and White Cross Drugs, just off the skanky end of the Strip. Loaded up with aspirin to soothe my pounding head, I had corned beef hash and eggs at the counter. At Tiffany's counter, you can see the other side of Vegas. There's no glitz or glamour here. Things must have slid pretty far if you're dropping your quarters into a slot machine at an all-night drugstore. I looked carefully at the weathered faces of my fellow customers—half expecting to see Ruhlman. I tried his cell phone. No answer. I trawled the Double Down Saloon, the somewhat downscale Golden Gate, Binion's, and Riviera casinos, looking among the desperate and downtrodden for my friend's face—with no success. I drank a pink, basketball-size Scorpion at local fave, the Fireside Lounge, hoping that Ruhlman might show up for a mound of nachos and a drink with an umbrella in it. But he never did.

The next day, still unable to reach my fellow doctor of gastronomy, I had a soul-restoring bowl of *menudo* (tripe soup) at the El Sombrero Cafe on South Main. The perfect antidote to the Casinos of the Damned. I put in a little pool time at the Wynn, watching the hardcore gamblers play blackjack in their bathing suits. I was crossing the casino floor when I felt my elbow enclosed in a steel-like, desperate grip.

"Money! I need money," said Ruhlman, in a pair of dirty shorts and a Dead Boys T-shirt covered with a mix of frozen daiquiris and deep-fried Twinkie from Fremont Street. "I've been at the Mermaid for the last forty-eight hours," wailed the one-time budding TV star. "I lost everything. Everything! I was jacked up on some hideous sugar high from those Twinkies.

And the Oreos! They *deep-fry Oreos* here, Bourdain! I was helpless under their influence. Now give me money. I'm on a roll at the keno. I'm almost back even." Only a week earlier, I'd seen a blazer-clad Ruhlman playing the Simon Cowell role on the PBS competitive cooking series, *Cooking Under Fire.* Now he was a shell of his former self, unshaven, eyes banging around in his skull like pachinko balls. Frankly, he scared me. I quickly handed him a wad of cash, figuring I could hide it in expenses.

"All right, Ruhlman. Here's your filthy money," I said. "But when you lose it, get up to my room and shower and shave. I'll lend you a proper jacket and some clothes. We've got a scene to shoot in the desert. And then Bouchon. Remember Bouchon? Thomas Keller? The guy you wrote those books with?"

The mention of Keller seemed to have a positive effect on my tormented friend. He stood erect, eyes focusing for what was probably the first time in hours, and wiped an Oreo crumb and a crust of what looked like dried blood off his cheek.

"Yes," he said. "Bouchon. Of course. You're absolutely right." He handed me back the money and strode with new strength and determination toward the elevator bank. "Don't know what I was thinking there for a while. Lost the plot momentarily . . . No matter. All right now, back to business. After all . . . we're professionals."

When you talk about expectations, none were higher than those surrounding Thomas Keller's much-anticipated Vegas version of Bouchon. The knives were out for the chef whom many consider the best and most respected in the world. That a chef of his unquestioned caliber and integrity—whose French Laundry seemed the very antithesis of everything Vegas stands for—would open a restaurant in the bizarro faux-Renaissance Venetian hotel/casino/resort seemed to many an abdication of greatness, even a betrayal of principles. Plenty of food nerds wanted to see him fail—*preferred,* from the safety of their desktop computers, to see him fail—as a punishment for daring to bring good food to what they see as The Worst Place on Earth.

Keller, by this school of thought, should be punished for thinking that gamblers and vacationers from middle America and the
South, in their ugly shorts and their socks with sandals, might
recognize and appreciate sophisticated, properly cooked French
food. To them, it was pearls before swine, a "sellout," an insult
to the proprietary instincts of the metropolitan dining "elite."
Ruhlman had made a good case, on a foodie Web site, that this
was pure snobbery. Why *shouldn't* the masses have access to fine
food? he argued. Why *shouldn't* they be invited to the same table
we—New Yorkers and San Franciscans and world travelers—
see as almost a birthright? Isn't that a great chef's ultimate
responsibility, to change things for the better? To seduce, coerce,
and induce people to eat better, try new things, experience joy,
even *enlightenment?*

I thought Ruhlman had made an unusually cogent case. In
fact, it was this plaintive argument that had won me over,
convinced me to put aside my own fear and loathing and come
to Vegas myself. Was he right?

To step into Bouchon is to step into a perfectly, seemingly
effortlessly recreated French brasserie. The long zinc bar recre-
ates Paris's famous La Coupole. The details are, typically for
Keller, without a false note. It's another world, a little bit of
France floating free of the grim realities only a few yards away.
The menu is surprisingly traditional. Nothing daring about it in
these early days. No *boudin noir* or tripes or even *foie de veau* or
other less accessible brasserie classics; just perfectly—superbly—
executed mainstream fare. A "Grand Plateau" of lobster, mussels, seasonal crab, shrimps, oysters, and clams, sourced from
the same boutique purveyors used by the French Laundry and
Per Se, was predictably awe-inspiring. Rillettes of smoked and
fresh salmon could easily have been served at either of the
motherships if scaled down and prettied up for their fancier
rooms. Beignets of *brandade de morue* were light and fresh and
as well seasoned and flavored as one could hope for. We ordered
poulet rôti, which is, as most professionals know, the measure of
a cook's ability. You can tell almost everything you need to

know about a kitchen by how they roast as simple a dish as a chicken. It was better than good. It was the best chicken ever. Moist, flavorful, inspiring in its simplicity. A flatiron steak *frites* made me miserable with its virtuosity. I had previously been comfortable with the idea that I served the best French fries in the country at my place, Les Halles in New York. I'm afraid we no longer hold the U.S. title. Needless to say, they know how to cook, and rest, a steak at Bouchon. Desserts (a *tarte au citron* and a chocolate mousse) were, yes, you guessed it, fantastic. They make it look easy. And it's easy to eat there. No behaving for the waiter. No jacket and tie required. Everything—the room, the service, the menu—conspires to make a beautiful argument that it *is,* in fact, possible to do it right in Vegas. That one *can* create a pocket of calm, casual, yet sophisticated pleasure, of culinary excellence smack in the middle of—yet comfortably removed from—the carnage and ugliness below.

I found, I think, my perfect metaphor, had my final Vegas epiphany on my last day in town, as I hurtled face-down at accelerating speed toward the surface of the earth, free-falling from two miles above the desert, a Flying Elvis strapped to my back.

When you jump out of a plane for the first time, the first thousand feet are pure adrenaline-pumping, endorphin-juiced thrill. Straight down, head first, your mouth stretched into a silent scream. Then you level off a bit, as Elvis taps your shoulder and you stretch your arms out, legs back, into the "banana position."

For a few long moments more, you actually sail through the sky. All your childhood dreams come true, as for second after glorious second you are—before the chute opens and yanks you back to reality—almost convinced you can fly. When you feel something touch your outstretched fingers, you almost believe that *one* of the spangled, ducktailed figures on either side of you, connected in formation as you fall through space, could actually be Elvis.

Maybe that's what it's all about. What Vegas has come to mean for chefs, for cooks, for gamblers, diners, for all of us who go there: While we may be rushing inexorably toward the hard realities of the ground, surely and inevitably arriving in the same place (unless our chute fails to deploy or we crap out, in which case we end up there sooner rather than later), for a few moments, or hours, or even days, Vegas convinces us we can stay aloft—forever.

ARE YOU A CRIP OR A BLOOD?

I JUST FINISHED READING Canadian author Timothy Taylor's *Stanley Park*, a brilliant, if irritating, novel with a chef as hero. Taylor's protagonist breaks down the world of chefs into two camps: the Crips—transnationalists, for whom ingredients from faraway lands are an asset, people who cook without borders or limitations, constantly seeking innovative ways to combine the old with the new—and the Bloods, for whom *terroir* and a solid, rigorous connection to the immediate region and its seasons are an overriding concern. "Crips" would describe chefs like Norman Van Aken, Nobu Matsuhisa, Jean-Georges Vongerichten, guys who want the ingredient, at its best, wherever it might come from and however long it might have traveled, practitioners of "fusion." The Crip relies on his own talent, vision, and ability to wrestle ingredients into cooperation, hopefully breaking ground, revealing something new about ingredients that we may take for granted by pairing them with the exotic and unfamiliar. We have seen what the Crips are capable of at their best, and also what they can do at their worst, the terrible sameness of some of-the-moment Pacific Rim, Pan-Asian, and Nuevo Latino menus, in which chefs misuse Asian or South American ingredients with the single-minded enthusiasm of golden retrievers in heat, humping blindly and unproductively at your leg.

The earliest and most notable example of a Blood would be Alice Waters, whose Chez Panisse in Berkeley remains the cradle of the "slow food" revolution, a restaurant whose ingredients

37

almost exclusively represent the bounty of northern California and the Pacific Northwest of America. Fergus Henderson is a Blood, his food a proud expression of both nation and culture. It's a compelling argument, to say I will cook what's available in season. I will cook what is here. It recognizes the incomparable joys of eating wild strawberries or white asparagus in France, fresh baby eels in Portugal, tomatoes in Italy. The Bloods, in my experience, rooted as they are to place and time, are more likely than not to cook with real, heartfelt soulfulness and integrity, seeking to nurture, sooth, comfort, and evoke, rather than dazzle.

I always liked to think of myself as a Blood. Having recently traveled the world, often to very poor countries where being a Crip is not an option, I was enchanted again and again by cooks making fresh, vibrant, hearty, and soulful meals, often with very little in the way of resources. Like with the early culinary pioneers of France and Italy, the engine driving great cooking in Vietnam and Mexico, for instance, seems to be the grim necessity of dealing with what's available *when* it's available—and making the most of it. I've yammered endlessly, tiresomely, on the desirability of food coming from somewhere, that the sort of regional, seasonal fare that so many French and Italians grew up with is what is missing from much of American and British culinary culture.

But now I don't know.

There is more than a whiff of dogma in the Blood argument. The French "Group of Eight" chefs who decried the introduction of "foreign" spices and ingredients into haute cuisine strike me as the same crowd who want every movie to be a bloated, government-funded costume drama starring the inevitable Gérard Depardieu. I once heard a Parisian chef, while watching a comrade from Alsace make *choucroute garnis*, comment, "Thees is not French." An element of jingoism hangs in the air when some chefs decry "outside" and "foreign" influences on cooking—a scary overlap between those decrying foreign-influenced food and those decrying foreigners. And the organics mob, so fervent in their recitations of the dangers of pesticides, hormones, antibiotics, and genetic manipulation, often sound as if their agendas are driven by concerns far from taste or pleasure. The "slow food" lobby, arguing for sustainable sources of food, organic and free-range products, cruelty-free meat, and a return to a photogenic but never-to-be-realized agrarian wonderland, seem to overlook the fact that the stuff is expensive, and that much of the world goes to bed hungry at night—that most of us can't hop in the SUV with Sting and drive down to the organic greenmarket to pay twice the going rate.

Don't get me wrong. I like free-range; it's almost always better tasting. Wild salmon is better than farmed salmon, and yes, the farmed stuff is a threat to overall quality. Free-range chickens taste better, and are less likely to contain E. coli bacteria. Free-range is no doubt nicer as well; whenever possible we should, by all means, let Bambi run free (before slitting his throat and yanking out his entrails). Since I serve mostly neurotic rich people in my restaurant, I can often afford to buy free-range and organic. I can respond to the seasons to a great extent. But at the end of the day, if I can find a genetically manipulated, irradiated tomato from the other side of the country that tastes better than an Italian vine-ripened one from Granny's backyard (not likely, but just suppose), even if it causes the occasional tumor in lab rats, I'll probably serve it. It's how it tastes that counts.

For instance: I like grain-fed beef. When talking about beef, I don't want some muscular, over-exercised animal with delusions of liberty providing the steaks. I want a docile, corn- and grain-fed jailhouse fatboy who has spent the latter part of his life standing in a lot doing nothing but eating, all that nice fat marbling rippling through the lean. If, as in the case of Kobe beef, some nice cattleman wants to give my steer regular rub-downs with sake (and the occasional hand job), all the better. The grass-fed Argentine stuff, shipped in a cryovac bag full of water and blood, tastes like monkey meat by comparison.

"Does the product *taste* good?" should probably be the chef's primary concern. To insist, to *demand,* that all food be regional, seasonal, directly connected to time and place can—in the case of some of the more fervent advocates—invite the kind of return-to-the-soil thinking evocative of the Khmer Rouge.

Not long ago, watching perhaps the greatest of the Blood chefs (a man with only the faintest and best-intentioned Crip tendencies), Thomas Keller, yanking fresh garlic and baby leeks out of the ground at a nearby farm in the Napa Valley, I felt a powerful, bittersweet frisson, a yearning for how things might, in the best of all possible worlds, be. On the other hand, standing in Tokyo's Tsukiji market, gaping at the daily spoils of Japan's relentless rape of the world's oceans, I thought: "Jesus! Look at all this incredible fish! Damn, that toro looks good! That monkfish liver is amazing! I want some." Fully conscious of the evil that men do in the name of food, I have a very hard time caring when confronted with an impeccably fresh piece of codfish.

So I guess I won't be stocking my restaurant's larder with exclusively Hudson Valley products anytime soon. When my customers want strawberries, I'll have them flown in from warmer climes. Though I use the New York foie gras for pan-seared, I will continue to order the French for terrine. My Arborio rice will come from Italy, my beans for cassoulet from Tarbes. Because they're better. When those cute little baby eels from Portugal are available again, I'll be ordering them; who cares if there'll be none left for the Portuguese? I will continue to occasionally drink caipirinhas with my sashimi at Sushi Samba in New York—and I'll try to not feel silly about it.

Perhaps the best thing chefs can do is to cook, whenever possible, with heart. Where poorer nations have a tradition of cooking well because they *have* to, we have choices. If we can take something lasting from the Blood cause, it is that it is always better to make the most of what's available, to cook well. If a chef's unique vision and identity is associated closely with a particular area or local culture, great. He's doing God's work. If there is good, local skate available, then there is no reason to fly in the endangered, mushy, and oft-frozen Chilean sea bass. A good chef imports an ingredient from the other side of the globe because it makes sense—not for its novelty value or its rarity. Why bother to make Mexican food in London if the end result is nothing but soulless sour-tasting caulking compound? Why spend hundreds of thousands of dollars creating a fashionable ersatz dim-sum emporium and then bleed out all the happy sloppy informality that makes the dim-sum experience so much fun?

However horrifying it might be to see some young, fresh-out-of-culinary-school novice bombarding his guests with dende oil, Thai basil, yuzu, and chipotles, it's nice to know that others for whom those ingredients are more familiar can find them at will.

But I'm not giving up my white Italian truffles until the last one is gone. Show me a bootleg ortolan and I'm there, crunching bones with only a minimum of guilt. I'll just be sure to not overcook it.

VIVA MEXICO! VIVA ECUADOR!

LET'S BE HONEST. LET'S be really, painfully honest: Who is cooking?

Who is the backbone of the American restaurant business? Whose sudden departure could shut down nearly every good restaurant, nightclub, and banquet facility in every major city in the country? Whose sweat and toil allows annoyingly well-known white-boy chefs like me to go around the country flogging books, appearing on TV, writing obnoxious magazine articles, and baiting their peers? Who, pound for pound, are the best French and Italian cooks in New York?

If you're a chef, manager, or owner, you know the answer: Mexicans. Ecuadorans. Salvadoran guys (and women) from south of the border, many of them with green cards they bought on Queens Boulevard for thirty dollars. Ex-dishwashers with no formal training, minimal education; people who have often never *eaten* in restaurants as good as the ones they cook in. Manuel, the brilliant saucier at your two-star restaurant, puts on his best suit, combs his hair, dresses up his family in their Sunday best, and tries to get a table at the one-star place across the street. The aspiring actor/model/part-time maître d' will break out in a flop sweat, trying to figure out where to hide him—if "La Migra" hasn't already grabbed him on the way to dinner.

There is no deception more hypocritical, more nauseating, more willfully self-deluding than the industry-approved image of "the chef." We all know who is doing the heavy lifting, who's making that nice risotto with white truffles and porcini mush-rooms, the pan-seared hamachi with *sauce vièrge*, the ravioli of beef cheeks with sage and *sauce madère* . . . We *know,* to our eternal shame, who is more likely to show up every day, dig in, do the right thing, cook conscientiously, endure without com-plaint: our perennially unrecognized coworkers from Mexico, Ecuador, and points south. The ones you *don't* see hurling around catchphrases on the TV Food Network, or grinning witlessly at the camera after the latest freebie for the Beard House.

What is the heart of the matter? The answer to this simple question: When was the last time you saw an American dish-washer? And if you saw one—would you hire him?

If you're like me, probably not.

The best cooks are ex-dishwashers. Hell, the best *people* are ex-dishwashers. Because who do you want in your kitchen, when push comes to shove, and you're in danger of falling in the weeds and the orders are pouring in and the number-one oven just went down and the host just sat a twelve-top and there's a bad case of the flu that's been tearing through the staff like the Vandals through Rome? Do you want an educated, CIA-trained American know-it-all like I was early in my career? A guy who's going to sulk if you speak harshly to him? A guy who's certain there's a job waiting for him somewhere else ("Maybe . . . like Aspen, man . . . or the Keys . . . I can cook and maybe hit the slopes on my days off, or the beach")? Or some résumé-building aspiring chef ("Yeah, dude . . . I'm thinking of like leaving here next month . . . maybe going to do a *stage* with Thomas Keller or Dean Fearing . . . He *rocks* . . . My uncle has a friend who says he can hook me up . . .")?

Or do you want somebody who's come up the hard way? A guy who has started at the bottom, worked his way up, educated himself, step by step, station by station in the intricacies of *your* particular operation—who knows where everything is, in every corner of your restaurant, who has been shown, again and again until it's implanted in his cell structure, the way *you* want it cooked? He may not know what a *soubise* is, but he can sure make one! He may not know the term *monter au beurre,* or know who Vatel was—but who cares? Vatel punked out over a late fish delivery and offed himself like a bad poet. Somebody had to cover *his* station the next day. Manuel would have shrugged and soldiered on. No shrieking and wailing and rending of garments for Manuel. He's a professional, not some flighty "artist" who can't handle a little pressure.

No disrespect to my alma mater. The CIA is, without question, the finest professional culinary school in the country, maybe the world. It has, in my lifetime, raised the level of performance, the expectation of excellence, to previously unseen heights. To graduate from the CIA—or any other major culinary school—ensures basic, standardized knowledge of history, terminology, and procedures of our trade. A CIA diploma should, and does, mean a lot to potential employers; it represents an accumulation of valuable classroom experience and impeccable standards. But it is no guarantee of character. It speaks nothing of one's heart and soul and willingness to work, to learn, to grow—or one's ability to *endure.*

The Mexican ex-dishwashers usually come from a culture where cooking and family are important. They have, more often than not, a family to provide for, and are used to being responsible for others. They are, more than likely, inured to regimes despotic, ludicrous, and hostile. They've known hardship—*real* hardship. The incongruities, contradictions, and petty injustices of kitchen life are nothing new compared to *la mordida,* wherein every policeman is a potential extortionist, and what was, until recently, a one-party system. You see an expression on the faces of veteran American cooks who've been around the block a few times, had their butts kicked, a look that says, "I expect the worst—and I'm ready for it." The Mexican ex-dishwasher has that look from the get-go.

As I've said many times, I can teach people to cook. I can't teach character. And my comrades from Mexico and Ecuador have been some of the finest characters I've known in twenty-eight years as a cook and as a chef. I am privileged, made better, by having known and worked with many of them. I am honored by their hard work, their toil, and their loyalty. I am enriched by their sense of humor, their music, their food, their not-so-nice names for me behind my back, their kindness, and their strength. They have shown me what real character is. They have made this business—the "Hospitality Industry"—what it is, and they keep its wheels grinding forward.

It was once said that this is the land of the free. There is, I believe, a statue out there in the harbor, with something written on it about "Give me your hungry . . . your oppressed . . . give me pretty much everybody"—that's the way I remember it, anyway. The idea of America is a mutt-culture, isn't it? Who the hell *is* America if not everybody else? We are—and *should* be—a big, messy, anarchistic polyglot of dialects and accents and different skin tones. Like our kitchens. We need *more* Latinos to come here. And they should, whenever possible, impregnate our women.

Lately, things have changed . . . a little. The off-the-books, below-minimum-wage illegal has to some extent disappeared from view, at least in the good restaurants I worked in. The strata of Latino labor has enlarged to include sauté, grill, and even sous-chef positions. But you don't see too many chefs of French or Italian or even "New American" restaurants with a last name like Hernandez or Perez or Garcia. Owners, it seems, still shrink from having a mestizo-looking chef swanning about the dining room of their two- or three-star French eatery—even if the candidate richly deserves the job. Language skills are not the issue. Chances are, Mexicans or Ecuadorans speak English a hell of a lot better than most Americans speak Spanish (or French for that matter). It's . . . well . . . we *know* what it is, don't we?

It's racism, pure and simple.

I'd go on, more than happy to open the *next* can of worms— the How come I don't see many African Americans in good restaurant kitchens? question—but I'll leave that to another, more reasoned advocate, hopefully one with better answers than I have.

What's the number-one complaint from chefs and managers in our industry? I can tell you what I hear in every major city I visit, and I've been visiting a *lot* of them lately: "I'm having a hard time finding good help!"

Solution? Simple: I suggest immediately opening up our borders to unrestricted immigration for all Central and South American countries. If the CIA grads don't want to squat in a cellar prep kitchen for the first couple of years of their career, or are too delicate or high-strung or too locked into a self-image that precludes the real work of kitchens and restaurants, then they should just stand back and watch their competition from south of the border take those jobs away for good. Everyone will end up getting what they deserve. It'll be a wake-up call for the home-team cooks and a boon to our industry—and the right thing to do. Perhaps the CIA should start a farm team in Mexico or Panama, like the Yankee organization. And every Mexican and Ecuadoran line cook in New York should get an immediate raise, amnesty from any immigration charges, a real green card—and the thanks of a grateful nation.

COUNTER CULTURE

FOR A WHILE, I thought it was just me. After years of eating well, in great restaurants, four hours at Alain Ducasse New York now felt like a year with an ugly mob. Sitting there in my high-backed chair, choking in my tie, oppressed by the dark dining room, the relentlessly hushed formality of it all . . . by the time my waiter pushed over the little cart and invited me to choose from a selection of freaking bottled *waters,* unironically describing the sources and attributes of each while I squirmed in agony, I felt ready for my head to explode with frustration. At Charlie Trotter's in Chicago, asking simply where I could find a bathroom, I had my napkin whisked away and was escorted to the bathroom with humiliating ceremony (all the way into the stall—where, as I recall with unease, I was also advised how I might find paper and operate a toilet). By the time the waiter had dutifully replaced the refolded napkin on my lap, surely no one in the dining room was left uninformed as to exactly where I'd been and what I'd had to do. There might as well have been a flourish of trumpets announcing "the customer at table seven has an urgent need for a piss!" While it's okay for Ferrán Adrià to tell me exactly how he wants me to eat each dish ("One bite! All at once!"—he is Ferrán Adrià, after all), some foam- and agar-agar-crazed wannabe in London or Chicago who tries to tell me how to chew my food is gonna get a pepper mill upside his head—if he even allows pepper near the table anymore. I've had it with the pomposity of it all. Restaurants are supposed to

be about the food, aren't they? They're supposed to be . . . well
. . . fun.

Call it a collective yearning, a simultaneous rush of welt-
schmerz, a sense of general exhaustion with the rigors of traditional fine-dining-style service, or simply a growing realization
that the previously de rigeur features of the high-end dining
room are too damned expensive to be practical; but thankfully,
more and more culinary gurus appear to harbor similar instincts
and are moving away from the idea that good food has to be
served in hushed temples of gastronomy. Some of the world's
best chefs, if not always entirely abandoning the churchlike
atmosphere of the Michelin-starred dining room are, at the very
least, successfully exploring other options. I think it's a long
overdue development.

Opening up more accessible, less formal, fashionably downscale outlets than their signature mothership operations(s) is, of
course, nothing new. Alain Ducasse spawned his Spoons for a
presumably less moneyed, more on-the-go crowd looking to
suck up a little reflected glory with their bento boxes. Charlie
Trotter's Trotter To Go enabled those who felt they weren't
paying enough for a potato to fulfill their dreams of haute
takeout. And Wolfgang Puck famously embraced the Beast
entirely, opening a vast empire of airport pizza joints. Jean-
Georges Vongerichten, while maintaining the impeccable Jean-
Georges mothership, has frenetically (and usually successfully)
flirted with a variety of dining styles and themes—everything
from family-style Chinese eaten at communal tables to Singa-
porean street food—without noticeably diminishing the
"brand." Even Thomas Keller has opened a (nonetheless Keller-
ized) bistro in the heart of ugly-shorts capitalist darkness, Las
Vegas.

But the most radical moves have been taken by chefs as far
apart geographically as Paris, New York, Chicago, and Montreal, chef–operators as different in temperament and training as
any could be. What seems to unite them is their willingness—
nay, eagerness—to dispense almost entirely with all they deem

unnecessary to the service of highest-quality food: the extensive glassware, the tablecloths, the expensive silver and floral arrangements, even the *table itself*. In this bold new vision of the way it could—and perhaps should—be, the finest ingredients, prepared by the very best chefs and cooks, are served over a counter, diner style.

It's a revolutionary shift, or more accurately, a reactionary one. Not so much about what chefs want to do as much as about all the things they don't want to do anymore. And the change from black-and-white-penguin-suited tableside service to counter service looks to be an almost entirely chef-led trend, reflective of what chefs themselves like to eat in their few hours away from their own kitchens and, as significantly, where they are eating.

I spend a lot of time in my nearly never-ending bounce around the world eating and drinking with chefs. It seems that in every city I visit, everywhere in the world, whether on a book-flogging tour, while making television shows, or just traveling for fun, I end up too late at night with the local hotshots and their crew, talking shop, talking food, talking about what we all really like to eat—and what we secretly consider to be bullshit. And I listen to what people tell me. I notice what they eat. When we play the "Death Row Game," naming those single dishes or ingredients that we'd choose if given only a few hours to live, as the last taste to ever cross our palates, I take note. Most chefs' choices for last meal are invariably simple. No one *ever* expresses a desire to experience a fourteen course degustation menu (or even any part of one) in an as-yet-unvisited three-star Michelin. Instead, the word *Mom* usually comes up. Bread and butter, steak frites, duck confit, and a bowl of pasta are popular answers. As frequently, the words *Spain* and *sushi* will be heard. More often than not, we're eating sushi or Spanish-style tapas while having this discussion.

It is no coincidence that so many chefs have been visiting Spain lately, only to return with an altered worldview. While most chefs first head off to Spain so that they can experience Ferrán

Adrià's El Bulli, on the Costa Brava, they do have to pass through the rest of Spain to get there. Many return dazzled by the casual Spanish approach to eating: dinner at midnight, the standup snacks at crowded tapas bars, the whole concept of the *poteo*—the multistop bar and food crawl from casual eatery to casual eatery, grazing for what's good, cherry-picking the best at each place ("a little bit, often") before moving on to the next place, and the next. The tiny-bite *pinchos* and unself-conscious approach to the very best ingredients come as both relief and revelation to the jaded chef on vacation. All those nonsensical, show-business aspects of "our thing" seem ever more burdensome, and extraneous, upon return.

And then there's sushi, and the sushi bar. To say that chefs have always been well disposed toward sushi and sashimi would be an understatement. No single development in Western gastronomy has changed our lives as drastically or as well as that first moment when Americans and English-speaking restaurantgoers decided they could let go of their instinctive wariness of raw fish—that sashimi and sushi were cool and desirable and worth paying for. From a marketing standpoint, the spread of sushi lifted all boats for all chefs. Now that there was always a Japanese chef willing to pay twice the going rate for quality seafood, standards shot through the roof. And more importantly, the choices of ingredients we could reliably expect to sell our customers expanded. Customers willing to eat eel, sea urchin, belly tuna, and monkfish liver meant that French and Italian and American chefs could now offer the neglected, nearly forgotten traditional items once almost impossible to sneak onto our menus; we were now free to serve the oily, bony, squiggly, and delicious delights like octopus, mackerel, rouget, and fresh sardines that we had always loved—and that had always been essential parts of our various "mother" cuisines.

Just as importantly, chefs liked to eat sushi. It was a flavor spectrum markedly different from what we were elbow deep in all our working days. Freshness and quality were immediately apparent—just look in the display—and gratifyingly devoid of disguise or extravagant technique. And after a long day dealing with waiters and floor staff, chefs could avoid further contact entirely, ordering the good stuff directly from the sushi chef. Raw fish also gave us a nice, clean, healthy protein buzz that went well with all the liquor we'd likely been swilling and made us feel better about the ravages of our various lifestyle choices.

Over the years, chefs have accumulated many happy experiences at counters. We liked them. We wished we could have one for ourselves. Maybe the earliest, loudest shot across the bow—and the one that caused the widest ripples—was the opening of L'Atelier de Joël Robuchon in Paris. Robuchon, of course, is one of the very best chefs on the planet, one of the French masters, and L'Atelier was, then, a radical departure. The elegant but casual space in Saint-Germain is almost entirely kitchen, with counter space and seats snaking at angles around its perimeters. Black-clad counter "help" act as combination server–sommeliers, clearing and setting, suggesting and pouring wines, and chatting informally with customers, as one would expect at a favorite diner. The precisely plated and delicious food would be perfectly at home in the dining room of a traditional three-star restaurant, but in fact benefits from the more comfortable ambiance. I recently sat alone and had a nine-course menu *découverte* and never felt the awkwardness of the solitary diner. The servers were friendly and talkative, and the usually jaded, seen-it-all Parisians on both sides and across from me were positively effervescing with pleasure, as if recently released from prison. Eating jewel-like fare such as *La Langoustine dans un ravioli truffé au choux vert, Le Cèpe en crème légère sur un oeuf cocotte au persil plat*, and *Cochon de lait en cotelettes dorées* (accompanied by Robuchon's ethereal yet butter-loaded mashed potatoes)—even an ironic tribute to the classic *Le Riz rond*—was a joy. Gone was the stodginess, the ceremony, the invisible straitjacket that usually accompanies a meal like this. Customers felt free to tear at bread from the baskets placed above them on the sushi-style display case and mop sauce with abandon. It felt liberating. I left feeling as if I'd seen the future. (Or at least very much hoping I had.)

I've been a fan of Paul Kahan's Blackbird in Chicago for years. Unlike some of the Second City's other practitioners, the place never seemed full of itself, as much a bar with surprisingly good food as a destination restaurant. With the opening of Avec next door, however, Kahan and his chef de cuisine Koren Grieveson moved into even more customer-friendly territory. The long, honey-colored cedar-walled room holds five communal tables and a long wine bar designed to encourage a "convivial atmosphere." Avec intends (as its name implies) that its impressive collection of wine be "best enjoyed *with* food, *with* friends, *with* company." From a wood-burning oven and single stovetop just across the long counter, an astonishingly good assortment of house-made salamis, artisan cheeses, and large and small plates like slow-roasted pork shoulder, smoked quail, lamb brochette, and whole roasted fish are slapped down by energetic and spectacularly knowledgeable servers who seem positively exuberant in their detailed descriptions of wine, cheese, and cured meat options. It's a great meal—and again, *fun.* As at L'Atelier, you look around and see people smiling, actually talking to each other, nicking food off each other's plates, and having what has been missing from so many moribund and pretentious dining rooms: a good time.

There was a "well, what were you waiting for" feel when Mario Batali and his chef Andy Nusser opened Casa Mono in New York. By now, it seemed entirely right that we needed a place to eat perfectly wonderful small plates of Spanish-style tripes and cockscombs, blood pudding, and cured hams at a bare lunch counter. Great ingredients done right, by cooks standing a few inches away. Order a lot and dig in. That Mario himself is often to be seen happily picking from plates with his fingers sets an inspiring tone.

But the boldest, wackiest, most reactionary of the defectors to casual counter-style services has to be Montreal's enfant terrible, Martin Picard. At the crowded, chaotic, and giddily retro Au Pied de Cochon, he's stood everything on its head. The one-time chef of the city's "best restaurant," the more twee and traditional "big plate/little serving/cappuccino of whatever" Toqué, Picard broke entirely from his precious, haute roots and opened a rude, crude, over-the-top fabulous ode to excess, specializing in insanely mammoth portions of Québecois sugar-shack-style indulgence. You know from the very beginning what you are in for: Bar snacks are *oreilles de crisses*, ear-shaped tidbits of fried pork rind. Picard himself, usually unshaven—looking more lumberjack than chef—is to be found, usually in food-stained T-shirt, presiding over the madness by a roaring wood-burning oven. Dino-sized plates of pot-au-feu (a whole game bird, four marrow bones, stacked with *boudin noir* and foie gras), cassoulet, pig's-foot stew, duck "in the can" (a half duck breast, foie gras, and cabbage, slow cooked in a can and poured over a crouton topped with celeriac purée), and *poutine*—the Picard version of the classic Quebec guilty-pleasure fave of *frites* drowning in demi-glace and cheese curds, topped with a thick slab of melting foie gras—all are prepared in front of you by Picard's fellow transgressors, a crew of T-shirted and funny-hat-wearing cooks with similarly impressive résumés. There are a few tables, stuffed between wall and counter, but the fun is to be had watching the dedicated but underdressed cooks in the crowded, nearly unworkable-looking open kitchen, gleefully lopping slabs of foie and throwing them around like cheap shortening. The signature dish of stuffed pig's trotters is exactly that: two enormous pig's feet, absolutely jammed with foie gras and sauced with a rich onion cream sauce.

It's too much. It's too loud. The kitchen looks like a train wreck. The portions are crippling. You won't want to think about foie gras for weeks after eating there. And it's an absolute joy to experience. Everyone—from customers, to cooks, to service staff, to the chef—seems happy to be there. The cooks will tell you so themselves, as they race to fill orders from postage-stamp-size work spaces, elbowing each other to get at one of the endlessly refilled crocks of mashed potatoes. There's no "attitude." It's about food—and company—and the enjoyment of both. It may well be the antidote to every other restaurant in North America.

A LIFE OF CRIME

"Why didn't you give him a beatin' then?"
"Well, 'cause . . . uh . . ."
"I told ya. Forget this other shit. Give him a fuckin' beatin'."
"Well, the uh . . . I was waiting to hear from you."
"I told you yesterday . . . What are you, Chinese? Hit him.
This guy's nobody, and if he's somebody, I don't give a fuck."
—John Gotti, former Gambino crime family boss,
discussing debt restructuring with an associate

I LOVE READING ABOUT crime. I like *writing* about crime. I like listening to wiretap recordings of gangsters, hearing the marvelously loopy, repetitive, elliptical, and wildly profane patois of two semiarticulate career criminals who think they just *might* be being recorded by the FBI, but have business to conduct anyway. It's poetry to me.

In my apartment, CourtTV, the twenty-four-hour criminal justice cable network, is always on; the sounds of badly miked witnesses, recorded emergency calls, droning coroners, and preening lawyers are the background music to my leisure hours. While I sip my morning coffee in bed, friends are betraying friends on the stand, pathologists coldly recite the particulars of damage to bones and tissue, stone killers affectlessly describe the circumstances leading up to murder, dismemberment, arson . . . and worse. Lawyers aggressively examine and cross-examine, shrieking with feigned outrage, while outside my windows, car

55

alarms whoop and wail—the occasional urban percussion of shattering safety glass when yet another young entrepreneur makes off with a car stereo. It's like jazz to me, and I miss it when I'm away. The familiar criminal sounds are almost comforting.

A lot of crime buffs favor the lone sociopath, the serial killer, the pathological narcissist. They like maladjusted teens who listen to Metallica, shave their heads, and then go on killing sprees, or former bed wetters who kill their mothers, then describe how they could still hear Mom's voice, chastising them as they flushed her vocal cords down the food disposal. They thrive on the special little moments in criminal trials when, for instance, the best friend of this month's latest juvenile mass-murderer balks at admitting on the stand that he saw his buddy cry—this just after cheerfully implicating him in the slaughter of ten of his classmates:

> Lawyer: *So, after emptying his weapon, am I to understand that Mr. Sprewell adorned his person with the blood of his victims? Is that correct?*
> Witness: *Huh?*
> Lawyer: *His face . . . he put blood on his face after killing them?*
> Witness: *Oh, yeah. He, like smeared blood on his cheeks . . . like an Indian, you know? Stripes like. He said it looked cool.*
> Lawyer: *And later . . . after you say you both went back to the defendant's home to play video games and kill his parents . . . did the defendant at any point cry?*
> Witness: *Cry? I don't know . . . I don't know if he like . . . cried. He was . . . you know . . . upset.*

Me? I'm bored by the lone nut and the sexual psychopath. I don't care to what degree Metallica recordings played a role in young Timmy's transition from honor student to thrill killer. I don't care "who dunnit" . . . or even "why he dunnit," and my tastes in crime fiction reflect that attitude: I'm interested in professional criminals. I'm interested in crimes where you know from the get-go *why* they did it: because it was *their job* to do it. As in the case of the mob-style execution of Gambino capo Paul Castellano, shot to death out front of a popular Midtown restaurant, it's the little things I want to know about: Before the killers loaded their weapons and dressed themselves in identical raincoats and hats, before they set out separately from their modest family homes in Staten Island and Queens, did the killers kiss their children, jot down brief shopping lists of groceries to bring back on their return? (One box Cheerios . . . half gallon milk . . . dozen eggs . . . tampons, large . . . two cans tuna, chunk style.) Did their voices tighten at all at the breakfast table when they told their wives that they might be a little late tonight? Did they program the VCR to tape their favorite sitcom? And what sitcom was it? It's the jargon of crime—the characters, the rituals, the workaday details—that fascinate me.

Crime is hard work, after all.

As a red-blooded American child, I always wanted to be a criminal. My heroes, like those of so many American children, were an unlovely assortment of back-shooters like Billy the Kid, bank robbers like John Dillinger, racketeers like Legs Diamond, capitalist visionaries like Bugsy Siegel, and innovators like Lucky Luciano. These were guys who did what they wanted, *when* they wanted, said whatever the fuck they felt like saying, and, in general, avoided the restrictions of societal convention—attractive qualities to a young kid weaned on the MC5 and the Stooges. Later, when I actually *became* a criminal of sorts, trying to support myself through a variety of harebrained drug-dealing schemes, sneak thievery, petty burglary, and fraud, I found to my dismay that a life of crime was difficult and unglamorous. It required that most dreaded trait, discipline, as well as a closed mouth and a lot of downtime, where money was going out and none was coming in. My coconspirators at the time were an unreliable lot, either talking too much or making dangerously stupid improvisations on our carefully hatched plans, and in my case, anyway, our few ventures into felonious activity were—at the end of the day—decidedly unprofitable.

Which is how I became a chef.

But that's another story.

Suffice it to say, when I finally buckled down to a life of legitimate toil in the restaurant business, I began to meet some *real* criminals, guys connected to organized crime, and I recognized right away that while *they,* apparently, had what it took to live a life outside the law, *I* did not. And I was curious about the differences between myself and these full-timers. What remained with me from my early, heady days of surreptitious entry was the love of conspiracy, an appreciation of clandestine meetings, the comfortably familiar phrase book, long ago codified and set down in Hollywood films, of the hard-core, professional bad man. La Cosa Nostra and, to a lesser extent, espionage, became obsessions. I wanted to know, for instance, how Kim Philby kept his mouth shut for all those years. How could a kid in his early twenties, still in college, keep quiet about his true loyalties? Especially when he was doing something as exciting as spying for the NKVD? How could he *not,* after a few beers, blab to his friends about his secret work for the Workers' Paradise—especially when he'd been loudly espousing unpopular political views to all and sundry? How could young Kim *never,* while trying to bed some breasty Marxist sophomore, have boozily confided that, "All this right-wing twaddle is a *sham* baby . . . I'm down with the International, bitch . . . and doing some serious motherfucking undercover shit! Now take off those panties!"

Guys who wake up every morning, brush their teeth, shower, shave, then go to work at the serious business of committing felonies, these are the characters who continue to dominate my reverie—and my fiction. Bank robbers, spies, enforcers, contract killers, loan sharks, confidence men, and racketeers . . . it's their consistency over time, their relentless adherence to the requirements of the job, that makes me, in my way, love them. Take a guy like Vincent "The Chin" Gigante, the former boss of the

Genovese crime family, who I used as an inspiration for a character in *Bone in the Throat*. Here's a guy who, for *thirty years,* played the public role of a doddering, schizophrenic old man, appearing on the street for walk-talks with his soldiers in bathrobe and slippers, talking to himself, behaving erratically, moving his eyes and head in such a way as to indicate insanity—and all the while was running with an iron grip the largest and most ruthless criminal enterprise in the country. This crazy act kept him out of jail for most of his life—though the Feds did catch up with him in the end. You have to admire that kind of work ethic. They never caught The Chin on tape, telling a subordinate to "whack somebody out" or "put a rocket in his pocket." You never heard The Chin's voice playing over the courthouse speakers, talking about how he was going to "sever [somebody's] motherfuckin' head off" (one of my favorite Gotti-isms). The Chin played his part to the end.

Gotti, to his detriment, surrounded himself with those other fascinating creatures of the criminal netherworld: informers. Listening to recordings of the embattled don in his Little Italy social club, berating his crew, bemoaning his gambling losses, contemplating the machinations and intentions of his rivals, there's a poignancy to the experience: Not only was the poor bastard being secretly recorded by the FBI, but sometimes three out of four of the close associates in the room with him were, or later became, government informants. It's hard these days, it seems, to get good help.

So for purposes of fiction, organized criminality offers plenty of drama, plenty of situations in which characters find themselves in extreme circumstances with presumably difficult choices to make: Should I shoot my best friend today? What happens if I don't? Can I trust Paulie? After I kill him, when his kids come over to play with my kids, what should I tell them about Daddy's disappearance? Should I cooperate with the prosecutors? Can I survive the rest of my life eating jail food? These are the Big Questions in my kind of crime fiction.

And of course, crime can be funny.

The line between crime fiction and real-life crime becomes fuzzy, often hilariously so. All the real gangsters have *seen The Godfather*, One, Two, and maybe Three. They've *seen Goodfellas*. And these films made a powerful impression. Recently I visited my favorite Web site, gangland.com—an online repository for up-to-date organized crime arcana—to find a transcript of New Jersey's De Cavalcante crime family members enthusiastically speculating on which among their number had provided inspiration for the Tony Soprano character on *The Sopranos*. Real-life gangster "Crazy Joe" Gallo, prior to falling down dead into his linguine with white clam sauce, is said to have practiced his Tommy Udo imitation in front of the mirror every morning. (You remember Tommy, the Richard Widmark character in *Kiss of Death*? The famous scene in which the giggling Widmark binds and gags an old lady into her wheelchair, then pushes her down a flight of stairs? "Heee-heee . . . heee . . . heeee"?) And there *must* be scores of aspiring Joe Pescis out there, taking the occasional break from the daily grind of extortion and murder to do dead-on impressions of Joe: "What? I *amuse* you? I'm a clown?"

There is a powerful element of pure comedy, of classic *schtick* in the business of crime. With so many natural wordsmiths, mimics, movie fans, and practitioners of a century-old oral tradition, is it any wonder? And as Monty Python so astutely demonstrated many years ago, the basic elements of comedy *all* come down to the unexpected head injury, repeated blunt-force trauma to the skull. Whether it's Oliver Hardy getting a good smack upside the nut with a mishandled ladder, or a Colombo loanshark getting his brains spattered all over the dashboard of his shiny new Buick, the principle is the same—and it spells *funny*.

Joe Pesci, thinking that today he's gonna be a "made guy," looks down at the floor, sees that the carpet has been rolled up—and has time only to say, "*Oh shit!*" before getting two behind his ear. Classic! Just like Oliver Hardy *should* know that a ladder will soon be bouncing off his face—because it bounced

off his face in the scene before, and in the scene before that—
Pesci's character *should* know that when a close personal friend
invites you to a sit-down with the bosses, or says that *you* can
have the front passenger seat ("That's okay . . . *you* sit in
front"), there's every likelihood that a fatal head injury is
imminent. There's a historic inevitability to both comedy and
organized crime, and the punch lines are often the same.

Times, sadly, are changing. Traditional criminal groups like
New York's Cosa Nostra, Boston's Winter Hill Gang, Chicago's
Outfit are being replaced by newer and less amusing stylists,
clever mobs of ruthless Russians, Serbs, Israelis, Asians, Jamai-
cans, Colombians, and Nigerians whose appreciation of the
classics seems lacking. Their crimes, for the most part, are so
sophisticated and so *boring* that simply reading about them
induces coma. Notoriously close-mouthed, even by professional
standards, these recent arrivals to America's shores are less likely
to provide the kind of recorded admissions that thinned the
ranks of their predecessors and entertained generations of readers and moviegoers. Some of these guys, I don't even know if
they've seen *The Godfather*—much less *Mean Streets* or *Goodfellas*! I doubt sincerely whether they will honor the tradition of
amusing movie audiences.

The bad guys of the future will probably look and sound and
act more like Bill Gates than "Fat Tony" Salerno . . . and the
world will be a bleaker place for it. No more "Gentleman
Jimmy" Burkes hijacking loads out of Kennedy airport. Tomorrow's criminals will simply move tiny blips from place to place
on their computer screens, theoretical felonies that take place
somewhere in the ether. Monies from the Bank of Smerzsk will
somehow find their way to another account in the Grand Cay-
mans, or to a shell corporation in the former Soviet Republic of
Torporistan. And the man who presses the "enter" key will have
all the seething menace and dangerous charisma of a certified
public accountant.

So I'm looking elsewhere these days. Crips, Bloods, La "M," the
Aryan Brotherhood, El Rukn—they just don't do it for me. They

kill like sharks, as remorselessly and predictably, for reasons as silly as choice sneakers. Our secret services, particularly the CIA, have such a long history of incompetence at the manly arts of assassination—and as organizations have come to resemble nothing more than Midwestern cow colleges—that there's little hope of returning to the fun-filled days of pragmatic killers, ideologically driven cold warriors, and Yalie pranksters. While the Israeli Mossad still provides the occasional item of interest (I particularly enjoyed the exploding cell-phone gag!), recent developments do not bode well for the future. The remnants of the KGB seem too preoccupied with stealing the silver and pilfering what's left of their former empire to actually whack anybody, so there's no help there either. As the modern-day ranks of the Five Families increasingly emerge from the shallow end of the gene pool, we see fewer and fewer instinctive funnymen like Gotti or Sammy Gravano (or even that kooky, kuh-razy Brit comedy duo, the Kray twins), and it gets harder and harder to imagine a modern-day Cosa Nostra killer with the wit, charm, and cold competence of *The Godfather*'s Clemenza, instructing his accomplice after murdering an incompetent and possibly treacherous coworker, "Leave the gun. Take the cannolis."

As John Gotti said, complaining (on tape, naturally), about people talking too much:

> *From now on, I'm telling you that if a guy just so mentions "La," and he goes . . . I heard nine months of tapes of my life (in court). I was actually sick and I don't wanna get sick. Not sick for me, sick for "this thing of ours," sick how naïve we were five years ago. I'm sick we were so fucking naïve.*

I empathize with John. His underboss, Sammy, to whom he made the above comments, turned cooperating witness and put John in the can for life without. The government generously rewarded Sammy by forgiving him his part in *nineteen* brutal murders, a small price to pay for his testimony and for a very revealing, very funny book.

For a while, I had an ex-mobster friend named Joe "Dogs," who after his best pal tried to kill him, also became a government witness. He called from time to time, late at night, wanting to talk about nothing in particular: the city, restaurants he used to be able to go to. He liked to gossip about recent arrests of old friends, wonder aloud about book deals—as he too has a second career as a writer. I think it's the New York accent he missed most, that he couldn't talk with anyone where he was now the way he used to talk when he was a functionary for the Gambinos. He missed the good old days.

I know how he felt.

ADVANCED COURSES

I HAVEN'T SEEN MUCH of America. I don't know much about my own country, but I'm learning fast. In between the airports, minibars, and newsrooms, the hideous sprawl of industrial parks, chain hotels, and generic food that make up the thirty-city journeys I've been on to promote my books, I've begun to glimpse the America they once wrote sappy songs about: the purple mountains, twisting rivers, mill towns, wheat fields, and wide open spaces. And I've met a lot of cooks.

They come to readings in their civilian clothes, but I know them from their faces—the gaunt, haunted, thousand-yard stares, the burns on their forearms, the pink and swollen hands, the way they hold themselves in that permanent defensive crouch. The look that says, "Expect the worst and you'll never be disappointed." In those faces there's pain, hope, and a deep appreciation for irony. And when they take me, as they often do, to eat and drink and drink some more, to talk about the thing we do, there are inevitably a few who distinguish themselves, a vanguard who wants to hear of chefs and cooks in other cities and what they're "selling." They want to know how far they can go. What's next? When will it happen?

"Monkfish liver! Can you sell them? How many people order them?" one will say. "I herda them," says another. "The fucking burger . . ." groans another, "I can't get it off the menu. I tried, but they scream." "Give them the damn burger," says another, "and fucking salmon if they want it too. Just slip them the good stuff slowly, when they're not looking. A little here, a little there, as a special. Choke them with burgers but slide them tuna rare. Give them their salmon, but make it ceviche. They'll come around. They're coming around."

In Milwaukee, where cooks complain of monstrous portions and demands for steak fries, one chef features an item called "Something Strange But Good" on his menu, sneaking a little something new to his regulars. The sirloin has already been replaced by onglet. The fish is being served rarer every week. It's a beginning. All over the heartland, lamb chops become lamb shanks. Calves' liver and onions give way to sweetbreads and tongue. Throughout the Midwest, foie gras is spreading all over the menu in mousses, *torchons*, in seared *amuse-gueules* given away free, readying customers for the sucker-punches of foie gras "cappuccinos" and "foams" to follow.

In Iowa City, they talk of "slow food," regional products, artisanal cheeses from nearby Wisconsin, local venison, wild duck, and range-free pork and lamb and beef. In Madison, chefs and cooks apologize when they tell me where they're working, places with predictable names and predictably grim menus, but they're all near hopping with enthusiasm, waiting for their chance.

In Kansas City, along with the high-end, white-tablecloth joints, they're still passionate about their barbecues. No two locals seem to agree on which place is best, whether sweeter or spicier is better, and they can discuss the subtle differences in style and flavor as it moves out from the city center to the suburbs. (Spicy in the center, sweeter as it moves farther afield.) Digging into ribs, chopped brisket, pulled pork, spicy slaw, and baked beans at Oklahoma Joe's (an unassuming cafeterialike space situated in a combination gas station–convenience store), I enjoy the most tender, inspiring barbecue I've ever experienced: greasy, sticky, served on plastic trays between slices of white bread. It's a revelation.

In Saint Louis, a goateed chef with a mountain drawl tells me he's thrown out his salamander grill and microwave. "Won't

have any a' that cheatin' in my kitchen. Nope. Won't have it."
He nearly tears up at the thought of cutting into a hunk of lamb
or duck before it's rested.

There's a curiosity about new food among the public, even
when it's coupled with apprehension. "Saw you eatin' that snake
heart on the TV. How'd that taste? That pho stuff didn't look
half bad, though, I gotta say." And they can find pho themselves,
because everywhere I go are Vietnamese restaurants; Thai,
Hmong, and Chinese markets; families of émigrés operating
small businesses, many looking and tasting just like the ones
back home. There are Mongolian, Japanese, Korean, Indian,
and Pakistani joints popping up everywhere. America's cool, if
you look hard enough, if you wander far enough from the strip
malls and theme restaurants and Starbucks and Mickey D's.
Things have changed. Things are different now. Every day.

SWEET

NAME DROPPING DOWN UNDER

HOLY SHIT, AINSLEY HARRIOTT is fucking huge!

I'm in Sydney, Australia, drinking vodka at Fix, the bar behind Luke Mangan's restaurant, Salt, when I look over and see Ainsley, whom I've said some very nasty things about in print (meant every damn word too), and realize that this guy, towering over the crowd, could—should he be so inclined—probably kick my ass. Watching him on TV, cudding housewives and doing the cooing, squealing Jerry Lewis schtick, I figured the guy had to be a shrimp. I figured a guy that flouncy wasn't the sort to maybe see me in a bar someday, reach down, smash a beer bottle against the wall, and then grind it into my neck. Now I'm not so sure. Jesus he's big! His shoulders are the size of basketballs . . . Maybe I should start worrying about Jamie Oliver too. Haven't been so nice to him either. He could be studying some lethal form of martial art; he's already got a fucking paramilitary, I heard. "Oliver's Army?" What is that? Are they like Saddam's Republican Guard? Do they do Oliver's bidding, up to and including eliminating his enemies? Is some glassy-eyed acolyte with a faux cockney accent gonna drive by on a Vespa and let loose with a full clip from a Tec-9? I'd really better think about this.

Fortunately, the evening progresses without senseless butchery. Ainsley even sits down at the same table briefly, gives me a friendly smile and a knowing tap at a copy of my book—which either means he has the forgiving nature of a saint, or I simply haven't been nearly enough of a shit. Rick Stein, the very likable celebrity chef, restaurateur, and serial pyromaniac, sits across from me. Rick is apparently on a mission to burn down Australia, one cooking demo at a time. No television chef is as charming when confronted by sudden, unexpected columns of smoke or flames leaping from a pan. I like Rick. He's a veteran like me, a chef with book deals and a television show, and over drinks we pondered the mysteries—as I often do with other chefs—of the "celebrity chef" phenomenon, both of us feeling maybe a little bit guilty about traveling around staying in hotels for free, while our comrades of old still sweat and strain day after day in the infernos of real kitchens, making real food, for real customers. Is it a good thing? Why now? What does it all mean?

First of all, what is a "celebrity chef"? Well, it's a celebrity—meaning well known, bordering on famous—who is, or was at one time, a chef. This definition would exclude amateurs, neophyte cooks, and sous-chefs plucked off the chorus line by TV producers and elevated through the magic of television to "chef" status. If you're a comely young fry cook with an adorably boyish forelock and you get yanked into a TV studio, given the moniker of, say, the Adenoidal Chef, and suddenly housewives in seventeen countries are squirming in their caftans while you make green curry, that doesn't make you a chef. After fame comes, if someone is silly enough to build a restaurant around your stupid, well-known mug, good for you. It still don't make you a chef. Britney Spears has a restaurant built around her persona and image. That doesn't make her a chef.

Why now, though? What the hell happened? What is wrong (or right) with society that even a son of a bitch like me gets a damn TV show? Why do people even care about chefs? What changed? When I started cooking back in the seventies, the prospect of it becoming a glamour profession was laughable in the extreme. Cooking was something you did between other jobs; it was the last refuge for scoundrels, misfits, and tormented loners. Full-time employees of the "Hospitality Industry" did not enjoy high status or require the services of publicists, voice coaches, elocution tutors, dermatologists, and hair stylists. They required only free liquor, as much food as they could pilfer, a few shekels at the end of the week, and maybe the occasional blow job from a sympathetic waitress. Now, my fry cook is pestering me all the time. He wants to know when he gets his "wide-screen TV, bitches and ho's." He's saving up for his own publicist—as soon as he learns to speak English.

Maybe people just aren't fucking enough. There was a definite upsurge in the fortunes of chefs with the early eighties discovery that indiscriminate sexual activity can kill you. Certainly people seem to be eating more—evidence, perhaps, of sublimated desire. As chefs rushed to acquire basic communication and diplomatic skills, thighs expanded in seemingly direct proportion. "Food porn" began to take hold around the world: buyers of lavishly photographed, expensively bound cookbooks gaped longingly at pictures of people doing things on paper, or on television, that they would probably never try themselves at home. Are celebrity chefs seen as safer, nonthreatening alternatives to, say, rock and rollers, or porn stars of the past? Given the choice between having that cute, perky Jamie Oliver in your kitchen or Tommy Lee, Jamie's presence would seem less likely to lead to penetration or the theft of prescription drugs.

But that can't be all, right? Maybe Rick Stein—and Nigella Lawson, for that matter—appeal to some other need, some deeper emptiness in our collective souls. Rick can honestly be called a celebrity chef. He's put in his time in professional kitchens. Like me, he's getting a little old to put in fourteen-hour shifts every day in a hot à la carte kitchen. Celebrity chefdom can be a pretty nice score, an appropriate payoff for years of toil and uncertainty. Nigella is a celebrity, no question about that, but is she a chef? Of course not. Which is fine. Her show is about eating well, not so much about cooking—about the good stuff, like pork fat and pork skin, becoming approachable, even fun. But Rick Stein and Ms. Lawson share a common and profound appeal, I think. If you're like millions and millions of others of generations X and Y, or a lingering boomer, maybe you left home for school or work when you turned eighteen, ran away to the big city, Mom and Dad an embarrassing reminder of childhood whom you occasionally phone up on holidays. As you sit in your lonely apartment, you feel a yearning, a longing for a sense of family, of belonging. Disconnected as you are from roots you still feel ambivalent about, those big family meals in movies are looking strangely good. A vestigial "nesting" impulse takes hold and you find yourself watching Rick or Nigella, thinking, "Gee, I wish he were my older brother, or dad, and he was cooking for me." Or "I wish Nigella were my sister, or mom, cooking me that slow-roasted ham. I wish that leftover scrap of pork she's nibbling on in the middle of the night were in my refrigerator."

Let's face it: Nigella probably cooks better than your mother. And she's a lot better looking, and cooler. Nigella wouldn't mind if you smoked weed in your bedroom before dinner, would she? She wouldn't criticize you if you came home with your nose pierced and a fierce, full-back tattoo depicting Saint Peter and Dee Dee Ramone shoveling coal down the crack of your ass. Of course not. She'd say, "Remember to clean that nose with alcohol—and wash your hands for dinner! We're having roast suckling pig with quince chutney."

So maybe the celebrity chef racket isn't all bad. Even Jamie Oliver at his most frenzied and annoying is probably, on balance, a force for good. The celeb chef thing, at its best, entices the unknowing, the fearful, the curious to eat a little better, maybe cook once in a while. And it provides much-needed late-career lucre for older, broken-down, burned-out chefs like, well . . . me.

Of all the food-crazy countries in the English-speaking world, Australia is perhaps the most rabidly enthusiastic. It's the Gold Rush for chefs Down Under. In Melbourne, chefs like Paul Wilson of Radii, Raymond Capaldi of Fenix, and Donovan Cooke of Ondine walk down the street after work like frontier-era gunslingers. There are chef-friendly drinking establishments that cater to the needs (and the propensity for bad behavior) of the alcohol-starved late-night chef posse. And all anyone wants to talk about is food and restaurants. Restaurants open and close, chefs bounce from place to place like Manhattan at its most capricious. Both Melbourne and Sydney boast scores of terrific restaurants, and everyone knows the names of their chefs. Chefs are like sports stars here: Everyone knows their stats, the teams they played on in the past. Tetsuya Wakuda, whose cookbook has—along with the *French Laundry Cookbook*—been considered prime "chef porn," meaning books that we professional chefs take to bed with a flashlight in our lonelier moments, is generally considered to run the best restaurant in Australia. His kitchen cranks out an absolutely amazing, jewel-like degustation menu that has to be experienced to be believed. Tetsuya, though shy and very serious, is more than ready for his media moment. It's only a matter of time before they get their hooks in him.

On the other hand, you've got Donovan Cooke, a chef from Hull, England, who can trace his culinary credentials back to early Marco Pierre White days. His Ondine in Melbourne is easily one of the best going; his tuna à la ficelle with horseradish cream, oxtail ravioli, fennel, and oxtail broth (a playful take on the beef classic) is one of the best goddamn things I've ever eaten in a restaurant. But it's very hard to picture Donovan with his own television show. While his contemporaries took elocution lessons and learned front-of-the-house survival skills, Donovan kept his thick accent, bounced around Michelin-starred restaurants in France (his French is an amazing thing to hear, believe me), and peppers his sentences with the real language of chefs and cooks. He cooks like a Michelin-starred Frenchman and looks like a football hooligan. When I dropped in on him unannounced, he was standing behind a busy stove, cranking out meals, personally working the sauté station. He is absolutely obsessed with flavor—and sauce making in particular—and seems to want to talk about nothing more than the nuts and bolts of emulsion, reduction, fortification . . . all in delightfully non-TV-friendly terms: "You reduce the fucking jus, right? And

you don't bloody skim it. You emulsify the fucking fat right in—
at the last second. If the sauce breaks? What do you mean if the
sauce breaks? If the sauce breaks—you're a fucking cunt."

That's a celebrity chef I want to see on TV.

MY MANHATTAN

I'M A NEW YORKER, so it should come as no surprise that I think my city is the greatest city in the world. I like living in the city where so many of my favorite films take place, where nearly every street corner reminds me of some piece of lurid personal or criminal history. "Crazy Joe Gallo was shot here . . . Big Paul Castellano got whacked there . . . Used to score there . . . That place used to be a speakeasy . . . My old methadone clinic . . . That used to be an after-hours club . . ." It may not be the most beautiful city. It's not the nicest city (though it is, sadly, getting nicer). And it's certainly not the easiest city to live in. One minute you're on top of the world, and the next—like when you wish to light up a smoke at a bar and can't—you're wallowing in misery and self-pity, unable to decide between murder and suicide. But it is exactly those famously manic highs and lows that make New York, and Manhattan in particular, like nowhere else. I mean, you can talk London or Paris or Barcelona all you like, but we're open all night: I can pick up the phone around midnight and get just about anything I want delivered to my apartment: Chinese food, Lebanese, sushi, pizza, a video, a bag of seedless hydro, a human head.

I think I know what I'm talking about here. I've been other places. I travel a lot—about eight months out of the year. And while I love London, Edinburgh, Dublin, Melbourne, Hanoi, Salvador, Saint Petersburg, Tokyo, and Saint Sebastian like old friends, I miss my city when I'm away too long. As much as I enjoy getting lost, disappearing into another place, another culture, another cuisine, there are places and flavors, sounds, smells, and sights I begin to yearn for after three or four weeks eating fish heads and rice.

When people from other cities, planning a trip to New York (or *the* city, as we locals are apt to call it), ask me where they should eat, where they should go, where they should drink during their stay, they are often surprised at my answers. Sure, we have some of the best high-end restaurants in the world here, but that's not what I miss when I'm wiping fermented bean paste off my chin, or trading shots of bear-bile-infused rice whiskey in Asia. When visiting Manhattan one should go for things that *we* do really well and the rest of the world doesn't.

Example? Deli. We have it; you don't. Even Los Angeles, with no shortage of Jews, can't get it right. For whatever mysterious reasons, no city on the planet can make deli like New York deli and the first thing I start to miss when away from home too long is breakfast at Barney Greengrass, The Sturgeon King, on Amsterdam Avenue and Eighty-sixth Street. Sunday breakfast at Barney's is one of those quintessential New York things to do: a crowded, ugly dining room, unchanged for decades; wobbly tables; brusque waiters; generic coffee. But their eggs scrambled with dark, caramelized onions and lox, served with a fresh toasted bagel or bialy, are ethereal, and the home-team crowd of Upper West Siders is about as "genuine New York" as you can get. Grab a copy of the Sunday *New York Times* and a copy of the *Post*, and dig in. If your waiter seems indifferent, don't let it bother you—he's like that with everybody. You can buy some of the legendary smoked sturgeon or Nova Scotia salmon at the counter to take away, but you will surely be committing a sin against God if, after breakfast, you neglect to purchase a pound of what is far and away the best chopped liver on earth. Hand-chopped chicken livers, schmaltz (chicken fat), sautéed onions, and hard-cooked eggs . . . it's the benchmark to which all others should aspire.

No visit to New York is complete without a proper pastrami

sandwich, and New Yorkers will argue over who's got the best like they're fighting over Bosnian real estate. But a safe bet is Katz's Deli on East Houston for a nearly-as-big-as-your-head pile of steaming hot pastrami, sliced paper thin and stacked between fresh seeded rye bread. The appropriate beverage is a Dr. Brown's cream soda or Cel-Ray. And be nice to your waitress; chances are she can kick the shit out of you.

Pizza is another subject on which New Yorkers have strong opinions. If you feel like humping out to Brooklyn, to Di Fara's, you can get the best of the best. But I like the white clam pizza at Lombardi's on Spring Street, when I don't feel like getting my passport punched for a pie. They serve only whole pies at Lombardi's, so if you want to master the manly New York art of walking down the street while eating a slice of pizza, you'll have to grab one at any of the ubiquitous mainstream joints. Just remember: feet slightly apart, head tilted forward and away from chest to avoid the bright orange pizza grease that will undoubtedly dribble down. Be aware of the risk of hot, molten "cheese slide," which has been known to cause facial injury and genital scarring.

Everybody has seen Central Park on television, and yes, it is dramatic and beautiful, but I love Riverside Park, which runs right along the Hudson River from Seventy-second Street up to Grant's Tomb. On weekends during warm months, there's a large Dominican and Puerto Rican presence, huge picnics with radios blaring salsa and soca music, large groups of family and friends playing basketball, volleyball, and softball while slow-moving barges and tankers scud by on the river.

Speaking of sports, the West Fourth Street basketball courts on lower Sixth Avenue host some of the best nonprofessional, street basketball in the world. Professionals have been known to drop by—and they get a game, much of it elbows and shoulders. A large crowd rings the outer fence three and four deep to watch some of the city's most legendary street players.

When I've been home for a while and I need to treat myself to an expensive spirit-lifting experience, I always think sushi. And

Yasuda on East Forty-third Street is the place to go for old-school Edo-style sushi and sashimi, the fish served—as it should be—near room temperature, the rice still warm and crumbly. I always book the *omakase* (the tasting menu, literally, "you decide") on a day when Yasuda serves up sublime, tasty bits of screamingly fresh, rare, hard-to-get, flawlessly executed seafood. I can spend a whole afternoon there, eating whatever comes my way, working my way through every available option: mounds of sea urchin roe; top-drawer fatty otoro tuna; sea eel; yellowtail; mackerel—and the occasional surprise. On a recent visit I was served some Copper River salmon roe, before season, from the chef's personal stash. If I find myself in the neighborhood late at night, just across the street, through an anonymous office building lobby, down a flight of fire stairs to a cellar and through a plain door, is Sakagura, a huge, nearly all-Asian late-night joint with a mammoth selection of sakes and accompanying snacks. Guaranteed to inspire exclamations of "How did you find this place?!" among your envious friends.

Sneer at hot dogs all you want. A well-made wiener is a thing of beauty. Actually, even a bad hot dog can be a beautiful thing—if you're eating it at Yankee Stadium washed down with a warm, watery beer (as long as the Yanks are winning). I'll go so far as to say you will never understand New York, or New Yorkers, until you've eaten too many bad hot dogs and drunk too much cheap beer at a night game at the stadium. Similarly, Rudy's Bar on Ninth Avenue serves terrible hot dogs too. Free ones. But ambiance counts for a lot, and after plenty of mid-afternoon drinks (never go at night) listening to their magnificent jukebox, watching the daytime drinkers slump over onto the bar, those lightbulb-warmed weenies suddenly seem like a good idea. If you want a quality hot dog, however, the best by consensus is at the legendary Papaya King on East Eighty-sixth Street. Be sure to enjoy your dog with their frothy delicious papaya drink—and if you put ketchup on your dog I will fucking kill you.

New York's subway system is certainly not among the best in

the world, and I miss the full-length graffiti pieces, the tribal markings that once made the cars so menacing and evocative of classic New York films like *Death Wish*. But I still love the people-watching late at night on the Number 9 or A train. The sound of people talking, that gorgeous, jazzlike mix of Brooklynese, Spanglish, Noo Yawk; the hard faces New Yorkers put on like masks to get through the day. There are, once in a great while, magical moments, when united by a shared laugh or outrage, passengers will let the veil drop and actually acknowledge each other with a sardonic smile, a shaken head, a caustic remark—or like one time, when a deranged drunk was harassing a tired-looking woman and the entire car rose up and chased him off the train, a momentary united front.

For late-night bad behavior, I am a devoted regular at Siberia Bar, located on Fortieth Street in Hell's Kitchen, a few doors east of Ninth Avenue. There's no sign. Just look for the unmarked black doors under the single red lightbulb—and leave your conscience at the door. If Satan had a rumpus room, it would look a lot like Siberia: squalid, dark, littered with empty beer cartons, the ratty furniture stained with the bodily fluids of many guilty souls. It's my favorite bar on earth; it has a great jukebox of obscure mid-seventies punk classics, and no matter how badly you behave at night, no one will remember the next day. The crowd is dodgy and unpredictable. You never know who's going to be draped over couches upstairs, or listening to live bands in the dungeonlike cellar; rock and rollers, off-duty cops, drunken tabloid journalists, cast and crew from *Saturday Night Live*, slumming fashionistas, smelly post-work chefs and cooks and floor staff, kinky politicos, out-of-work bone-breakers, or nodding strippers. It's heaven.

If I gotta put on a tie or a jacket, the food better be damn good—and the food at Scott Bryan's Veritas on East Twentieth Street is always worth struggling into a shirt with buttons. It's also got the best wine list and one of the most knowledgeable sommeliers in New York. (Not that it matters to me; I usually drink vodka.) Scott's a friend, so I often sit at the bar and snack off the appetizer menu, but his braised dishes and seafood mains are always exceptionally good. Eric Ripert's Le Bernardin on West Fifty-first Street is, in my opinion, the best restaurant in New York, but then Eric is also a pal, so don't trust me. (The Zagats, Michelin, and the *New York Times*, however, are similarly enthusiastic.) Le Bernardin is my default special-event destination—even though Eric busts my balls fiercely every time I dine there: "What are *you* doing here? You sell-out! This ees not your kind of place! What ees happening to you? You've changed, man. You used to be cool!"

The ultimate New York dining experience, however, may not be in a restaurant at all. For me, it's a rainy, lazy night at home in my apartment. I'll smoke a fat spliff, lay out some old news-papers on the bed, and call out for Chinese. I'll eat directly out of that classic New York vessel, the white cardboard takeout container, and watch a rented movie from nearby Kim's Video. Kim's specializes in hard-to-find exploitation, genre, cult, and art-house favorites, organized by director, so I can say, give me a Dario Argento, an early John Woo, *Evil Dead II*, *The Con-formist*, or that Truffaut film where the two guys are both fucking Jeanne Moreau. Food never tastes better.

HARD-CORE

GABRIELLE HAMILTON, AT THIRTY-EIGHT, with no expression on her face, gazes out the open French doors of Prune, her restaurant on New York's Lower East Side, and considers my question: "How has kitchen culture changed since you got in the business?"

"No one has sex with each other anymore," she replies, almost wistfully. "It's no longer 'Mom and Dad divorce and you have to wash dishes.' Now, it's 'Mom and Dad sent me to cooking school.' People now *choose* to be chefs. It's clean, educated, squeaky."

Though she is seven months pregnant, avoiding alcohol (and the smoke from my cigarette) assiduously, Hamilton clearly still misses the bad old days. She misses "sitting at the bar after closing, drinking for a few hours. It's amazing how you can get a third wind after you've been covered in meat juice all day."

Her particular road to becoming a chef and owning her own restaurant was not an easy one. Hamilton grew up one of five kids in Lambertville, New Jersey, an industrial town of lumberyards and factories (now undergoing something of a renaissance as a weekend getaway). Her father, a theatrical designer, and her French mother split up when she was eleven. After a year with her mother in Vermont, she returned to New Jersey to live with her father. By age twelve, she was working in restaurants.

"Were you a problem child?" I ask.

She gives me a very dry, sardonic smile and replies, "Only if you consider kleptomania and drugs a problem." After school, and for summer jobs, she began washing dishes at The Picnic Basket in New Hope, Pennsylvania. "I needed the money," she says. "I wanted the money." Restaurants were "the only thing I knew how to do." Fortunately, her mother, an excellent cook, had given her and her siblings "a lot of skills already." At various establishments, she continued to wash dishes, bus tables, wait on customers. "I did everything," she says, "bartended, pastry . . . everything." At fifteen, she got her first cook's position. She rolled into New York in the early eighties and worked as a food stylist and catering employee until 1999, when she opened Prune.

When Hamilton says she did "everything," it's sort of like Keith Richards with sleepy understatement telling you he "used to party a little"; her description is tantalizingly inadequate. Stories of Hamilton's long hard road of "wilderness years" between dish jobs and later chefdom have become something of an urban legend. According to who you talk to, there were brief stints in everything from stripping to murder-for-hire. Of course, I believe them all. She's hard-core. Example? Much later, when I ask her what she first looks for in a potential employee, she responds with, "First thing? If I'm standing there in my whites in the dining room, and they ask me 'Is the chef here?' They're not getting the job."

You should probably know that she is, by turns, ardently feminist, reactionary, and refreshingly (even painfully) candid. She is absolutely devoid of artifice, and she has a very low tolerance for bullshit. New York's freebie paper, *The New York Press*, included her in its list of New York's fifty Most Loathsome People last year, and it's not hard to imagine her stepping—if not stomping—on some toes. It's no surprise that I like and admire her tremendously. Had she written her version of *Kitchen Confidential* before I did, I'd probably still be flipping steak *frites*.

Her original concept for Prune? "It was a reaction to years of shitty catering," she admits. Prune was about "what it wasn't.

New York, in '99, was still in long menu scrip mode." Hamilton says she wanted to open a place where everything wasn't stacked and drizzled. The menu was "everything I grew up eating. I wanted the food to have a close, familiar feel . . . like in a household. I'm not an inventor."

The celeb chef thing "bums me out," she complains, before admitting that she doesn't even own a TV. It's easy, however, to read the above, or experience Hamilton's withering gaze of disapproval, and miss the heart of the matter. Chefs reveal their true natures with their menus, with their food, and with the nature of the environments that they choose to serve it in.

Prune is a cozy, warm, inviting, and informal restaurant with a tiny, open kitchen, a few plainly appointed tables, and an ancient zinc bar. The menu is pure, unvarnished sentimentality, soulful comfort dishes pilfered, plucked, and remembered from the childhood she had—and from what is also, perhaps, the childhood she wished she'd had.

Pasta kerchiefs with poached egg, French ham, and brown butter is straight from Hamilton's own past. Roasted marrow bones with parsley salad (my favorite dish in the world, by the way) is a lift from London chef Fergus Henderson's St. John (Hamilton was kind enough to call him and tell him she was appropriating his signature dish). Fried sweetbreads with bacon and capers, monkfish liver with warm buttered toast, and lamb sausages with escarole and romesco sauce join Italian wedding soup on the appetizer menu. The bar menu sports radishes with sweet butter and kosher salt and sardines with Triscuits and mustard—a dish that Hamilton loves because "it got me through every poor time in my life."

For main courses, Prune offers roast suckling pig with pickled tomatoes and crackling, whole grilled fish, braised rabbit legs, rib eye with parsley shallot butter, ruby shrimp boiled with sausage, potatoes, and corn; as for the daily specials, even the most cynical professional would find them as inviting and comforting as slipping half-drunk into a warm bath.

"I like no garnish, noncomposed plates," she says.

She loves Asian food, particularly Thai, Burmese, and Sze-chuan, but refuses to incorporate any of its influence into her own cooking. "No. Won't allow it. *Can't* have cilantro on the menu. That's not what this place is about."

So what, then, *is* Prune about?

Like a lot of American chefs, Hamilton is conflicted on the subject of the French.

"I hate the fucking French," she snarls unhesitatingly. When pressed, she grudgingly concedes a fondness for "their cheese, wine, and perfume." But here, I think it's Hamilton who is full of shit. Prune exudes France from every pore. She can run from French terminology and French menu descriptions, she can lard her menu with nostalgic Americana of long-ago summers and still-remembered meals with friends, mix in some rural Brit and a little country Italian. But Gabrielle's French mother's cooking hangs over the place. Prune looks French. It feels French. Before the smoking ban, it was a smoker's paradise. Even the laid-back bistro attitude is stealth French.

Perhaps eager to put the boot in again, she agrees enthusiastically that Spain is indeed "the New France" but shrinks from the tiny bite, *pinchos*/tapas thing: "I still have an attention span. I can eat a *meal*." At the end, "I want to feel *fed*" (words most Frenchmen would probably agree with). Pressed to name some chefs she admires, she gives me the biggest, warmest smile of the day as she names Veritas's Scott Bryan (heavy French influence) and his one-time underboss Mark Ladner (okay, he's cooking Italian at Lupa, but there's a French cook in there somewhere). "I love what they do."

Like a lot of chefs I know who can date their careers back to the good old/bad old days of the eighties, Gabrielle Hamilton is a survivor and a cynic, and like all cynics, a failed romantic. Sorry Gabrielle. I can smell the French on you. It's the radishes with butter and salt on the bar that gave you away. You can run from the past, but you can't hide. None of us can.

She feeds me some braised lamb before I leave, and once again (and I've been trying for years) I attempt to convince her to write the women's version of *Kitchen Confidential*. "You'd make me look like a freakin' manicurist!" I insist. "This is a book that *needs to be written*. Isn't there *enough* testosterone in this genre?!" I point out that she's already a writer, having been published many times in *Food & Wine* magazine, and that publisher pals of mine have been asking.

She waves away the idea and stands up, ready to get back to the downstairs prep kitchen where her crew are setting up for dinner service.

"I'm not going to write the Great American Novel," she sighs. "But we'll feed a few people."

WHEN THE COOKING'S OVER
(TURN OUT THE LIGHTS, TURN OUT THE LIGHTS)

FOOD AND SIN ARE two words that—in the English-speaking world, anyway—have long been linked. Food is a matter of the senses, a pleasure of the flesh, and when one anticipates eating a good meal, one's body undergoes physiological changes similar to those experienced prior to . . . other functions. The lips engorge, saliva becomes thick, the pulse quickens. Early moralists who believed that taking too much pleasure at the table led inexorably to bad character—or worse, to sex—were (in the best-case scenario, anyway) absolutely right. Everything about a restaurant setting conspires toward that end, be it the peach-colored mood lighting that makes you look more alluring and attractive, to the floral arrangements and decor, to the vigorous upselling of wines and spirits. Like rock and roll, the desired end result is to make you happy—and to get you in the sack.

The same folks (or their more recent equivalents) who looked disapprovingly at unrestrained gourmandism were just as quick to identify music—particularly jazz, rhythm and blues, and rock and roll—as the enemy, an evil force likely to lead their sons and daughters to unsuitable mates, unwanted pregnancies, and "wild" behaviors. And in this too, as has long been established, they were right.

Good food *does* lead to sex. As it should.

And in a perfect world, good music does too.

It is surely no coincidence, then, that the kind of music most chefs and cooks like to listen to, especially after work, is exactly the kind of stuff, heard in exactly the kind of places, that Mama was afraid of. Chefs, whose own personal appetites are rarely confined to food, have always, often notoriously, had a healthy enthusiasm for life's other pleasures. We are, after all, in the pleasure business. It is our job to give pleasure to our customers. How can we be expected, one might ask, to regularly and reliably *give* pleasure if we do not ourselves fully experience it and understand it—in all its strange and fabulous permutations?

Perhaps you should keep that in mind next time you find yourself out late and spy a chef, after work, drunkenly and maniacally bobbing to an old AC/DC tune, well on the way to being seen in flagrante delicto with the hostess from your previous dinner. The chef isn't fooling around, or letting off steam, or even behaving inappropriately. The chef is just fulfilling a responsibility to fully understand the subject: doing research.

If food can lead to sex, and if music can lead to sex, and if the three have often been seen in each other's company . . . is there a direct connection between food and music? Does the music that chefs listen to while they cook—and in their off hours when they are free to roam like the savage, unrestrained beasts we know them to be—lead in some direct way to culinary creativity? Do chefs see music and the places and lifestyle surrounding music as inspiration, or merely as release?

After years of personal introspection and research, and close questioning of some of the country's more accomplished chefs, I arrived at some conclusions.

In my own career, there have always been two soundtracks for each kitchen: one for the workday and another for the late hours after work, when, pumped up with excess adrenaline, my fellow culinarians and I would head out to the clubs or the bars, where we'd drink and review the events of the day. We'd tell stories, share our pain, gripe about bosses and customers, and do what chefs and cooks do when they travel in packs: talk shop. The things I cooked, like the people I knew, I associate with certain songs, certain bands, nightclubs long gone, bars both nearly forgotten and still with us. The places and the songs changed, but certain patterns have held true over the years.

During the mornings, while prep cooks roasted bones and chopped vegetables for stock and the line cooks set up their stations, portioned fish, and made sauce, it was a time for fairly melodic fare. The kitchen sound system, usually a food-encrusted boom box with considerable functional eccentricities, would play nothing too jangly or nerve-racking: Curtis Mayfield, Isaac Hayes, Depeche Mode, Neil Young—sentimental, atmospheric fare likely to make us feel good about ourselves while cleaning squid or tearing the abductor muscles off scallops. The service period (when, admittedly, most chefs don't allow music, but read on) was usually given over to the large and usually omnipresent Latino contingent: salsa, soca, mariachi, and Mexican pop. When the rush was over, while last orders dribbled out and the cooks began to break down their stations, I usually stepped in with louder, more nihilistic sounds, designed to get us through the last hours of cleaning drudgery and off to the bars with hearts still pumping: mostly mid-seventies/early-eighties punk: the Clash, the New York Dolls, my beloved Ramones, and others whom I still associate with my first happy years of cooking professionally in New York. Those were the bands we went to see then, after our kitchens closed and we'd had a few freebies at the bar. Most of those places—in fact, all of them—are closed now: Max's Kansas City, CBGB's, the Mudd Club, Club 57, Hurrah, along with after-hours venues like AM/PM, the Nursery, and the Continental. All day long, the job was about *control* and maintaining command of one's ingredients, environment, and personnel. After work it was about *losing* control.

One constant, then and now, is my still ironclad ground rule regarding music both during and after work: In any kitchen where I am in control, there is a strict NO Billy Joel, NO Grateful Dead policy. If you are seen visibly enjoying either act, whether during or even *after* your working hours, you can clean out your locker now. You're fired.

Like a lot of my peers, I'm much older and maybe even a little nicer now and pretty much done with nightclubs and any place where there are likely to be crowds or dancing. People I drink with, and listen to music with, tend to gather not at clubs but at favored dive bars where the music and ambiance suits our taste and our demographic. A good jukebox is vital.

In every city in America where there are restaurants, there are bars where chefs and line cooks go to relax and kick back. It's never sleek or swank; it's usually a dive, someplace nonjudgmental and forgiving of the occasional bad behavior (and with a liberal pouring policy). It's always open late, as it must be to accommodate cooks' hours, a place where cooks are likely to meet others in their field who share their peculiar half-lives, people who understand what they've accomplished and endured during the last ten or twelve or seventeen hours, and who don't mind the lingering scent of smoked salmon or garlic.

In New York, there's Siberia Bar, a dark, shabby, nearly undecorated dump on West Fortieth Street in Hell's Kitchen. No sign on the door, just a red lightbulb. Inside are sagging, hideously stained couches, friendly bartenders familiar with restaurant folk and their peculiarities, and—on both the ground floor and in the dank, brick-lined cellar—jukeboxes brimming with classic Dead Boys, James Brown, Stooges, Modern Lovers, and Velvet Underground. In Chicago, there's the superbly grotty Rainbow Club and the tiny Matchbox, where you're likely to find cooks from Tru or Blackbird or hotel kitchens listening to head-banging anthems. In New Orleans, the last stop for bar-crawling cookies is the supremely squalid and at times terrifying Snake and Jake's Christmas Club Lounge, where winking Christmas lights, a shotgun-shack motif, an esoteric playlist, and "flexible" hours of operation attract some of the Crescent City's finest practitioners of the culinary arts.

Miami has the magnificently unreconstructed Club Deuce in South Beach, where original members of the "Mango Gang," among them Douglas Rodriguez and Norman Van Aken, used to congregrate, presumably to discuss early experiments with fusion. During the recent South Beach Food & Wine Festival, after the official parties ended, numerous celeb-chef attendees found themselves propped up at the Deuce's serpentine bar watching off-duty ladies of the night play pool. As I lurched back to my hotel, the lion-hearted and still-going-strong Nancy Silverton (of La Brea Bakery in L.A.) was considering grabbing some greasy tacos across the street.

But it's Atlanta that can lay claim to the best of the best (which is to say worst) chef-friendly dives in America: the legendary Clermont Lounge, a sort of lost-luggage department for strippers, who perform—perfunctorily—on a stage behind the bar. An Atlanta institution, attended at one time by nearly every citizen high and low, the Clermont changes character somewhat after midnight. The seemingly lost and hopeless give way to a hipster/restaurant trade contingent. Control of the jukebox (maintained strictly by the performers until then) is given over to a DJ. Though the dancers remain, there is decidedly nothing at all erotic about the spectacle. Cooks, male and female alike, applaud the Clermont's legendary headliner, the decidedly Rubenesque "Blondie," who recently celebrated nearly two decades at the venue. More than one chef and many cooks in Atlanta cherish their personally crushed and autographed can of Pabst Blue Ribbon from the veteran entertainer.

Well, *of course*, some of you might be saying at this point. This kind of degenerate, libertine behavior in marginal establishments is to be expected from this writer and his ilk. What about our better, more accomplished chefs—the ones who are actually known and celebrated for their *cooking*, not some obnoxious memoir? Surely the three- and four-star hotshots, the guys we read about in the *Times* and *Gourmet*, have more refined tastes in musical venues? The French gurus, like Daniel Boulud, for instance, they're retiring after their shifts to sip a little wine by the fire, maybe listen to old Serge Gainsbourg, right?

Wrong.

Boulud's tastes run toward the Black Crowes and the Rolling Stones. He's even had speakers installed in his kitchen, though he says, "I've yet to work on a playlist for them. I've focused all my energy on music for the lounge." After work, he likes to run up to Harlem to St. Nick's Pub or to Luci's Cocktail Lounge to listen to electric blues. Listening to the Devil's Music even influences his craft, he admits. "I let music set the mood when I'm cooking at home or traveling—and thinking what I'd like to cook."

Laurent Manrique of San Francisco's Aqua and fellow Glimmer Twin Eric Ripert of New York's Le Bernardin are, probably unbeknownst to their more restrained clientele, both dance club maniacs who claim that staying up all night listening to techno and trance music at skull-vibrating, molar-rattling volume is a vital part of the creative process.

"As much as in the kitchen there are boundaries—in the nightclub there are no boundaries," says Manrique. "It's two strong extremes. In the clubs, you let yourself go. With dance music, like with food, you go from simplicity to complexity: strong rhythm, one melody, then another. Dishes can be like that. First fish, then spice, then sauce. In harmony." Both chefs have loyalties to specific DJs. In San Francisco, Manrique is partial to DJ Deep Dish at dance club Ruby Skye, while with Ripert in New York it's DJ Junior Vasquez at Twilo.

Given the heaving throngs, the ear-splitting volume, and Ripert's well-known penchant for expensive tequila, do they ever come up with any actual dishes during these bacchanals?

"It's happening all the time," says Manrique.

"Music has never led me to a finished dish," says Laurent Gras, formerly of San Francisco's Fifth Floor and the Waldorf Astoria's Peacock Alley in New York—now at Bistro du Vent. While like Manrique and Ripert he likes dance clubs and dance music—naming DJs Danny Tenaglia, Sander Kleinberg, Paul Oakenfold, and Sasha as favorites—he specifies that they give him "inspiration . . . the freedom and creativity to remove a concept from tradition and express pure emotion. The depth

and combination of flavors—like sounds—can be easily tran-
scribed as a succession of ingredients and harmony. Bass
evokes dark colors. Treble, clear colors. Music can move
my eye from materials and pictures to forms and colors."
As an example, Gras describes the effect of one dance club
mix from DJ Tiësto called "Open Your Eyes" on his cooking:
"It had a beautiful and powerful melody that made me think of
combining cocoa and tomato. I put these flavors onto the main
ingredient, swordfish. I felt it needed these powerful, powerful
combinations and yet needed to be very delicate and light.
With a beautiful presentation, of course. The (eventual) dish
was a tomato and duck consommé, a touch spicy, with
swordfish coated with cocoa nib and grilled on the barbecue.
It turned out to be a beautiful dish."

Hubert Keller of Fleur de Lys also likes to stay up late at
nightclubs. He too names Ruby Skye as a favorite venue, along
with Matrix and Swig, in San Francisco, and the Tabu Ultra
Lounge and Ivan Kane's Forty Deuce in Las Vegas (where he
recently opened a Fleur de Lys at the Mandalay Bay Resort).

"I often get my best inspirations for a new dish by listening
to music. And when I develop a dish I tend to do that late at
night."

Keller is not content to just go to nightclubs and let someone
else do the DJing. "My wife, Chantal, bought me an incredible
DJ setup a few years ago, truly state of the art. To my knowledge, Fleur de Lys in Las Vegas is the only four-star restaurant in
the country that has a DJ booth. When I went to Vegas, my
commitment to music was nonnegotiable. I insisted. Most people don't know that on some Thursday nights, I actually take a
turn as DJ."

Of those chefs who claim music as an inspiration, Rick
Tramonto of Chicago's Tru uses music to inspire not just his
cooking but his spirit. Though he likes, on occasion, to go out to
listen to blues at Buddy Guy's or House of Blues, and says
that, when cooking at home he listens to "Frank Sinatra when
cooking Italian, rock and roll—like Van Halen and Eric

Clapton—when making Asian food," most of the time after work he says he listens to "contemporary Christian or gospel music."

It should be pointed out that chefs' hours are similar to musicians'. Marcus Samuelsson of New York's Aquavit says that not only is music "definitely an inspiration and helps [his] creativity on many levels" but that he listens to music "all the time. I go to listen to friends who play in bands. It's part of my social scene as well as my professional life."

There are those chefs who are inspired by music and claim their after-work hours as a time conducive to a fertile imagination, and then there are those (like me) who seek only escape and distraction.

Tom Colicchio of Craft says that after work he goes out to New York's Alphabet Lounge when Toke Squealy, the band of his guitar teacher, Alan Cohen, plays, or to Arlene's Grocery "to check out [his] friend Becca's band, Thin Wild Mercury." But, he adds, "I don't think it has any effect on what or how I cook. But it does provide time away from thinking about food or my restaurants."

The more you're chained to the stove, the less likely you are, it seems, to claim music as an inspiration. WD-50's wildly creative chef–owner, Wylie Dufresne, who is still in nearly constant attendance at his sole operation, does allow music in his kitchen. "All day long," he says. The playlist is determined by "whoever gets to the radio or CD player first. It's a democracy in the kitchen. It can be anything from hip-hop, the Grateful Dead, Wilco, reggae, lots of mixes made by those in the kitchen and friends." But after work, he confesses, "I don't get out to see live music as I once did. But we do enjoy the jukebox at Doc Holliday's [a neighborhood saloon] after a long day."

Maybe Norman Van Aken of Norman's in Coral Gables best captures the enduring spirit of what music, and after-hours music-related activity, mean to chefs. Though he too plays in a band (with fellow chefs Dean Fearing and Robert Del Grande) when he can, in his hours away from his restaurant he says he likes to "go down to Key West and look around for stuff that happens off Duval Street, back in the alleys. I love jukeboxes, roadhouses, or dives. Doesn't matter."

He sums things up simply.

"After family, two things saved my life. And cooking was one of them."

THE COOK'S COMPANIONS

COOKING PROFESSIONALLY HURTS. I'M not just talking about the aching feet, the tormented back muscles, the burns and cuts; I mean also the spiritual pain, the disappointment and self-doubt that comes with being a cog in a large and ever-whirring machine, the crushing sense of futility one feels when working in an operation that is clearly doomed, or the feelings of isolation and frustration one experiences after a seventeen-hour day peeling shrimp and tournéeing vegetables in a less than hygienic cellar prep kitchen.

I'm not complaining, mind you. We've all been there, those of us who've chosen this life. We knew, or had a pretty good idea, what was expected—and chances are, the professionals who are reading this have spent plenty of time at one point or another in their careers hunched over a fifty-pound load of fresh squid, yanking quills and pulling out ink-sacs, or enduring the tirades of a despotic and unhinged chef. We've got the scars to show for it: grill marks on our wrists, pink and faded lines where knives nicked flesh, the telltale hump of yellowing callous at the base of the index finger of our knife-hands. We know what it's like to work all day and all night, finally tumbling exhausted into bed, still reeking of salmon and garlic. We have, all of us, made careful observation of the hierarchy around us, wondered, in moments of extremis, why, for instance, the boss just bought himself a new Porsche Turbo when yesterday he said that checks would be late this week—and sorry, but we need to cut overtime.

We've all, at some terrible moment, peered through sweat and pain, and the constant noise and clatter of the kitchen, and wondered how come that lazy chef got to swan around the dining room in a spotless new Bragard jacket while we toiled and cursed and broke ourselves on the wheel of commerce.

At moments like this, I have always taken refuge in some old friends—in this case, four books whose simple existence has always given me comfort, books that every time I read them remind me that I'm not alone, that even with all the stupidity and occasional squalor one encounters in the span of a long career in the food-service industry, one is part of a grand tradition. It is nice, so nice, to find that one's labors, even one's early moments of abject misery as an overworked *commis* or prep drone, are part of a continuum. And it is pleasantly surprising, even reassuring, to discover how little has changed since the early part of the century. After revisiting one or more of these old friends, I can again feel proud of what I do. I am reminded of what it took to get here, of what I have endured, and can breath the thick, steamy kitchen air again with assurance, even defiance, because I've survived. Because I'm still here.

Down and Out in Paris and London by George Orwell was a revelation to me when I first turned its pages and encountered Orwell's descriptions of his life as a *plongeur* (dishwasher) and prep cook at the pseudonymous Hotel "X" in 1920s Paris, and of his later misadventures at an undercapitalized and slightly shady bistro. "I *know* these people!" was my first impression, drawing an immediate parallel between the gargantuan cellars of the Hotel X and the hangar-size kitchen of the 1970s Rainbow Room, where I was then working as a *tournant*, buffet cook, prep flunky, and general dogsbody. Here's Orwell, describing after-work drinks with his crew.

We threw off our aprons and put on our coats, hurried out the doors, and when we had money, dived into the nearest bistro. ... The air seemed blindingly clear and cold, like arctic summer, and how sweet the petrol did smell, after the stenches of sweat and food! Sometimes we met some of our cooks and waiters in the bistros, and they were friendly and stood us drinks. Indoors we were their slaves, but it is an etiquette in hotel life that between hours everyone is equal, and the engueulades [put-downs] do not count.

Sound familiar? Orwell goes on to describe, painstakingly, the elaborate and time-honored pecking order, which rang true to me even in 1978. The language and worldview of Orwell's cooks matched perfectly with my experience of the time.

Undoubtedly the most workmanlike class, and the least servile, are the cooks. They do not earn quite so much as waiters, but their prestige is higher and their employment steadier. The cook does not look upon himself as a servant, but as a skilled workman; he is generally called "un ouvrier" [a workingman] which a waiter never is . . . He despises the whole noncooking staff, and makes it a point of honor to insult everyone below head waiter.

Orwell's later adventures in a *faux-Normande* bistro, a filthy, corner-cutting, ill-equipped cesspit, make for hilarious reading for anyone who's worked in a failing Mom and Pop operation where sanitation and quality were not premium considerations; and his portraits of foul-mouthed cooks, nearly insolvent owners, opportunistic waiters, and oblivious customers strike a chillingly familiar chord.

Nicolas Freeling's *The Kitchen* takes place in the late 1940s Grand Hotels in France. Describing his rise from lowly *commis* to chef, the author creates lovingly detailed portraits of chefs, sauciers, grillardins, entremetiers, pâtissiers, and *commis*. For its enduring relevance and accuracy to the world of cooks, Freeling's entertaining, near-perfect recreation might just as well have been written today.

The king-hell, jumbo foodie bible, however, the Talmud and Dead Sea Scrolls combined, has to be Émile Zola's gargantuan masterwork, *The Belly of Paris*, a work of fiction set in the then spanking new central market of nineteenth-century Paris, Les Halles. Our hero is an escapee from Devil's Island, a starving, desperate ideologue and socialist who finds himself, improbably, a food inspector. Zola describes an entire universe of food, traveling through the bowels of the marketplace, describing, beautifully at times, the live poultry markets, the fishmongers, the produce vendors, butchers, charcutiers, and market gardeners of that time. Once again, the reader will be surprised by how little has changed. Anyone who has spent time preparing old-school bistro and/or brasserie classics will recognize, in a glance, the preparation of *boudin noir* or the marketing of trimmings, hooves, snouts, and offal as pâtés and galantines; and anyone who loves food for its own sake will find much enjoyment in Zola's loving descriptions of meat, fish, and produce as they wend their way from source to market, from market to vendor, from vendor to customer. At times, it's nearly food porn, as Zola's hero gazes longingly at unattainable heaps of perfect vegetables glistening in the early morning sunlight, plump sausages in the pork butcher's window, the play of color and light on a still-living trout in the hands of an attractive fishwife.

Finally, there's David Blum's painfully hilarious *Flash in the Pan,* a savage and painstakingly documented account of the life and death of an American restaurant. Owners Bruce Goldstein and Terry Quinn, rather inadvisably, allowed the author to sit in on the planning, staffing, equipping, and opening of their fashionable restaurant, The Falls, at one time situated on Varick and Vandam streets in Manhattan. Blum describes every step from empty construction site to jam-packed model and celebrity hangout to floundering failure. It's an invaluable book for anyone who's ever opened a restaurant, or worked on opening a restaurant, and a cautionary tale, filled with the kind of hubris, stupidity, vanity, and desperation many of us may have seen, at one time or another, in our own checkered careers. Agonize over the menu with an in-over-his head chef and a capricious but determined owner! Watch as floor staff are hired and fired!

Commiserate with unpaid vendors as they get the word—after everybody else—that they won't ever be getting paid! Dig in for hectic, overbooked dinner rushes, computer meltdowns, psychotic episodes, internecine squabbles, petty feuds, bizarre and obsessive behavior. This book actually saved a friend's life. He was about to go to work for one of the principals in *Flash in the Pan*, long after The Falls had closed, and I said, "Maybe you'd better read this book first."

As is so often the case, the real joy is in the details. Here we have:

A packed restaurant every night . . . a catastrophic service situation . . . a French laissez-faire personality managing the floor on busy nights . . . and an owner who is happiest ignoring both and fiddling with the dials on his stereo system . . .

Or,

. . . they've been giving too much food away. "Comping" your friends is one guaranteed way to keep food revenues to a minimum . . . It is a practice that is widely discouraged in the industry. It is not, however, a practice that has been discouraged at The Falls. And yet, in the opening days of the restaurant, no doubt feeling generous and expansive, [the owners] have frequently given away food and drink. How much? Difficult to say, in that no one particularly wants to keep a close count of the giveaways. One night in the first week, Henry guesses that [the owners] gave away half the meals served.

And maybe some of you chefs have been here:

[The chef] diligently follows Bruce and eagerly awaits his boss's latest brainstorm. Bruce gets straight to the point. "I've got a great new dessert idea," he says. "Banana cream tart!"

"Banana cream tart?" [the chef] asks. "What exactly is that, Bruce?"

"It would be like a banana cream pie," Bruce explains, allowing his hands to form an imaginary tart-like circle, "which is everybody's favorite dessert . . . only we'd make it into a tart, so it'd be smaller and healthier."

[The chef] has no response except to roll his eyes, which he can do subtly yet with precision.

After a long pause, he finally mutters, "I guess I can make that."

Having worked in a few knuckleheaded operations like this in my time, I can tell you, it's fun reading Blum's account in the cold, clear light of years later. I may come home after a particularly hellish night feeling like a whipped animal, but *hey,* at least we're busy! My current bosses may take an unusual and annoying interest at times in unpleasantly gamey wild hare and less-than-universally-popular organ meats, but at least they love food. They know what the hell they're talking about! The vodka we're pouring at *my* restaurant is what it says on the bottle.

The function of all four of these old friends, tattered and broken-spined as they may be, is ultimately to make me feel better about myself and the way things are going. And to make me laugh. In our business, you'd *better* have a sense of humor. We flirt with disaster every day—particularly during busy dinner rushes, when one screw-up, one mistake, one broken piece of equipment or ill-prepared cook can send the whole night's service careening into nightmare. We chefs take pride in our work, both in whatever degree of artistry or craft we bring to our product and also in the grim business of cranking out table after table of hot, properly prepared food. We know the sheer terror of running out of food, of being short-handed, and if we can't laugh about it when it happens—afterward—we eat ourselves alive. The torment of seeing a witless customer destroy a cherished fish special with bizarre dietary requirements, or with a misguided urge to design their own meal, can cut like a knife. A waiter who describes that lovely pheasant as tasting "kinda like chicken" can cause a chef's brain to boil, pushing his pulse rate into that red zone where all humanity seems aligned against him—every customer, every owner, every coworker an emissary of pure evil. A good laugh, a little context, they go a long way to bringing one back from the urge to shave one's head, climb a tower, and start shooting at pedestrians.

We should know. As citizens of the world, we should know what came before. How we got here. Why we do things the way we do them. Where our food comes from. We should know what it was like for our humble predecessors, sweating and struggling in unrefrigerated larders, unventilated kitchens, the septic madhouse and twisting, low-ceilinged subcellars of restaurants past. We should remember the way it felt, scraping potatoes onto a garbage-strewn floor, scrubbing grease-caked pots with cold water, bending to the will of crazed and increasingly parsimonious masters. And we should understand not just how much has changed, but how much has stayed the same: the *character* of the business we have chosen as a lifestyle—the way people who do what we do have endured, have learned, have risen and learned to love this thing of ours.

CHINA SYNDROME

FINALLY. CHINA.

I'd been nibbling around her edges for years, eating Chinese food in Malaysia, Singapore, Hong Kong, Taipei—and, of course, New York. But I'd never been to the mainland, to the Source. I'd been, to be honest, intimidated by the largeness and importance of the subject: the oldest, greatest, most influential and varied of the world's mother cuisines. Unlike other places I'd written about, China, with her eight distinct regional cuisines, seemed a subject for whom enthusiasm alone would not be enough. A certain . . . expertise, surely, would be required.

I needn't have worried. Few people on earth are as enthusiastic about food and eating as the Chinese. Show up with an open mind and an empty stomach, willing to try anything that comes your way, and enthusiasm is indeed enough. You will find yourself welcomed—and well fed—again and again, a passenger on a deliriously colorful joyride.

The old joke that the Chinese will eat anything inadvertently reveals what is best about them: There are few "good" ingredients and "bad" ingredients in China. There are the often expensive ingredients that are easy to cook, and the other stuff, the tongues, feet, and odd bits that take a little time—a few thousand years of trial and error—to figure out how to make good. Like any great culinary tradition, the driving engine is the need to transform the humble, the tough, the unlovely into the delicate and sublime, or to figure out what was good about an ingredient all along.

In this way, it can be said that deep inside every good cook, be they French, Italian, or American, beats the heart of a Chinese. With this in mind, I recently ventured my first few little bites out of a very large country.

At Huang Cheng Lao Ma restaurant, in Chengdu, Szechuan's frenetically developing capital, a large cauldron of murky and bubbling palm oil sits center table: the notorious Szechuan hotpot. Bobbing on the roiling surface of the dark, viscous liquid is a logjam of tongue-scalding dried Szechuan chilies. Less noticeable, but just as plentiful, are a fistful of *hua jiao*, smaller, darker "flower" peppercorns. The dried chilies are pure burn. The peppercorns, though aromatic, are pure freeze. They numb the mouth, at times the whole face, as they go down (which explains why they are a popular remedy for toothache). My friend David, a Chengdu native, points at the spicy hellbroth with his chopsticks and says, "It gets stronger as it cooks."

He points across the large communal table at a family of locals gathered around a similar witches' brew. The mother is red faced and holds a fist to her chest. The father is mopping sweat from his neck. David grins and dips a slice of raw beef into the hotpot, swirling it around to cook for a few seconds before a secondary dunk in cooler oil, then pops it in his mouth.

"Diarrhea tomorrow," he promises.

"For me, or for you?" I ask, assuming that it's my delicate Western metabolism he's concerned about.

"Oh no. Everybody pays tomorrow," he laughs. "Still. We come back again. You'll see. It's addictive."

Plates of uncooked chicken, shrimps, sliced kidney, quail eggs, noodles, and vegetables arrive. Each will find their way in increments into the increasingly volcanic oil before disappearing down our throats. It's like a lethal fondue. We've ordered the strongest, "hottest" variety, in a town famous for its profligate way with peppers, and it hurts so good. The perfect mixture of pleasure and pain. I feel strangely in competition with David.

They say "never let them see you sweat," but it's way too late for that. We're both in full lather. David swallows another slice of kidney, rubs his solar plexus, and grimaces, and I feel—to my shame—gratified by his pain. I'm surviving Szechuan. I'm making it through this most incendiary of incendiary meals in the fire capital of the world. And I'm loving it. The effect of all the peppers is almost narcotic in its endorphin-producing qualities. In fact, early hotpot chefs were rumored to lace their concoctions with opium, to keep customers coming back. It wasn't necessary. Those who survive their initial exposure to the dish can't help but return to it, like a beautiful but bad girlfriend. (Later, when I return to the States, I'll secrete two kilos of those magical *hua jiao* in my luggage, wanting never to be separated from them again.)

The next day, at Chen Ma Po Dou Fu (which translates loosely to "Pockmarked Granny's Tofu"), I happily submit to another glorious if painful scourging and devour the restaurant's namesake dish: a bowl of meat and spice-stippled tofu awash in more palm oil, named for its likeness to its creator. I pick cautiously through a Szechuan chicken that is easily 80 percent dried chilies (one tries to pick around them) and 20 percent chicken, and, like so much of local fare, awash in yet more pepper-infused palm oil. As David said, even knowing my inevitable unpleasant gastroenterological destiny, I don't care. It's too good. My palate—if it doesn't burn out of my skull entirely—will never be the same again.

The relatively friendly flavors of Beijing are a welcome change. And I concentrate, in the limited time I have, on what the capital city is best known for: duck. Duck so crispy, flavorful, juicy, and unctuous that it will ruin you for "Peking Duck" anywhere else. Li Qun Roast Duck Restaurant, located in an old *hutong* neighborhood near Tiananmen Square, is a crowded, ramshackle home turned eatery. Eager customers are squeezed around a central courtyard, jammed into small former bedrooms, their tables brimming with stacked plates of food. In the kitchen, the chef carefully positions head-on ducks over open peachwood flame in an ancient brick oven, turning them and moving them constantly to expertly crisp the skin. The meat is sliced and presented with the de rigueur pancakes, sliced scallion, and hoisin sauce—but it's better, *much* better, eaten straight and unadorned. In keeping with the mantra of "nothing potentially delicious shall go to waste," a plate of savory duck tongues and fork-tender duck feet arrives hot on the heels of the duck itself, all of it revelatory in its wonderfulness.

I could easily have spent my entire ten-day trip to China eating at—and writing about—one square block of restaurants, or a single strip of wet market, and never have scratched the surface. China is *big*. And one lifetime is not enough to fully or authoritatively explore her. But it appears increasingly likely that in future, more of us will have the opportunity to try. In modern China, there are construction cranes everywhere. Roads are widening, dams being built, hotels going up, Western businesses pouring in, along with dollars and more dollars. New street signs are in Mandarin and English, and China projects an impression that she's getting ready to fully assume her role of financial superpower. So, perhaps it's not necessary to go to China. She'll be coming to you.

NO SHOES

Understand this: I always hated those articles, like the ones in *Vanity Fair,* featuring the Lifestyles of the Rich and Despotic, where some chicken-brained Hilton kiddie, shriveled Sukarno relative, or Scientologist movie star lets us into their swanky digs to show off their collection of expensive motorcars and Tiberius-inspired plumbing. I don't know why they really publish this stuff. Do the writers actually admire these no-accounts and wish us to emulate their wastrel behavior if we can? Or are the writers, in fact, hard-core Maoist provocateurs, hoping secretly to rouse us ordinary schlubs to a murderous rage with these glimpses into the profligate spending of capitalist grotesques?

That said, where I'm sitting right now is a rented villa on the Caribbean island of Saint Martin. Directly in front of me, through open French doors, is a coconut palm, gently straining in the breeze, its fronds brushing against a whitewashed balustrade. In the distance, green-covered mountains, a vast expanse of blue sea—so many shades of blue it looks like a child's crayon box (the jumbo collection)—and beyond, the hazy, distant shapes of the islands of Saint Eustatius and Saba sit on the horizon under puffs of white, gold, and purple clouds. A rooster crows somewhere. Birds cheep in the garden. The caretaker's dogs gnaw lazily on leftover bones outside the front door . . .

Jesus! I think I may have crossed the line into Terminal Michael Winner Syndrome. ". . . While Ricardo, the capable maître d'hôtel, had urged me to dine in the grill room, I opted instead for Le Bateau Rouge, a charming brasserie by the port that Michael Caine had recommended on an earlier visit. I had the sole. And something white and starchy. I think it was a potato."

I've been in the West Indies for two months now, and for that entire time I have not once worn shoes or socks. I keep a pair of flip-flops in my rented Jeep, for when I have to pop into the market for some stinky cheese, or the local paper; but I have yet to eat even one meal in a restaurant that requires footwear of its guests. It has been my sole, overriding criteria for this vacation: I refuse to eat anywhere where shoes might be required.

In that wonderful, creamy, narcotized state of sunstroked semiconsciousness that comes from the drinking of alcoholic beverages in direct tropical sunlight, the idea of making it through multiple courses and a bottle of wine in a white-table-cloth restaurant, with its inevitable snail-paced service, does not tempt. I eat almost all my meals in barbecue shacks or *lolos*, little corrugated tin-roofed lean-tos with nearly identical menus of grilled chicken leg, barbecue ribs, grilled spiny lobster, spicy Creole boudin, conch sausage, grilled snapper, meat patties, johnny cakes, bullfoot soup, plantains, rice and pigeon peas, and beer. Cutlery is plastic, napkins—if any—are paper. Music is provided by a boom box tuned to the local station. Food arrives when it arrives, in no particular order. There are usually some insects involved, but the 10-percent DEET I'm slathered in keeps them from eating me alive. Stray dogs hover by the table, waiting for an unfinished chicken leg or spare rib bone. There are always ashtrays on every table.

I am very happy here.

Largely, I am happy because while I eat, there is sand between my toes—great pillows of it, large-grained, pebbly, with bits of surf-smoothed shell mixed in; or fine-grained, white, and pow-dery. On the rare occasions when the establishment has a floor, it's either smooth, cool terra-cotta tile, or the weatherbeaten planks of an imperceptibly swaying dock, all very pleasurable, as if by brushing my toes constantly and directly against the surface of the earth, I tap into some primitive vein of perfect happiness.

Food tastes better without shoes, I have come to believe.

And I am considering testing my theory at a yet-to-be determined two- or three-star fine-dining establishment on my next trip to London. Surely my good friend Gordon would not eject me from his wonderful restaurant at Hospital Road if I showed up shoeless in Hawaiian shirt and cut-off jeans, would he? Not when I explain that my outfit has been strategically designed to enjoy his artistry to the fullest degree possible. Undistracted by underwear riding up in my crack, or the pinch of garters, I shall surely discover heretofore overlooked dimensions of his fine works. I'll cite historical precedent, if need be, to keep the maître d' from hurling me through the door: the Romans, for instance, who ate in the prone position, raised up on an elbow, dressed in comfortable garb—a toga thingie, easily pulled up mid-meal so as to allow a friend or paid companion to more easily fondle one's genitals between courses. Who understood the elements of a good meal, or a good party, better than those kooky caesars? Who can deny the desirability of experiencing pure flavor, texture, and culinary technique free from the constraints and intrusions of restrictive modern garb? It's an insult to the chef, isn't it? Like trying to eat in a straitjacket or fuck through a shower curtain.

I don't know.

Maybe I'd better pack one pair of Hush Puppies. Just in case.

THE LOVE BOAT

TOMORROW, THERE WILL BE blender drinks and citron presses and fluffy towels by the pool. Smiling attendants will cool us with chilled white washcloths and spray our overheated, sun-browned flesh with refrigerated mist. The *New York Times*—or the newspaper of our choice—will be waiting in our mailboxes when we wake, our names printed on each page, and if we like, there will be tea and cakes, aromatherapy, a massage. We will glance at each other briefly, wordlessly, across the cigar room or the library or the whirlpool and know that we have made it, that we have put aside the cares of the world, that we have only to rest, to read, to play, to sleep—and that when we wake, we shall be in another time zone, another country.

But tonight, seventy-six very rich people are pressed deep deep deep into their custom-made Italian sheets, squeezed down into their mattresses by the rise and fall of the rooms around them—then lifted, as if weightless, momentarily above their beds—then pressed down again. The vast living rooms, dining areas, foyers, bedrooms, and marble-appointed bathrooms that surround them tilt and sway, climb and dive as their floating condominiums negotiate force-seven near-gale-force winds and high seas of eighteen- to twenty-seven-foot swells. Mashed and elevated ever so gently in their beds, most surely sleep. The ship does not protest. No groans or squeaks or creaking beams. She handles like a brand new Mercedes 600—large, yes, but *solid,* and smelling of new wood and new money. Through the airtight, soundproof sliding doors to our long outdoor private verandas, the wind and surf, the crash of waves against the hull are barely audible. The rat-tat-tat of raindrops on our outdoor jacuzzis goes unheard.

I'm making osso buco and wild mushroom–black truffle risotto. I'm chopping orange gremolata for garnish in my spacious and well-equipped kitchen as the floor pitches and rolls and threatens to deposit me face-first in the simmering pot of veal shanks on my spanking new, four-burner range top. A load of laundry hums behind me. The dishwasher does its business beneath a long expanse of counter, and when I toss a few herb stems, orange scraps, and vegetable trippings into the food disposal, it devours them without complaint. Tasteful but efficient railings keep my saucepots, plates, and glassware in place while I pick and weave unsteadily to the refrigerator, where a vichyssoise cools beside a constantly restocked supply of imported beer and juices. In the sleek, comfortable Danish Modern bedroom, my wife watches a film from the double bed. In the large, well-appointed living room, on an enormous flat-screen TV set among book-lined shelves, a CNN anchor drones on about a world that seems, right now, very far away. A bottle of champagne chills in a silver ice bucket on the suitable-for-six dining room table.

But I don't think I'll be drinking it tonight.

Welcome to the world of ResidenSea—or *The World*, as our remarkable vessel is named—644.2 feet long, with 106 private residences and fifty-nine rental apartments and studios. Not a cruise ship. Not a mega-yacht. She is, as the literature proudly states, "a floating resort community of like-minded persons who will settle for nothing but the very best," the "ne plus ultra of voyaging," a self-sufficient neighborhood of luxury homes "at sea continuously circumnavigating the globe."

In short, it's a big, swank, ridiculously well-fitted-out boat on which rich people can buy their own homes, dropping in or jetting off as they see fit as it wanders from continent to continent.

"We'll be trapped like rats," protested Nancy, my wife, when I told her where we were going.

"The rich are more boring than you and me," she said. "You want to be penned up in a floating prison with a bunch of mummies in cruise-wear? Are you insane? I am *not* playing shuffleboard. I am not going to see Red Buttons or Kathie Lee. And I am *not* contracting the Norwalk virus so you can write some stupid story. And I am *not* going to be your comedic device again." She was right in the middle of reading Mark Twain's *Innocents Abroad,* about a luxury cruise with similarly grandiose claims, a book I now regretted giving her.

"This ain't the *Love Boat,* sweetheart," I protested. There are no organized dinner seatings. No limbo contests on the Lido deck. Gopher and Julie are nowhere to be found. "It'll be great, honey! And it's free! The magazine'll pay for it! C'mon! Think of it like . . . like Gilligan's Island. Only it'll be a five-day cruise, not three hours, and with what they charge, you can be assured we won't end up trying to build a desalinization plant out of coconuts. You know how much money you gotta have to take a trip on this thing? C'mon! Let's live large!"

Residents of *The World,* I hastened to point out, do not sleep in anything remotely resembling a "cabin." Residential apartments (and we'd be staying in one) range in size from 1,106 to an astonishing 3,242 square feet, each with "state-of-the-art kitchens," two to six bedrooms, living and dining areas, and a veranda. Four full-service restaurants, a gourmet market and deli, shops, numerous bars, a nightclub, casino, library, business center, theater, health spa, swimming pool, putting greens—and, believe it or not, a tennis court—awaited our attention should we care to make use of it.

"C'mon! We'll pretend we're a retired South American dictator's idiot son and wife! Let's live a little! Work on our suntans!"

The idea, I explained, was for me, loudmouth professional utility chef and obnoxious memoir author—and wife—to board this magnificent sea-beast at Curaçao and spend five nights between there and Costa Rica, fending for ourselves: buying food at Fredy's Deli, *The World*'s on-board market and provisioner, and cooking in our "state-of-the-art" kitchen. We'd rough it—as much as one *can* rough it in a multimillion-dollar apartment with twice-a-day maid service—buying groceries and then preparing our meals from scratch, and I'd report on the experience in the kind of sober, dispassionate, objective terms for which I am well known.

"If I see a limbo contest shaping up, I'm going over the side," said Nancy. "And if you come down with some ship-borne gastrointestinal complaint, I'm gonna be the first one to say 'I told you so.'"

Who, you might ask, would actually live on such a vessel? I think it's fair to say you have to be very, very rich to own a home on board *The World*. How rich? Apartments run from 2.5 to 7.5 million dollars each, with residents having to pony up an additional 5 percent of purchase price per year to pay for fuel and operating costs. Imagine owning a Fifth-Avenue apartment—only this one moves—making leisurely ports of call in the Mediterranean, the Caribbean, South Pacific, Asia, South America, and Africa, scheduling itself so as not to miss significant events like the Cannes Film Festival, the Grand Prix at Monaco, and the British Open in Saint Andrews. I was enthusiastic. My only reservation was that I didn't think I owned the clothes for this venture. I couldn't turn to Nancy and say, "Honey? Could you lay out my deck shoes, my blue blazer, my khakis, and my cabana wear?" I didn't own any of those things. I thought I might have once owned a Greek fisherman's cap, but I hadn't seen it since I spilled bong water on it back in college.

I cheerfully signed on, and a few weeks before we were scheduled to join the ship, two sleek leather and woven-linen document cases arrived in the mail along with some briefing material.

"See, Nancy? See?" I said, waving the objects in front of her nose. "Class."

On the date of departure, we flew to Curaçao, were met by a ResidenSea representative at the airport, and soon got our first look at *The World*, an impressively big, newer, sleeker, more dramatically sharp looking version of the floating cities you see disgorging day-trippers all over the Caribbean. After being photographed and X-rayed, we were issued ID cards and escorted to our quarters.

There was a bottle of Piper on ice waiting in our spacious two-bedroom, two-bathroom apartment when we arrived, and, exhausted from the plane, we gratefully sucked it down before passing out in the master bedroom. The next morning, after a room-service breakfast of fresh-squeezed orange juice and still-warm-from-the-oven croissants and pastries, I went out to explore.

Perhaps you remember the sixties television series *The Prisoner*? In it, Patrick McGoohan, a secret agent (only and forever referred to as "Number Six"), wakes up to find himself incarcerated in a kooky, futuristic, utopian/totalitarian—yet very comfortable—community-cum-prison called "The Village." The similarities kept coming to mind as I wandered the mostly deserted halls, vast lobbies, lounges, and grand but empty spaces of *The World*. Though there were seventy-six passengers currently in residence, along with a something less than bare-bones complement of 260 plus crew, it didn't feel like anywhere near that many. Passengers apparently kept to themselves, and crew, when passed in the common areas, gave brief, cheerful greetings, much like the "Be seeing you" and "Have a nice day" of *The Prisoner*. Like "the Village" on the series, *The World* publishes its own daily paper. As in "the Village," no currency is exchanged. One's room number (as on the series) serves as credit reference enough, and one's photo ID card serves as room key. As in "the Village," there is a general store, Fredy's Deli, its shelves stocked with pretty much what you'd expect to find in a small Upper East Side gourmet shop/deli, with a friendly and obliging shopkeeper who is happy to provision you from the ship's stores. There even *is* a village on the ship: a small cluster of shops and facilities along and above a wide walkway referred to as "The Street" where you can buy clothes or jewelry, smoke a

Cuban cigar, check your e-mail. There are maps—as in "the Village"—showing only the immediate community surrounded by water; and, like McGoohan's apartment, *The World*'s apartments are impeccably, perfectly cleaned and maintained, modern and comfortable (as is everything on the ship). In fact, one thing I never fully understood about the prisoner on the show was why he wanted to escape so badly. He seemed to have it pretty good.

As the plan was for me to cook, I would not be dining at Portraits, *The World*'s "contemporary French Fusion" restaurant (jacket and tie or formal wear required), nor at The Marina, where "seafood, steak, and rotisserie specials" are the thing. And while I might give myself a break for lunch with "Mediterranean cuisine with a Northern Italian flair" at The Tides, I would certainly not be venturing the "oriental delights at East restaurant and sushi bar." As I was soon to have confirmed during a tour of the ship's antiseptically clean kitchens and storerooms, *The World* may be a floating enclave of very rich people who expect and demand the very best, but in this case, the rich eat a lot of frozen food. Until I saw a sushi chef hanging a fishing line off the far end of the putting green, I was staying away from the sushi bar, thank you very much. Ironically, considering they are surrounded by water, ships—even luxury ships—are seldom good places to enjoy fresh seafood. At sea for days at a time, they are provisioned at ports with varying concepts of refrigeration and resupply. The bacalao and salt fish of earlier times has been replaced by frozen fish on larger vessels. It may not be "the very best," but it's safe.

When Nancy and I were summoned to meet with the safety officer, in the ship's cinema/theater, and told him that I'd be doing a lot of cooking in the apartment, he explained—among other useful things, like how to inflate our life vests—that at the first signs of smoke, our kitchen would automatically seal itself up Bond-villain-like behind sliding fire doors that would emerge from tasteful concealment in the walls. Overhead sprinklers would discharge, and an alarm would notify the bridge. I instantly made a mental note to avoid making any dish requiring deglazing, or likely to create a lot of smoke. The safety officer seemed like a nice man. But I did not want to see him again in his pajamas wielding a fire extinguisher, an "I told you so" look on his face, in the middle of the night while holding a scorched pan or a burned bagel. That would be embarrassing.

This consideration, and the fact that all the ranges were electric (there was, of course, no gas on board) were major factors in determining my menu and provision list. I'm a gas guy all the way, having worked exclusively with direct, immediately responsive flame my whole professional life. Because my only experience with electric stoves before my kitchen on *The World* had been in college—one of those hideous slide-out range tops with ancient coils that stank of old food and burning circuitry as it slowly, slowly came up to heat—I had nothing but bad memories and low expectations now. So I figured: Assume the worst. Start slow and keep it simple. Steak and potatoes. Pan-seared entrecote, perhaps, with a baked potato.

I needn't have worried. Our kitchen was larger and better equipped than most New York City apartment kitchens. The four-burner Schott range heated up very nicely, the burner glowing fiercely deep beneath sexy-looking black ceramic, and was surprisingly responsive to every twiddle of the dial. Though the chef had kindly offered to "thaw out anything" from a vast walk-in freezer containing every conceivable cut of meat, poultry, fish, and game, my entrecotes were in fact faux-filets (sirloin), but I wasn't bothered. They were nicely marbled and of good quality (if recently frozen) and seared up nicely in one of the thoughtfully provided nonstick pans, forming a lovely crust studded with brown sea salt and crushed black pepper. Any worries about smoke faded with the efficient whirring of the overhead stovetop range hood. I handled the gentle, slow-motion cantering of my kitchen floor well, I thought, for a landlubber, and when the time came, the steaks joined the potatoes in the reassuringly named Competence B-300 oven until medium rare. Soon, Nancy and I, in fluffy white ResidenSea bathrobes, were sitting at our dining room table, a towering floral arrangement dead-center, eating perfectly respectable Black Angus steaks and crispy-skinned potatoes, accompanied by an astonishingly affordable bottle of Brouilly.

Emboldened by this early success, I rose early the next morning and confidently made omelettes aux fines herbes, chopping the fresh herb and parsley with the delightfully sharp knives provided. I'd seen a pretty impressive selection of stinky French cheeses at Fredy's and had over-optimistically ordered an Époisse and an Alsatian Muenster. But when I went to fold a slice of the Muenster into my omelette, it became clear that this particular cheese had seen better days. My omelette tasted like a dead man's feet, with a dreadful ammonia aftertaste, and ended up in the food disposal (which worked like a charm). Nancy, however, was very pleased with her cheese-free omelette, happily poring over the day's *Times*.

Later, in that happy, hazy, lazy, semisunstroked state that comes with too much time spent drinking banana daiquiris (made with real bananas) poolside, I was in no shape to cook much for lunch. I padded down to Fredy's for a fresh baguette and some cold cuts. Though dress during the day was casual (there is a dress code after six), passing a few silver-haired gentlemen in crisp khakis, handmade bespoke linen shirts, and thin timepieces, I felt like Gilligan, crashing a party for the Howells. Back in my apartment, I made sandwiches, soppressata and *jambon blanc* for me and sliced steak (leftover from the previous night) for Nancy. Suffering from an inferiority complex while shopping in my jeans and T-shirt, I'd overcompensated by buying a bottle of Roederer Cristal to wash the sandwiches down. I may not have been rich, but I was, after all, living as if I were—if only for a few days. Feeling on top of the world as only the drunk can feel, a here-today-gone-tomorrow-what-the-hell kinda rich, I finished my sandwich and the champagne and staggered through my living area, past the couches and armchairs and cocktail table, out onto my veranda and flopped into my jacuzzi. The perfect end, I thought, to a perfect meal.

Before dinner, Nancy and I watched a video from the ship's extensive library on our big-screen TV, the wretched, incomprehensibly awful *Arabesque*—the only positive effect of the film being that after eighty minutes with Sophia Loren, I was in the mood for Italian. (No matter that in the film she played some kind of weirdly generic cartoonish Arab character.) I made penne in fresh pomodoro sauce, preceded by woody but welcome steamed white asparagus. My knife was sure as I filleted perfectly acceptable plum tomatoes and slivered slightly older than vintage garlic. I picked fresh basil leaves, cracked a can of Italian plums, another can of paste, sweated, swirled, simmered, and seasoned, all without a moment's seasickness, the kitchen behaving brilliantly. It had everything, didn't it? A microwave with broiler, a food disposal that could have handled Jimmy Hoffa, a dishwasher, all the appliances and doodads one could hope for, including vertical slicer/grater, blender, food processor, manual juicer, and blending wand. And so clean! Always clean! How could it not be? The whole place was scrubbed down, polished, and tidied twice a day, first in the morning while we drank and sweated by the pool, and again later, by a hurrying duo of charming yet focused Scandinavian girls, cute as buttons but with the work ethic of Sherpas, who'd arrive at six bearing chocolates, towels, and replacement staple items and give the whole place a quick going over. Fredy's had been, on balance, very good to me, managing to come up with everything on my provisions list but fresh chives. For chicken stock, I received a fresh batch from *The World*'s kitchens. A "small amount of flour" arrived portioned in a paper cup, sparing me the burden of a five-pound bag.

The kitchen was pretty damn stylish too. Recessed lighting, elegantly concealed washer and dryer, shiny new refrigerator with ice-maker. I cooked al dente penne in one of the heavy-bottomed sauce pots, drained it quickly into a colander, and dragged it, still leaking a little of the starchy pasta water, into the waiting sauce. A few tosses, that magic moment when the pasta took in the sauce, a last glorious shot of extra-virgin olive oil, and onto the plates. No one alive could have cooked better pasta that day. I was sure of it. As we ate, the sea moving by outside our long expanse of windows, the sun setting on the horizon, I felt like Emperor of the Sea. Not wanting this alcohol-inspired sense of mastery to end, when I finished my penne, I diced up the complementary platter of tropical fruit, tossed the mix in balsamic with a little fresh mint and sugar, and served macerated fruit salad for dessert.

Ham omelettes for breakfast the next day, followed by a visit to The Tides for a very decent lunchtime artichoke risotto for me and a gnocchi for Nancy. I made herb-roasted chicken and ratatouille for dinner and got ahead on the next day's menu by preparing another blast from my personal past (a long-ago trip on the *Queen Mary*), vichyssoise, and socking it away into the spacious refrigerator to cool overnight.

By now feeling perfectly (if artificially) at home with my swank surroundings, the next morning I again padded down to the neighborhood grocer for another freshly baked baguette and some cocoa powder. I had a plan, another cherished golden oldie from childhood. When I returned, Nancy had squeezed fresh orange juice, and we followed that up with steaming bowls of bittersweet hot chocolate into which we dipped long buttered halves of the baguette. As a few drops of buttery chocolate dribbled off my chin, I half-noticed the sky turning steel gray, the sea picking up, spindrifts of foam and spray beginning to trail off the tops of the swells. The up and down motion of the ship began to be more pronounced, with an occasional dull thud as the ship's bow muscled through a particularly big wave.

I did not, for some reason, feel like lunch that day.

It grew dark, then darker, rain becoming constant, the sea getting rougher by the hour. I woozily cleaned portobello, cremini, and oyster mushrooms and fine-diced black truffles for my risotto. I braised recently thawed veal shanks and made the sauce for my osso buco. I zested orange and minced fresh herb for gremolata, all the while lurching dizzyingly around inside the spacious but increasingly claustrophobia-inducing kitchen. Stumbling wearily to the bedroom for a brief lie-down—as my stomach was beginning to feel less than terrific—I felt the ship lean to one side, threatening to propel me through the windows. The ship's movements didn't seem to bother Nancy at all; she watched me moaning on the bed with a pitying look. As long as I lay there I was okay. But among my many unlovely aspects, I am a degenerate smoker, and as smoking is prohibited indoors (except in designated areas, my apartment not among them), I had to pay periodic visits to the now rain-swept veranda to smoke, huddling against wind and spray in a sodden deck chair or clinging to the rail before tottering back inside again to collapse. Feeling really wretched now, I tried to keep trips to the kitchen brief.

When the veal shanks were tender and the sauce reduced, I shut off the stove and put the pot aside to cool. I muttered something to Nancy about putting everything away for tomorrow as there was no way I was eating anything tonight. Thankfully, I had not started the risotto, or anything that wouldn't be better tomorrow. As *The World*'s information channel informed us that winds were now approaching gale force and seas rising to eighteen feet, the captain's voice suddenly issued from hidden speakers over my bed (more shades of *The Prisoner*), assuring passengers in a casual, conversational tone that conditions would "probably" not get too much worse and chiding those among us who had apparently been complaining that the seas had been too calm and unexciting. This is another difference between you and me and the very rich: The very rich, among them most residents of *The World*, for instance, have previously owned yachts. They know what it feels like to have your stomach rise up into your rib cage every few seconds while the floor heaves and pitches around you. And they seem to like it.

I have to admit, the ship managed the seas beautifully. Even when swells reached the occasional twenty-seven feet, my sleep was undisturbed by groaning or creaking, the shriek of protesting beams or stressed rivets. The hull, as if surrounded by shock absorbers, handled every crashing wave with a solid, well-muffled authority. Nothing in the apartment moved or dropped save an occasional book flopping onto its side. Pots and pans stayed on the stove, lamps stayed on tables, doors remained shut, cabinets closed. As the ship rose and fell, the most violent movements were inside my stomach as I was squashed and lifted (rather gently I confess) above and into my firm and expensive bedding.

I don't know that I would ever buy a residence on *The World*, regardless of what lottery I might someday win, or that I would ever book lengthy passage in her rental suites or studios. Most of her residents own two or three homes, which suggests a net worth unattainable in my lifetime and the lifetimes of all my friends put together. As delightful as it sounds to drop by one's floating home-away-from-home in say, Sydney, sail for Ho Chi Minh City, disembark for a few weeks, then rejoin her at some other port of call by plane—or private jet, as some surely do—I am not, I think, a seafaring man. I wish *The World* well, and all the intrepid souls who sail within her. They know better than I the ways of the deep blue sea—and how cruel a mistress she can be. They are used to solitude and are, I think, surprisingly self-sufficient for a demographic no doubt used to much pampering. Rather than living behind high walls on the Riviera, or in some faux agrarian-wonderland compound in Napa, or getting their faces and buttocks stretched taut in LA, here they relax, read, spend time with a few select loved ones, looking comfortably untaut and unattractive in their swimwear by the pool: a little mist, a blender drink, a nice nap, some frozen fish for dinner, remaining in contact with their faraway empires via Internet and satellite phone. I will always remember an elegant, silver-haired Frenchman who, during lifeboat drill, looked warily at the rather extravagantly appointed emergency launches and wanted to know only if there was plenty of red wine stored among the provisions. I liked him for that.

We ate the osso buco after the ship tied up at Puerto Limón, Costa Rica. And it was delicious.

My risotto was perfect.

SOUR

IS CELEBRITY KILLING THE GREAT CHEFS?

THERE HAS ALWAYS BEEN an element of the hustler/showman in the great chef. From Carême's extravagant *pièces montées,* best-selling books, and careful career management through Escoffier's shrewd partnership with César Ritz and on into the television age, smart chefs have known that simply cooking well is not enough. The chef in the dining room, mingling with the guests in an impeccably white starched jacket and toque, is a different man than the chef his cooks see. All chefs know and accept how much of the business of fine dining is artifice: The mood lighting, interior decoration, uniformed service staff, the napkins and silver, background music, and erotically descriptive menu text all conspire to create an environment for customers not much different than a stage set. Chefs have always written books, multiplatformed, and performed—to one extent or another—for their public. Whether coddling their customers or snarling at them, a chef caters to expectations, creating an image, hopefully one that will sell more food and attract more public.

With the advent of the Food Network and expanded media interest in chefs worldwide, however, the bar has been raised considerably. Speaking well and being good on television, giving good interview—these skills now seem almost as important as knife work. Even the Culinary Institute of America, the prestigious professional cooking school, now offers media training as part of its curriculum.

Perhaps, then, they should teach the cautionary tale of Rocco DiSpirito as an example of A Chef Who Went Too Far, one who went over the line—messed with the bitch goddess celebrity and got burned. Before television, Rocco was the well-respected chef of the three-star Union Pacific, a bright, charismatic guy with the world on a string. He was known for his skill in the kitchen, his innovative style, and his insistence on quality. As he became more recognized, he began expanding the "brand," consulting to other restaurants, signing multiple endorsement deals, showing up at openings and promo parties. Now, after his hideous, high-profile, post-ironic "reality" television venture, *The Restaurant*, has run its humiliating course, he's no longer the chef of his once excellent Union Pacific; he's banned from his own eponymous eatery (the cynical and soulless Rocco's); he's finally settled protracted litigation with his ex-partner, Jeffrey Chodorow (famously the last guy in the world anyone would want to face in court); and he can presently be seen hawking cookware with his mom on QVC. When last heard of, the once great chef was hosting a local call-in radio show in which he directs little old ladies to the best kosher chickens. It's been a long, hard, and painfully public fall. In a highly competitive business, a certain amount of backbiting and schadenfreude is to be expected. But, in Rocco's case, the reaction from his fellow chefs has been positively gleeful.

Where did he cross that line? When did Rocco go from being talked about by his peers as a hugely talented but ambitious knucklehead to a betrayer? Why is he seen to have broken faith with his profession?

Culinary students of the future will no doubt look deeply into this question, as it's an important one. They might ask as well, "Why not Emeril?" Emeril Lagasse would seem, at first blush, to have invited an even worse fate. Like Rocco, he is outrageously overexposed: two cooking shows, a line of cookware, a restaurant empire extending into Vegas and theme parks. He's famously inept at cooking (on television); can barely speak grammatically; still has a thick, working-class Massachusetts accent; and while hunched troll-like over his cutting board with gut ballooning over apron strings, he looks like a publicist's nightmare. More amazingly, he dared star in perhaps the worst television sitcom since Lancelot Link, Chimp Detective. Yet he's survived—and prospered. Why did the handsome, intelligent, and more culinarily gifted stud-puppet Rocco crash and burn, and not Emeril?

Maybe it's because Emeril's real. (Tellingly, chefs *like* Emeril. They may hate his show, but they like him personally, and continue to respect him.) Like Rocco, he came up the hard way, in his case starting out in a bakery in Fall River, Massachusetts, making his bones as first cook, then chef of a number of well-regarded restaurants before landing a cooking show on the Food Network. But unlike Rocco, Emeril presides over a successful empire of very good restaurants. Unlike Rocco, Emeril looks like he's enjoying being famous (not whining about it all the time, or trotting out his poor mom for sympathy). Emeril's awkwardness on camera, his goofy delight in playing to an audience, is, well . . . kinda endearing. Unlike Rocco, when Emeril puts on a white chef's jacket, he bothers to remove the expensive button-down dress shirt he was wearing before—so on camera, he doesn't look like he's ready to bolt for a meeting with his agent or a date with a model should the opportunity arise. And Emeril caught a break: His ludicrous sitcom was canceled almost immediately, thereby saving celebrity chefs everywhere from being last week's fad. On television and in person, Emeril looks like a guy who *likes* to cook. Rocco looks like he'd rather be anywhere else. Though far more successful and famous, Emeril projects a public image completely devoid of greed, vanity, lust, or ambition—sins to be found in obvious abundance all over Rocco's more handsome but need-riddled face.

Or take the case of Mario Batali. Before he became "Molto Mario," Batali cooked soulful, eclectic, and delicious Italian favorites at Pó, a tiny restaurant in Greenwich Village. He was a man of many appetites, a guy who liked to cook, to eat, to drink . . . to live. He loved the neglected hooves and snouts and guts that form the heart and soul of much of traditional Italian cuisine. Now? Mario is still a man of Falstaffian appetites. Only he's an empire too. And what has he done with his celebrity? Other than enjoy it? Well, he still serves his beloved hooves and snouts and guts—only now, with the bully pulpit of television celebrity to add authority to his argument, he's seducing thousands more diners into giving them a try. He still serves soulful, eclectic, and delicious food—only now he does it all over New York. Every Batali restaurant has a different concept; and every one of them fulfills a need we might never have known we even had. Rare among chefs, Mario has used celebrity to do good works, to continue to do what he loves. Mario on TV is the same as Mario in person. (Except for the smoking and cursing, of course, but we all do that.) I asked Mario about his relentless drive to open more and more restaurants. I said, "Dude! If I were you, making your kinda bucks? You'd never *see* me again. I'd run off to an island! It would take a week to even find me by *phone*! Why do you do it?" His answer was simple. And honest: " 'Cause I *love it.*"

Chefs have publicists and agents these days. Alain Ducasse likely has a legion of them. The restaurant has one publicist, and the chef often has his or her own. As I pointed out to a four-star chef friend of mine who was having a hard time adapting to the rigors of book tour and self-promotion, there is nothing shameful about it. "It's not just for *you* that you're doing this! The insipid three-minute cooking demos on morning news shows, the posing for photos, all the self-promotion. Sure it's undignified! *But it's good for business!* Now stop whining and get out there and take one for the team!" I meant it too. It's not just you, the chef, out there, puffing himself up; it's all who sail within: the owners, the investors, the cooks, the long-suffering sous-chef, the floor staff. They like money too. They could use having the restaurant's profile raised a little. They'd like to move up too. All that work, all those hours, all that loyalty, in a business where the overwhelming odds are that you will fail; almost any strategy that helps tilt the scales is a good thing. Cooking professionally is hard. It ravages the mind and body. Hard-core purist foodies may gripe that a chef is not "keeping it real," but I invite them to try working a busy sauté station six long shifts a week on forty-five-year-old legs. Chefs who are still doing that beyond fifty don't look forward to living much longer.

But where does one draw the line? Where, exactly, does a chef go over to the dark side?

I think that, as with any celebrity, it comes when you forget who the hell you were to begin with. When you forget that at the end of the day, even if you're not actually doing much of the physical cooking anymore, you're still just a *cook*.

When celebrity chefs get too far away from the food (which is what got them all this way, wasn't it?), they run the risk of entering that terrible and transitory zone of D-list reality-show freakazoids. (Does anyone remember any of the original "stars" of *Survivor*? Or of last season's *Apprentice*? Should anyone even *care*?) We like our celebrity chefs to still be, at the end of the day, *cooks*. This is not to say that Mario, or Jean-Georges Vongerichten, or Thomas Keller spend much time sweating behind the line these days. How could they? But presumably, they don't wander too far for too long. They *still* like to cook. They still like other cooks. They clearly love the business they're in. They haven't relaxed their standards. They first want people to eat and enjoy the food they love—in however many venues they serve it.

It may not be *all* about the food in the harsh, unforgiving business of celebrity chefdom, but it *is* still about cooking, about the pleasures of the table. Those who forget that, even the prodigiously talented, do so at their peril. As a TV chef/guy myself, I have always found it useful to remember that the good times could end at any second, that the next book could tank, that the TV thing could come crashing down with the arrival of the very next ratings book—or the next data from a faraway focus group—and that I could well end up right back behind the stove, flipping steaks and dunking fries until I keel over from the heat or alcoholism. I loved my time in professional kitchens, and it would not be a terrible thing to go back to it. The restaurant business, after all, is the greatest business in the world. Cooking is noble toil. And fun. No supermodel or television producer is *ever* going to say anything more interesting than my line cooks and sous-chefs. In the end it comes down to the very first question you ask yourself when enduring the hazing and drudgery of your first cook's job, or your first days at cooking school, when you look long and hard in that mirror and say, "Do I *really* want to be a chef?"

If you'd rather be an actor, or a spokesmodel—or even a writer—it's time to get out.

WHAT YOU DIDN'T WANT TO KNOW
ABOUT MAKING FOOD TELEVISION

IT CAN'T BE THAT bad, can it? I mean, let's face it, I'm doing another season. I know I have one of the best jobs in the world. A few weeks ago, as I was sitting on the porch of an old Antillean house in the Caribbean, waiting for my stuffed conch and Creole chicken to arrive, my waiter, a ten-year-old kid, asked me the kind of guileless, painfully illuminating question only a ten-year-old could ask: After watching me knock back around four beers, huff down a few smokes, and stuff my face with appetizers—pausing occasionally to babble witlessly at the cameras floating around like drunken hummingbirds—he looked me straight in the eye and asked, "Mister? What's your job?" I was absolutely flummoxed. What is my job? What the hell is it I do for a living? Am I a chef? Well . . . not really anymore, am I? My hands are so soft and tender from avoidance of manual toil that I could be a spokesmodel for overpriced emollients. Am I some kind of writer guy? I dunno. Don't like writers much. Given a choice between being trapped on a desert island with a group of writers or a family of howler monkeys, I think I'd pick the monkeys. At least I could eat them. And what the fuck is a "television personality"? Jesus! I hope I'm not that. I'd rather write "habitual masturbator" on my visa applications than admit to that.

Whatever it is I do these days, whatever you might want to call it, I do get to travel all over the world, going anywhere I want, eating what I want, meeting admired chefs who only a few years ago would have thrown me out the door had I wandered into their kitchens looking for a prep job. I get to do a lot of cool stuff that not so very long ago I never dreamed I'd live to experience. I've made friends all over the world. And I get paid for it. All I have to do is make television, maybe write about it all once in a while. Compared to cleaning spinach and draining the grease trap, it's a pretty good gig.

But you don't want to hear me gloating about nibbling Ibérico ham with Ferran Adrià at a table in the back of a little Spanish ham shop, or describing the feel of tiny Asian feet working my back muscles in some faraway hotel, or weighing the comparative merits of Moroccan *kif* versus Jamaican *bud*. You don't really want to hear me moaning about the cheese course at Le Manoir aux Quat'Saisons, or how Dale de Groff really does make the best goddamn martini on the planet. You want to picture me crawling across a cold tile floor, coughing stomach lining into something that only the hotel manager could refer to as a toilet, begging for mercy as my brutal overlords arm-twist me into choking down yet another mouthful of "pork ring" before submitting me to some new video-friendly humiliation, right? Who wants to read about some undeserving mutt having a good time for free when you actually have to work for a living? I wouldn't, believe me.

The show is produced, shot, "written" on a sort of fly-by-night basis by me, Lydia Tenaglia, and Chris Collins working for a production outfit called New York Times Television (they also produced and shot the Ruth Reichl shows). Working from a wish list (mine), we storyboard a kind of comic strip, blocking out the scenes in such a way as to incorporate the various destinations, dishes, restaurants, chefs, and cooks we seek to shoot. Assistant producers back in New York, researchers, and an on-site translator/fixer "enable" whatever unwise plan we make (often while intoxicated). Two shooters, usually Chris and Lydia, an assistant producer, and I set off to the destination, meet up with our translator, and try, as best as possible, to shoot what we need for a show. My impromptu ravings are recorded on camera, whether used in final cut or not, and a post-shoot interview serves as a basis for a later voice-over. We usually shoot about two meals a day. Each show takes about a week to shoot, anywhere from six to fourteen hours a day. There is no stunt food. If you see me eating it on camera, I'm really eating it. *All* of it. Often with seconds. A lot of very nice people go to a lot of trouble to give me their best, and I try to be a good guest. If I look happy on TV, I'm probably happy shooting the scene. If I look cranky, sweaty, nauseated, and unhappy, then that's probably my mood at the time. There is no makeup, obvious from the ever-changing panorama of pimples, bug bites, and scars visible on my rapidly aging mug, and if I haven't shaved for a scene, it probably means I just couldn't get it together that morning, 'cause my hands were shaking too badly.

Chris, Lydia, and I spend a lot of time together on the road, both working and hanging out. After all the hours in crummy hotels and airports, shooting scenes that just don't "work" but that we continue to "French shoot" (meaning they turn off the camera but mime shooting anyway to be polite), a sort of hysteria sets in. Some tiny little detail will become endlessly hilarious. While in Japan, the word *chanko*—for no good reason at all—had us all spastic with uncontrollable laughter for hours. I am now often referred to in internal memos—or when being difficult—as my evil, egomaniacal action-film-star alter ego, "Vic Chanko"—as in "Vic doesn't want to come out of his trailer" (though we of course don't have trailers). If I'm unhappy, I will torment them by referring to myself in the third person, as in: "Vic doesn't like this scene. Vic is checking out and checking in to the fucking Sofitel down the road." For episodes with a disturbingly homoerotic subtext (as in the Rio show), I become Vic's porn-star brother "Tad Chanko." It doesn't—as you've probably guessed—take a lot for us to laugh, not after we've been softened up by countless "hang-yourself-in-the-shower-stall" hotel rooms.

Speaking of hotels, you definitely *don't* want to know how much time we spend talking about lower intestinal activity and the peculiarities of the local plumbing. In Brazil, for instance, the "capacity" of the hotel toilets is lamentably weak. Used toilet paper, horrifyingly, is to be deposited in a plastic bucket next to the crapper. This goes against the grain of everything we've come to believe in in American urban upbringing—who wants the room-service maid giving you the thumbs-up on a good day, or looking worriedly at you after the results of too much dende oil? Such matters should be between you and your porcelain, *n'est-ce pas*? Not on the road. We are all-too-familiar with our respective contributions, and the viability of our flushing apparatus. Checking in and being greeted with a toilet that roars and whirls like a turbine engine is a much-prized event, discussed with a fervent appreciation that borders on the tragic.

Additionally, when a subject/host/restaurateur for what was supposed to have been an important scene turns out to be as exciting as a slice of American cheese, or exhibits webbed fingers, an unpleasantly ripe odor, evidence of inbreeding, or an inclination to sweaty embraces, the theme from *Deliverance* is often heard under somebody's breath. You will notice in season two the occasional humming of the particularly annoying and ubiquitous incidental music we endured throughout season one—a private joke between us and the editors back in New York. *Simpsons* references, Cher jokes, shameless cribbing from movie scenes are slipped in whenever possible. Chris and Lydia love shooting nightmare/dream sequences—as they get to play with their toys in post-production—and they also love to see me looking ridiculous whenever possible. Head injuries, blunt-force trauma, scenes of me on boats or looking like Mister Roper in a bathing suit are much enjoyed by crew and editors alike.

Why do I love working with this particular couple? 'Cause they're really talented. 'Cause I think they're really good at what they do. 'Cause they make the show look good on the cheap. 'Cause they like the same movies I do, will eat grubs if I insist they share my pain, and drink like champions. Both are absolutely fearless in the cause of good "B-roll," leaning out of moving cars, walking backward in mine fields, bullshitting their way through roadblocks, shoving their way through some very scary streets in favelas in nighttime Rio or in red-light Phnom Penh. We're considering a "chowing with the warlords" show in Central Asia and I know they're the right folks for the job.

At the end of shooting, back in New York, we watch rough cuts, argue about revisions, rewrite, tweak, and do final voice-overs in a studio. (By the way, recording studios are one of the last workplaces where I can *still* smoke! Sound engineers know that smokers' voices need the occasional hit.) The episodes then go to the network, which usually asks for surprisingly few revisions: a couple bleeps, cut out the sodomy jokes, the direct drug references, the offensive-to-major-religion stuff, the McDonald's-as-center-of-all-evil type of thing. "They're sponsors, for Chrissakes! You can't say they cause rectal tumors in lab rats! This isn't *60 Minutes*!" You know, reasonable.

In short, shooting the shows is a dysfunctional family affair—much like working in my old kitchens.

WARNING SIGNS

FOR THE LAST FEW years, I've become increasingly fascinated by a particular chain of London steakhouses (two related chains, actually). Taking up vast chunks of prime real estate on what sometimes seems like every other corner, they appear to be advertisements for What You Don't Want In A Restaurant, a rude, even proud demonstration of How Awful Things Can Be. Steakhouse franchise number one (let's call it The Chuck Wagon) often sits directly across from its sister outfit, steakhouse number two (let's call it The Feed Bag), and at eight-thirty on a Saturday night, both of them are defiantly, even extravagantly empty. They are everywhere in central London, inexplicably still open each time I visit, their large, red neon letters reading CH K W GON and EED AG, the view through their large picture windows revealing empty faux crushed velvet booths, ugly flock wallpaper, and a single, abject waiter staring hopelessly into space.

"How do these places stay open?" I always wondered out loud, and as my interest grew into an obsession, a friendly journalist took me to one of them for dinner, allowing me to probe their dark inner workings from close up.

What I found that night was a fascinating working example of nearly all those things you don't want to see when sitting down to dinner in a restaurant, a real-world, life-size museum diorama representing Restaurant Hell, a pavilion of shame where an entire restaurant chain decides to flush money down a hole, night after night, so that we, the casual dining public, can learn the many shades of hideousness, the warning signs of what will surely be bad food—and apply this newfound knowledge elsewhere. The Chuck Wagon exhibited the following classic restaurant crimes for our consideration; all of them can be taken as indicators of Nothing Good Will Come of This.

1) *A big, bright chain operation—loudly advertising VALUE.* How good can "cheap" steak be? Especially when the place is completely empty?

2) *A big, bright chain operation—directly across from an eerily similar operation.* The place seems to have, at one time, planned for regular arrival of entire herds of spectacularly stupid, undiscriminating diners. That the owners don't bother to replace the dead neon letters on their signs does not bode well for what's inside.

3) *Dead-eyed waiters, sitting in empty booths, looking bored, unhappy, and defeated.* This alone is reason to flee. The waiter knows, better than anybody, how bad things are. At my meal, as soon as my journalist pal and I sat down and a photographer took a picture of us from outside, our waiter inquired of our affiliations—and the purpose of the photographer—then immediately made a covert, whispered phone call. (A guilty conscience, and a procedure in place for dealing with too much interest, can never be a good thing.) Accompanying the waiter were a busboy (who apparently doubles as bartender), a dishwasher, and one cook. Now, how can *one* cook make all the food on an absurdly, even dangerously, *huge* menu, one might well ask oneself. And how long has that Duck à l'Orange been kicking around that quiet kitchen, waiting for me to come along?

4) *Signs of quiet scaling back and cost cutting.* A forlorn dessert cart, half-filled with hardy, not-too-perishable fruit variations (nothing that will oxidize or get too ugly too quickly—probably because it will be used again tomorrow and the next day) sits right by the front door, subtly blocking access to what might once have been an upstairs dining room. What don't they want us to see? Clearly a sign saying "Section Closed" is not

enough. It has been deemed necessary to seal off the stairs, preventing even the casual drunken tourist, hunting for the restroom, from stumbling upon whatever hidden horror lurks above.

5) *The trick menu.* Wow! It sure *looks* big! But, wait! There may be ten or twelve appetizers—but half of them seem to contain prawns! This strategy allows the lone cook to quickly whip up a variety of no-doubt once-frozen delights from a single box of thawed prawns. And there sure seem to be a lot of deep-fried nuggety, breaded thingies . . . I regard the chicken "Cordon Bleu" with the same suspicion I cast on the prawn nuggets; they very likely originated in the same far-away blast freezer.

6) *The telltale "DING!" of the microwave.* Is it a coincidence that I heard its woeful tolling just before my limp, watery, gray, and completely uncaramelized duck arrived? I think not.

7) *The table tent display offering festive party drinks with umbrellas in them.* I don't know about you, but when I sit down in an empty steakhouse—whether in London or anywhere else in the world—a piña colada, a grasshopper, or a Singapore sling are *not* the cocktails that leap immediately to mind. Their presence is evidence of a disturbed mind, as if some cargo cult of South Seas natives had found the menu of a fifties-era American diner and after hitting the lottery and moving to the UK, decided to re-create it from memory. "Oh yes! Americans *love* drinks that look like fabric softener—as long as they have cherries and umbrellas in them!"

8) *The mixed metaphor.* The shotgun marriage of New Orleans/Chicago/Virginia City Gay Nineties/Cathouse theme with framed prints of the Scottish Highlands seems strangely . . . inappropriate, as does the mélange of "California Burger" (even Californians would not recognize this as food), Prawn Cocktail, Duck à L'Orange, Chicken Cordon Bleu, and Steak and Chips. I believe I saw a Hawaiian Burger offered—a warning sign all by itself. How good can they be at *all* of these? Answer? No damn good at all.

9) *The universal garnish.* When the same brown and limp

premixed salad and woefully unripe tomato slice pops up on nearly every plate, it's solid evidence that there is no budding Robuchon in residence.

10) *The "Why Is This Place Really Here?" factor.* Do the math. The place is empty. It's *always* empty. Even if they fill once a day for lunch (which they don't), the place was clearly designed to make money through high volume and turnover—and they *can't* be making enough money to pay the rent, much less electric, wages, gas, and so on. So *how do they stay open? And why?* What are they really doing upstairs, past the barrier of decaying desserts? Cockfighting? Craps games? Illegal importation of exotic snakes and birds? Human sacrifice? I can't help but think about this as I listlessly chew a bloodless, flavorless, too-tough steak, without even a sharp steak knife (the secret of every successful steakhouse) to mitigate the miasma of awfulness.

I urge the reader to patronize, if only once, one of these shining examples of Restaurant Hell. Sit down in one of the oversized booths, breathe deep, suck up the ambiance, peer deep into the waiter's eyes. Take notice of the details. Carefully study the menu, a veritable field manual of the submediocre. Nearly everything you want to avoid in a restaurant is right there for you to see. Just don't order the duck.

MADNESS IN CRESCENT CITY

THREE O'CLOCK IN THE morning and I'm sitting (or am I standing?) with the kitchen crew from Lee Circle Restaurant at Snake and Jake's Christmas Club Lounge, a favorite after-work haunt of the New Orleans chef/cook demi-monde. It's a dark, crumbling, and septic shack where the decor is always Christmas. Colored lights wink through cigarette smoke behind the bar as a very large bottle-blonde in a tight latex bustier pours what must be my sixth or seventh Jägermeister shot and pushes it toward me. This is not my chosen beverage, but Snake and Jake's owner, Tony "Mr. Hospitality" Tocco—who looks like a Fun House-era Stooge—is insistent, eyeballing me through lank, greasy hair, a scowl on his face. It's all about "hospitality" at Snake and Jake's, he assures me for the fifth time. Proof? Naked people drink for free. A few weeks earlier, more than forty of New Orleans' finest culinarians and their enables had shown up at the front door and stripped buck naked. I'm glad I missed that.

In my quest for "authentic local" food in New Orleans, I've managed to completely avoid the French Quarter. No boobs, no beads, no Bourbon Street for me. No cloud of fryer grease, hordes of slow-moving tourists, no eggs Benedict or oysters Bienville in the famous coliseums of Galatoire's, Brennan's, or Commander's Palace. Okay, I did nick into the quarter for a quick dozen oysters at the Acme; and I did call out from my hotel room to the legendary Verdi Mart, where locals can order a quick, late-night delivery of bourbon and cigarettes and the bigger-than-your-head muffuletta sandwiches. But otherwise I've managed to pretty much stay away from the usual suspects. That said, every time locals ask where I've been eating and I tell them, there is disagreement. "Why didn't you try . . ." or "You should try . . ." is pretty much the standard reaction.

But I think I've been doing pretty well. I had a fabulously greasy breakfast at the grim flophouselike Hummingbird Hotel and Grill. I ate sublime sno-cones at the legendary Hansen's Sno-Bliz Sweet Shop, where the ice is shaved on a nearly century-old hand-cranked device, flavored in stages, and heaped in a cup topped with sweetened condensed milk. I had the crawfish pie, pralines, and jambalaya at Tee-Eva's; the "Feed Me" red-sauce-heavy assault at Tony Angello's; the tweaked classics and gumbo variations and best-in-world fried chicken at Jacques-Imo's; and the ham hock with collards and grits at the Harbor. Before arriving to face imminent destruction at Snake and Jake's, I drank local beer and ate red beans and rice and listened to jazz and blues at Vaughn's, an ancient bar in the Ninth Ward, and when the trumpet player took a break between sets to grill rabbit sausage and ribs on an outdoor pickup-truck barbecue, the other customers filling the streets, drinking from "go-cups," I met Tony, grinning evilly under a streetlight. Some of the cooks with me shook their heads. They knew what came next.

Oh, what a wonderful town. Bars are open twenty-four hours. Nearly everyone seems to drink heavily (I'm told that if you mention New Orleans as a residence, you go right to the head of the line at Betty Ford), and at a few bars, like Checkpoint Charlie's, you can wash the blood and hair from last night's misadventures off your clothes in the conveniently located on-premises launderette while you begin new ones out front. Fried batter is a menu item. And everybody, it seems, either cooks, eats seriously, or has opinions about both.

I'm enjoying the Jäger shots. My brain needs cleansing. Two days earlier, I was the guest of a man called Wild Bill of Zam's Swamp Tours, sitting on his cramped houseboat in the bayou as he deep-fried alligator nuggets. His nephew, a delightful young tyke with an impressive blond mullet, kept sticking a baby gator's face into mine, provoking it to snap at my nose. Mosquitoes clogged my ears and nostrils and nearly blocked out the light from the bare lightbulbs as I sampled alligator piquante and grilled alligator kebabs and listened carefully for the first strains of dueling banjos. The smell of frying alligator still clogs my pores.

But I've confirmed my hypothesis about enjoying yourself in a new and unfamiliar town. First rule: Run away from the hotel, as far and as fast as you can. Rule Two: Avoid anyplace where people like you (meaning out-of-towners or tourists) congregate. Rule Three: When you find a crummy bar clogged with locals who seem to be enjoying themselves, go in, sit down, and start drinking. Be sure to buy a few rounds for your fellow drinkers. At the appropriate moment, inquire of the best places to eat, emphasizing your criteria to go where no tourists have gone before. "Where do *you* eat?" is a good starting point. If you hear the same name twice, take note.

Rule Four: If in New Orleans, call Hazelden ahead of time and make a reservation. You'll be needing it.

A VIEW FROM THE FRIDGE

I AM A CHEF. Though I can be a terror in my kitchen, in the dining room of other restaurants I'm a pussycat. I am scrupulously polite and effusive in my praise. And I always tip twenty percent (at least). I'm also, I am told, not the most attentive of dinner companions. I can't help but be attuned—almost painfully at times—to every nuance around me: the ebb and flow of waiters and busboys, hosts and sommeliers, bartenders and cooks. After twenty-seven years in the restaurant business, the choreography of dining room service, any dining room's service, has become hard-wired into my nervous system.

I know that there are a number of simple, avoidable things that can throw off the rhythms of even the best-run places. When that happens, a memorable evening can be remembered for all the wrong reasons. I've learned plenty about what makes a wonderful dining experience from eating at great restaurants, but not nearly as much as I've learned from working in them. What have all my hours of standing before a stove taught me about sitting at a table? I'll tell you.

If the people at the table beside mine summon a busboy (the first available person in a uniform), unable to distinguish him from their waiter, I cringe. I can tell you with near certainty that additional communication will now be required: The busboy, a member of a profession largely comprising newcomers to America's shores, will have to take aside the already harried waiter.

"Table seven. Lady say chicken cold. No like-a spinach."

The waiter then must consider whether clarification, not to mention confirmation, is required before braving the chef's wrath. This means a trip back to the table, annoying the already annoyed customers by asking them to repeat their complaint. If you speak to the busboy, you might just ask him to locate your waiter. Better yet, try remembering your waiter's face.

I also feel the waiter's pain when, without warning, a patron seated with friends at a table for four (a four-top) suddenly bolts to the bar (or outside) for a cigarette. This often seems to occur just when the entrées for that table are about to be served—or, as waiters say, are "in the window, ready for pickup." I know the electric shock that travels through the restaurant's spine and into the brainstem of the kitchen: The chef has that table's food up! It's sitting perilously under the destructive warmth of the heat lamps. Other orders are coming up around it, new ones are coming in, and the chef is beginning to freak: His lovely food is dying in front of him. And he's got a difficult choice to make. He can push the orders for the four-top to the side and squeeze other outgoing orders around it for a while, in the hope that the smoker will return before the food gets cold and ugly, a skin forming on the sauce that the chef was once so proud of. Or he can yank the whole order, move the "dupe" (the kitchen's printed copy of an order) back to the "order" position, and start all over again. It's a tiny, inconsequential move for the customer—a cigarette at the bar—but for the kitchen, particularly in a good restaurant, it can cause mad panic and much misery. It's polite to schedule your breaks ahead of time—as in asking the waiter, "Would now be a good time to grab a smoke?"

The people at the two-top (a deuce) on my other side are friends of the house . . . or people with whom the house wants to *become* friends. I know this because I saw the military-type hand signals between the maître d' and the front waiter when the couple arrived. I saw the brief, whispered conversation along the service bar. I can recognize the body language for "notify the kitchen" and "comp." These customers will be monitored as if they were in intensive care, with *amuse-bouches* and careful recommendations of the chef's best efforts tonight.

I hope the cosseted duo will be suitably appreciative and that they understand that when the house picks up a check, it is appropriate for the guests to leave a cash tip, preferably a damn big one. Waiters, for all practical purposes, live on tips. The twosome is eating up valuable real estate in the dining room (space and time, representing a considerable chunk of potential earnings). All that extra-special attention necessarily robs attention from others. For these two to walk out without tipping would be a punishment to their waiter. If the floor staff pools tips, it would be a punishment to the whole team.

The same principle applies if a table, especially a large one, is late for a reservation. You want to see real suffering? Look at the face of a beleaguered maître d' with an unseated eight-top in the middle of a very busy dining room at eight-thirty on a Saturday night. He's already cleared a huge block of valuable time in the reservation book, probably turned away two four-tops (who generally spend more money than one eight-top) from a seven o'clock seating. He's also kissed off any hope of turning the tables at nine or even ten o'clock, for that matter. The party of eight yet to arrive represents a major leap of faith for him, an investment of not only the house's but the waiters' and busboys' money. Such no-shows are sticking it to the entire staff. (Along these lines, clowns who book at three or four restaurants on a given night and then neglect to cancel in a timely way are the blood enemies of restaurateurs and their staffs alike.)

Now, you might find this a bit disingenuous if you're thinking back to the night you arrived promptly and the restaurant wasn't able to seat you for fifteen minutes. Certainly, apologies are in order. But all I can tell you is that it's in the restaurant's best interest to seat you as soon as possible. No one on my side of the business willfully creates delays; after all, it's bad for business when drop-ins see an overcrowded bar. Maybe I'm asking too much, but think about the imprecise science of seating the next time you're lingering over your coffee and nobody seems inclined to give you the bum's rush.

Should you behave in a restaurant? Should you care what your waiter thinks of you? Does it matter if you show your appreciation? I know well how accurately and in what terms the mood and behavior of customers can be tracked. I know that cranky, rude, or capriciously demanding customers can be given—in the ongoing triage of restaurant toil—cruel nicknames and be quickly dismissed as lost causes. They are viewed as a liability, and this information is passed on to the kitchen in ways subtle and unsubtle: "Rush table twelve, will ya? I just want to get these jerks out!"

Does this mean table twelve will get lousy food and service? No, not necessarily. I have seen four-star kitchens in which the customer's every reaction is tracked, course by course, with pictograms or cuneiformlike code on the dupes or on a blackboard. If the smiley face from course one turns to a frown for course two, the kitchen might dispatch free *amuse-bouches* or a tiny glass of chilled Sauternes with a square of foie gras.

It's particularly loathsome when a customer who is displeased with his entrée vents his unhappiness on his waiter, as if willfully betrayed by his server. The simple distinction that his waiter did not himself cook his food is lost. Problem with the food? Ask nicely to have it replaced. Most times, you'll be surprised at how quickly and eagerly everyone responds. If the kitchen has made a mistake, it's never a good idea to take it personally. No, nothing untoward is likely to happen to your entrée when it returns to the kitchen. Customers who behave spitefully, angrily, simply flag themselves as rubes—even if they're wearing two-thousand-dollar suits. The whole restaurant will heave a sigh of relief at their exit, and on their next visit they will be relegated to the newest and possibly most inept waiter. The veterans won't want any part of them.

Polite complaints or criticisms? By all means. They will be recorded, probably in the manager's log, or at the very least conveyed at the appropriate moment to the chef, who will, especially if he's heard the same comments before, do something in response.

If the meal was good, should one send compliments to the chef? Yes! Believe it or not, the message will almost always be conveyed to the kitchen. We like it when our labors are appreciated. We remember it. And should we see you in our dining room again, we'll have a better picture of what you like and we'll be able to tip you off to what's new or special. We'll more than likely send free stuff your way. I'm always happy to hear from the floor staff: "Table six are regular customers, man. Really good people. Can you send them something? . . . What should they have?"

Sitting at my table, watching the action around me, I snicker at the miserable deuce a few tables away. They've been bullying their waiter mercilessly, and I can already see that he's conspiring with the busboy to clear their table as soon as the last forkful disappears into their maws. Later, over drinks with the waiters from the restaurant across the street, the terrible two-top will be discussed. *Named.*

In the extended, inbred family of restaurant workers, the duo has been identified, their faces and names burned into the consciousness of a growing number of servers as irrevocably as the mugs gracing those Wanted posters at the post office.

We all like places where they know our names and are familiar with our likes and dislikes. And, as in any complex relationship, one can with just a few smiles and nods or the occasionally muttered thank-you, become special: a genuinely appreciated patron, a customer in good standing, a friend of the house. To *demand* special treatment is counterproductive. You simply banish yourself to the ranks of the undesirable herd. Most servers and chefs are grateful when given a measure of trust, and they would feel lessened if they betrayed it. The favorite customer at all restaurants is someone who by word or demeanor says, "I know you. I trust you. Give me your best shot." My decades in the business tell me we usually will.

For those few, those happy few, every extra effort is made.

They are welcomed as warmly as fellow employees; advised frankly and honestly on the best menu selections; and in every way treated like the home team instead of the visitors: "Great to see you . . . Let me send you dessert? . . . A nice snifter of Calvados? . . . Thanks, and please come again."

NOTES FROM THE ROAD

I WALK IN OUT of the roaring midday heat into the air-conditioned lobby of the Goodwood Park Hotel in Singapore, my damp clothes quickly becoming a freezing straitjacket. It's high tea in the lobby. Waiters plate pastries and pour tea; they're making coffee in sinister-looking glass urns, liquid bubbling over gas burners, like you'd expect to see in the laboratory of a mad scientist. Beyond the French doors, no one is swimming in the vast pool, not a single red-faced German lying on the chaise lounges—it's just too damn hot. A quick vodka tonic in the hotel bar and then I limp up to my suite to change. I'm tired, having flown in from Sydney late the previous night, jet-lagged, my brain and liver still struggling with the vast amounts of alcohol I consumed Down Under. My tooth aches, a dull throb threatening to take over my head, and my throat is sore from talking about myself nonstop for the last year and a half. In my hotel room, I kick off my sodden clothes in the damp chill and take a wary look at myself in the mirror.

It's an uninspiring sight. My stomach is distended like a just-fed python's from an eating binge that began early in the morning and will, I am informed by Ilangoh and Bee Ping, my escorts, continue into the late hours. My eyes look like dark sinkholes, my skin is erupting from the tropical heat, and my guts are roiling like those coffee-brewing contraptions I just saw in the lobby. I hate myself . . . and I don't feel good. I grimace for the mirror and see something black stuck between my teeth.

It's scorpion.

Tail, to be exact. A single, crunchy, black stinger—lodged prominently up front. Perfect.

The morning began early with a journalist, at the Tiong Bahru market; we met over coffee and *chwee kueh,* a savory rice cake with dried vegetables. This was quickly followed up by curried fish roe, spicy *sotong* (squid), and prawns at the casual eatery, Nasi Padang River Valley on Zion Road, and then a full-on meal of chicken tikka, fish head curry, Mysore mutton, side dishes, and Kingfisher beer at Banana Leaf Apollo restaurant in Little India. (Everything is eaten off a banana leaf with the hands.) The food was tasty and fiercely spicy, and I wished I were hungrier. Then I was hurried over to the Imperial Herbal Restaurant near Raffles to meet another journalist.

Here's the downside to having written a book about eating adventurously around the world: People want to feed you stuff. And not just any stuff. They want to see you nibbling on the nether regions of unusual beasties. They want to photograph you chawing on small woodland creatures previously believed to be indigestible. They want to dazzle you with turtle parts you didn't know existed, chicken feet, hundred-year-old eggs, snake snacks, fried bugs . . . and they want to watch you eat every little bit. At the Imperial, I was honored with a whole cooked turtle, then urged by the owner to try the gelatinous fat ("the best part—very good for you"), alligator soup, sea cucumber, and a plate of fried scorpions cooked into shrimp toast. The scorpions sat proudly atop golden brown squares, fried into aggressive attack position, tails raised threateningly. I ate as much as I could, and as I was in an "herbal" medicinal restaurant, inquired about something for my aching throat. Over an aromatic, herbal tea—which did help somewhat—I was given a holistic checkup by the resident herbalist. He took first one wrist, then the other in between thumb and forefinger, and concentrated gravely. He asked me to stick out my tongue before passing judgment. "Good," he said. Yin and Yang were pretty much in alignment.

Maybe a bit too much yang on the left side—where my throat felt like it had a baseball lodged in it. I just wanted to know if it was a tumor. Apparently my karma was out of whack. But then, I knew that already. Finishing the last jellylike hunk of turtle, I got a text message on my phone from New York. *Dee Dee Ramone is dead.* I nibbled distractedly at another scorpion toast, feeling myself sink into a deep, dark depression.

Before returning to the hotel, I waddle around Singapore, a kooky, unbelievably clean, very crowded expanse of lush vegetation, stately colonial-era houses, and magnificent trees poking through and between vast, multileveled modern shopping malls and new office buildings. It's the world's largest food court, with major chains like Mickey D's, Starbucks, and KFC sandwiched between vendors selling fish balls and curries. There seem to be a Prada, a Ferragamo, an Hermès, and a Burberry on every corner and millions of people shopping shopping shopping. No cops in sight. Not a one. I am surprised by the seeming total invisibility of police presence. I guess the famously severe penalties really do discourage potential violators. I do not, by the way, necessarily see the widely publicized policy of caning as a bad thing. The rotten American kid who received a few desultory whacks for vandalism a few years back should have gotten another ten, just for stupidity and bad manners. After Clinton appealed to the government, his number of smacks was reduced—unfairly, I think, as his alleged coconspirators from Hong Kong had to bend over and take the full freight. While I'm in town, Singaporeans keep warily inquiring what I think of this, expecting, no doubt, for me to be appalled. But I can think of no punishment more appropriate for, say, the Enron bunch, than a public caning (after being stripped of all their assets and sentenced to a little prison time, of course). All those investors and employees who lost their life savings while their bosses cashed out should at least have the pleasure of seeing Lay, Fastow, Skilling, et al. publicly bent over a sawhorse and flogged with a rattan pole. Even the pillory would seem appropriate—as these weasels will still, inevitably, remain rich. It would be a feel-good event for everybody. In fact, while we're at it, a few whacks for people who order egg-white omelettes, no butter, no oil, might be enlightened policy . . .

The next morning, I'm up early to go to the Tekka wet market to shop, then to the Butterbean Bistro, to cook for another journalist. There is no part of me that doesn't hurt, and it's been quite a while since I've stood behind a stove. I dread having to prepare food from unfamiliar ingredients, in an unfamiliar kitchen, with unfamiliar tools—but the bistro is remarkably well equipped with mise en place, and I manage to soldier through a workmanlike meal of steamed razor clams and pasta, followed by a roast lemon and herb chicken with vegetables and citrus beurre blanc. Foolishly, I eat my own food, using up valuable storage space I should be reserving for professional purposes. A few hours later, we're on to a faux Spanish restaurant in a new-made-to-look-old food court for sangría and another interview, then to Geylang, where yet another journalist waits for me at a Chinese joint. Ilangoh and Bee Ping, who have been escorting me around, eating what I've been eating, and waiting for me in the freezing bar watching the World Cup in between events (Mexico loses to the USA, which does not make me happy, as this means my cooks back in New York will be getting savagely drunk), look bleary-eyed and tired as we enter the last place on the itinerary. A platter of roasted duck stuffed with cured egg, some chicken, soup, and rice await. Ilangoh and Bee Ping ignore the food. I am barely able to speak. I can't even drink my industrial-size Tsing Tao beer. My eyes swim around in my head like drugged minnows, and my stomach is in full warning mode, signaling "one more thing, Tony—and it's curtains." I know what the penalty is for publicly urinating in Singapore. What, I wonder, is the penalty for lurching into the street and spraying vomit into the gutter? Then collapsing into a gibbering, crying, spastically shaking heap? I don't want to find out. For the first time in a book tour of thirty-two American cities, God knows how many countries, countless interviews, and equally countless meals, I break things off after only a few minutes. "I'm sorry. man," I rasp. "I just can't go on. I'm dying here. I need sleep." I have no idea what I said to the journalist—though I think I remembered to slag Jamie Oliver before slumping into my rice.

It's a twenty-hour flight back to New York, with a short layover and plane change—and I ain't eating no plane food. I don't care that the food is designed in consultation with Gordon Ramsay. Unless I see him pushing the trolley down from the galley himself, I'm not touching it. The man next to me scarfs every course like it's his last fucking meal: appetizer, main, cheese course, desserts, and even port. I'm loaded with tranquilizers and liquor and am still awakened every time the flight attendant leans over to serve the guy another course. I eye his utensils, hoping to shank him with his butter knife—but it's plastic.

The next meal I have is a bowl of noodles at Narita Airport in Tokyo, something light and soothing and thankfully reptile-free. I'm sitting in the corner, trying to get down a little broth between puffs on a cigarette, when an American tourist recognizes me from TV. He's been traveling in the East for a long time, he tells me. He's eaten many strange things. He wants to talk about the delicious rat he had in China. The braised dog he was served only a few nights ago. The delights of tree grub. My cigarette doesn't taste so good anymore. I feel the blood leave my head and the room swims and when (as Ross Macdonald once said) I go to brush something off my cheek—it's the floor.

THE DIVE

THE SINISTER INTERNATIONAL MANAGEMENT Consultant Group that hired me gave me an extra day in Greece to kick back after the travails of singing for my supper the previous night. I don't remember asking for it, but I've been working like a rented mule, making television all over the Med for so long that, hell, I guess I can use the extra beach time doing sweet fuck-all. Things could be worse. Thirty minutes of talking over dessert and I pick up a fat check and then it's front-of-the-the-plane back home. Not a bad deal, especially when you consider I was still slinging hash only five years ago. The company drones and their wives all shipped out this morning, so here I am, alone again, on the deck of a ludicrously luxurious resort on a Greek peninsula, looking out at the Aegean Sea, smoking duty-free Marlboro reds and waiting for my Negroni to arrive. There are a few very dodgy Russian shipping types and their underlings around—Speedos, thick necks, and thin watches—but otherwise it's just me: the nearly lone resident of a mammoth, empty resort.

My discreet "bungalow" has its own gym, steam room, whirlpool, a heavy bag (which I've found is a lot of fun to punch), a beach ten feet away, view of the Greek islands—and a wide-screen TV that would be right at home chez MC Hammer. Naturally, I'm misanthropic. But the Negronis are helping considerably.

I'm coming off the toughest, most maddening, frustrating shoot of my undistinguished television career, a frantic ten-day bounce through the outlying islands of Sicily (all of them lovely, by the way). I was not with my usual close-knit dysfunctional family of producers and shooters. Camera One, Todd, is still new and I've yet to really get to know him. Tracey, whom I've worked with a lot, was along, but no Chris or Diane— instead, the nice but indecisive producer, Global Alan, and an annoyingly hyperactive assistant. It was a bad mix, and our local fixer, an aristocratic lout/bullshit artist (let's call him Dario), ensured that about fifty percent of our carefully planned scenes evaporated in front of our eyes.

"The helicopter . . . she no coming. The weather. Is too windy . . ."

"The helicopter she coming maybe ten minutes . . . okay, maybe she no coming today . . ."

"The sea urchins . . . fisherman say they no more . . ."

"The restaurant closed today . . ."

"The giant turtles . . . they-a sick maybe. No coming. We cannot shoot . . ."

The Greek amphitheater at Taormina, in which we'd planned a scene extolling the glories of antiquity, was booked with a film festival, meaning that it was jammed with modern festival seating, a spanking new stage, and a JumboTron screen.

Mount Etna was socked in with clouds. Zero visibility.

The "squid fishing scene," in which I was to head out at night with a local fisherman to later triumphantly haul my still-wriggling catch onto the heaving deck for the cameras, ended with me desperately pinning a dead stunt-squid to a hook and feigning a catch. After two hours of waiting futilely aboard a violently pitching scum-boat, the entire crew was green and engaged in projectile vomiting. Poor Tracey, though heroically still shooting, looked ready to die.

Dario: "The moon. She no good for squid tonight . . ."

No shit.

My on-camera subjects were equally disastrous. In Trepani, at the salt flats, the only drama was whether my dining companion would die of old age before the scene was over. He could barely eat without drooling, and appeared ready to nod off halfway through. The "adorable squid fisherman's family" with whom I was to share my "catch" of the night before in a "rustic, home-cooked Sicilian meal" hated my guts on sight. We were two hours late (after waiting futilely for the turtles) and they just sat there throughout the meal, glaring at me.

All these disasters left our increasingly desperate shooters with no alternative but to try and squeeze entertainment out of my every embittered, drunken utterance, my every nap, walk, and private moment: "C'mon, Tony! This is a scene! The 'I'm stuck in the airport and can't find the bathroom' scene! It's comedy gold!"

Sicily was stunningly beautiful. But as is becoming a recurring theme in my life, so much useless beauty unspooled in front of my eyes like a half-observed, half-felt movie. Just out of reach. Can't stop. No time to really look or breathe it in. Pantelleria, a tiny volcanic island off the coast of Tunisia: black lava petrified mid-flow into wild, jagged, majestic shapes; crystal-blue sea; green vineyards; olive trees; my house a thousand-year-old Arab-style *damoussa* with white-domed roof; the sirocco from Africa blowing constantly but gently. You can smell the continent, the spices, feel the Sahara in the air—and I was off all day making fucking television.

Yet, I learned something important about myself in Sicily. (And I'm not being melodramatic here. Really . . . Okay, maybe I am.) One afternoon, Dario, the useless "fixer," took us for an impromptu cruise on his yacht. It was intended as a quick substitute scene to make up for the ultralight that couldn't land. ("Too much-a wind. Sea. She is . . . too rough.")

Try to visualize it in Antonioni black-and-white: Dario and his bored aristo friends and their mistresses—all in their tiny little bathing suits and wraparound sunglasses—and me and my Ugly American crew, at sea on a seventy-two-footer, sails up. Islands in the distance, a clear day. A few miles out, Dario gestures to the high, sheer cliff face on the shore of a nearby island, a magnificent edifice where waves pound against rock and coral.

"I jump from that cliff all the time," he says, pointing at a hundred-fifty-foot climb straight up, with a vertical drop between reef and rocks. "When-a you go up . . . there's no way down but to jump," he says. And then he dares me, *dares me*, to do it with him.

Now . . . you know me. There's no *way* I'm gonna let this cocksucker get away with this. Especially as I'm cranky, not a little bit drunk, and by now in the mood to squeeze his neck until his eyes pop out of their sockets. I figure it's worth it, if only for the possibility that I'll get to see him split his pointy fucking head open on a rock. Plus, we're desperate for a scene for the show, and I figure the "Tony Foolishly Breaks His Spine" scene will definitely spell Emmy Award—for somebody. So I hear myself saying, "I'll do it."

We take dinghies over to the cliffs. Dario shows me where we have to get off and where to climb. Todd takes a camera position on a reef opposite. Tracey, who'll be shooting the jump from a dinghy, is weeping behind the lens as they ferry us over. "Are you sure you want to do this, Tony?" She knows I'm on beer number eight. And that cliff, the closer we get, is looking higher and higher. I'm not making things easier with my drunken bravado, jokingly babbling good-byes to any and all whom I've ever loved, or who have loved me. (Just in case.) This makes her cry more.

We clamber off the dinghy and Dario leads me slowly and precariously straight up the crumbly limestone cliff, both of us free-climbing in bare feet, picking our way up with fingertips and toes, hanging and traversing along crevices and not, repeat *not*, looking down. After about half an hour of climbing, and a few hairy moments, we reach the top. Dario slides into position for his jump, clinging to a slight hump behind him with both hands, his weight supported by a tiny, brittle-looking protrusion the size of a large bar of soap.

It's a straight drop down, he says. Between that rock there . . . and that shallow reef . . . there. Make sure to keep your arms tightly at your sides or you'll break them when you hit the water.

"I know you gonna wanna flap your arms. Everybody does," he says. "But don't. Really."

I'm perched above him, as there's only room on the jump position for one at a time. And let me tell you: One hundred fifty feet looks a lot higher off the ground looking *down* than it does looking up. I can't even really see where I'm supposed to land through the white water and the waves below.

Dario starts to push off.

And freezes.

He leans back against the rock and says, "I have to think about this . . ."

A moment later, he starts to push off again.

And then freezes again. He leans back, says, "Turn the cameras off"—as if they can hear us all the way down there. "I'm not-a ready. I have to think. It's been a long time since I done this . . ."

Now, I'm not feeling too good about this near-suicidal enterprise myself at this point. Here I am, clinging to a rock high above the sea, and the formerly confident Count Dipshit is going wobbly on me. And that narrow space between rocks is looking narrower and narrower. Tracey, in the dinghy below, looks like a toy bobbing about in a faraway bathtub.

I remind Dario what he told me: that there's no other way down. And I suggest that given his lack of success so far with aerial conveyances, signaling for a chopper is not a viable option.

After yet another aborted attempt, his feet trembling spastically now, I revert to schoolyard persuasion and tell him we'll look like fucking pussies if he doesn't get his shit together and fucking take the fucking leap. I have to admit, I'm more than anxious to see him jump. If only to see if, once he does, his head reappears—and I therefore have a shot at surviving this lunacy.

Finally he goes. First straight out, then a straight drop. And then, a few long seconds later, BOOM!

A few more seconds and I see his head resurface, and he's swimming for the dinghy.

I slide down into position.

I do *not* want to spend any time thinking about what I'm about to do.

One more look down. Two seconds. Dario still in the water . . .

And, God help me, I push myself straight out into blue sky and drop, drop down toward blue and white water.

And you know what surprised me? While airborne, as I flew out, and then plummeted down toward rocks and sea?

I didn't care.

I was not afraid.

I've known love.

I've seen many beautiful things.

And it was enough.

That was what I was thinking. Stone cold. Serene. Yet . . . happy, as I dropped, and the water rushed up to meet me at sixty miles per hour.

Needless to say, I survived the experience. It's hell on the soles of your feet hitting the water at that speed. But jumping into the void made for an illuminating few seconds.

And we got the shot.

BITTER

A DRINKING PROBLEM

THERE ARE FEW ARTICLES of faith in my admittedly jaundiced worldview, precious few things that I believe to be right and true and basically unimprovable by man or God. This, however, is one of them: a properly poured beer or ale—in my case, a hand-cranked Guinness—in a clean pint glass of correct temperature is God's Own Beverage, a complete and nutritious food source, a thing of beauty to be admired, a force that sweeps away, for a time, all the world's troubles.

One does not drink Guinness in a vacuum-sealed pod. Context is important. The best place to fully appreciate the state of enlightenment that comes with a fine English, Scottish, or Irish beverage is, of course, that all-important institution, the pub.

So I am contentedly watching the foam settle in my glass at the Festering Ferret in London's East End, momentarily at peace with the world, contemplating life's mysteries, planning future good works. I'm smoking, admiring the cracked leather seats, the moldering century-old carpet, the box-shaped, nearly toothless, geriatric bartender. I'm running my hand over my worn wood table as if it were the Rosetta stone, deciphering with my fingertips the cryptic, possibly pre-Druidic messages inscribed there—"Stiv is a cunt," "Bay City Rollers," "Jamie is a mockney shite"—their echoes resonating through the ages, connecting me with poets and thinkers of another age.

A waiter approaches, draws my attention to a blackboard on

the wall, and says, "Would you care for something to eat, sir? The osso buco of Chilean sea bass is particularly good today." I look up with horror. There, just to the right of a well-punctured dartboard, is a portent of True Horror. A real menu! I read it with growing apprehension and dismay, an icy tendril of fear probing my gut: "Soup of fresh green peas with chiffonade of crisp prosciutto and pumpkin froth"; "Tartelette of foie gras with apricot chutney and house-made brioche"; "Cruelty-free noisette of pork with snow peas and caramelised shallots."

Even worse, there is an entire vegetarian section, segregated to the left side of the board. Just before I collapse, shaking, to the beer-sodden floor, I read in the dessert section: "Green apple sorbet with wasabi." Then everything goes black.

The next thing I am aware of is my fingers being pried from the fleshy folds of the bar hag's throat. A large fellow in a chef's coat and apron is doing the prying. A well-scrubbed young *commis* is assisting by beating me about the head and neck with a saucepot. (Copper, I notice, and well maintained at that.) Through broken teeth and a foam of bloody spittle, I manage to splutter, "What? When? How? Why?" before breaking down into convulsive sobs: "Oh God! Oh Jesus! It's awful! The end is here! It's over! My life is over!" As I release my grip, the bald fellow explains, while keeping a knee on my thorax, "We're a gastro-pub now. Can I fix you up with some tofu and wild mushroom beignets? They're lovely." Which is when I make a futile grab for the nearest blunt object and the *commis* lets me have it with the saucepot.

Gastro-pub? What the fuck is that? For me, fancy food in a traditional old pub is about as inviting as the phrases "Hot male-on-male action" or "Tonight! Billy Joel live!" or "Free prostate exam with every drink." A good pub should *never* have fine food. What's wrong with a good meat pie? Black pudding? Sausages? Shepherd's pie is a beautiful thing. I don't want truffles in it! And a vegetarian menu? In a pub? Vegetarians in a pub? For their own good, vegetarians should never be allowed near fine beers and ales. It will only make them loud and belligerent, and they lack the physical strength and aggressive nature to back up any drunken assertions.

The British pub is one of the last great bastions of goodness, civility, and decency in the world. Who wants annoying foodies in their local? They'll infest the place. They'll multiply like cockroaches. Soon, a sip will barely have passed your lips before you overhear, "Have you tried the salmon confit with tomato water? It's fabulous!" or "I'd like the basil gelato, please."

There'll be no place to run then, friends, and no place to hide. The enemy might as well be camped in your sitting room, buggering your pooch, biting the heads off your budgies, and playing Kylie CDs at ear-splitting volume. Good beer and fancy food should be kept separate. A firewall between them, like church and state. That wall crumbles and all will be chaos.

WOODY HARRELSON: CULINARY MUSE

THEY CALL US "COOKS." And we—meaning everyone who's ever shaken a pan or dunked a spud in a professional kitchen—can trace our proud lineage directly back to our apelike predecessors, clustered around a fire, searing hunks of flesh over the flame. In Roman times, we were slaves (pampered ones, yes, but slaves just the same). In Ottoman times we were janissaries. Later we toiled in the kitchens of cruel and capricious monarchs, sweated in the cellars of grand hotels, bounced from restaurant to restaurant. Those in our clan prepare pho in makeshift food stalls at night markets, peel chicken from the bone to roll in freshly fried tortillas in mercados, flip eggs behind lunch counters. Through guile and persistence and desperation, using the knowledge passed down to us by those who came before, we turn tough, unlovely bits of meat and scrap, produce and legume, into beloved national dishes. This thing of ours was always about *transformation,* about the strategic application of heat to make what was available somehow better.

But some would have us believe that the flames around which we have gathered since the beginning of our species do *not* make things better. They make them worse. Less healthy. Impure. More likely to cause "mucus" (a bad thing), toxins, lowered enzymes—and generally diminished grooviness. According to some extreme practitioners, if cooked food—or animal flesh of any kind—finds its way into our mouth, it should be followed by fasting, and a thorough colon-cleansing.

Advocates and practitioners of "raw food" eschew all meat, poultry, fish, dairy, refined or processed staples (like flour and sugar), and anything cooked, preferring only those remaining foods that are still raw or "living." Until recently, they have been viewed as a lunatic fringe, espousing a philosophy so extreme and ascetic as to make ordinary vegans look like pleasure-seeking libertines. One typical work on the subject, Victoria Boutenko's tellingly titled *12 Steps to Raw Foods: How to End Your Addiction to Cooked Food*, assures us that "because cooked food does not have enzymes, our body cannot use it. Therefore the body treats cooked food as a toxin and is only concerned with getting rid of it." Who knew? I always thought my body treated food as a pleasure. Strangely, Ms. Boutenko later claims that "our body never makes mistakes. We all know what we need if we listen to our body." I can only imagine that if I hear my body calling out for a cheeseburger, signals have somehow been crossed. (Apparently what it *really* wants is a Boutenko patty of ground and processed nuts, carrots, onion, yeast, and banana, thickened with dried herb, yeast, psyllium husk powder, and ground flaxseeds.)

Fortunately for most, the literature on raw food has provided unpersuasive visuals: The cover photo of Boutenko's manifesto displays a truly hideous spread of such unappetizing, clumsy butt-ugliness as to frighten away any but the most fervently devoted; it looks as if some fifties-era Betty Crocker got titanically drunk and decided to lay out a buffet for the Symbionese Liberation Army. A starved Weimaraner would turn its nose up at such appalling fare.

Unfortunately, things have changed.

Raw food has gone legit.

Charlie Trotter is probably the nation's most internationally celebrated chef—an artist, an intellectual, and the author of some truly groundbreaking and beautiful cookbooks. His eponymous restaurant in Chicago is one of the country's best. Roxanne Klein is a veteran of many fine kitchens, the chef/owner of Roxanne's in Larkspur, California. She is, perhaps, the leading innovator and proponent of "raw food." Last year, the two collaborated on *Raw* (Ten Speed Press), a real "cookbook" in which absolutely nothing is cooked. It's imaginative, pretty to look at, and (largely because of Trotter's preeminence) a direct poke in the eye of the entire culinary profession.

Raw represents a radical (yet aesthetically compelling) abrogation of the basic principle that "cooks" presumably cook. The stove, the oven, the open can of propane, the roadside grill, the barbecue pit, the hearth are where *food is made*. Right? The place of heat is where cooks and eaters congregate, *will always congregate,* to share food and stories. Thus it has always been. Thus it will always be.

Maybe not.

Trotter has served a vegetable tasting menu for some time. Noticing that most restaurants tended to cobble together a plate full of side dishes and odds and ends when confronted with vegetarian customers, he rose to the challenge and raised the bar significantly for others inclined to improve their own veggie offerings. Charlie Trotter likes vegetables. He understands them. Though he surely knew that many of his vegetable offerings would taste a lot better married to a fat lardon of bacon, or tossed in duck fat, like most great chefs through history he made the very best of limited options.

In his introduction to *Raw,* he is careful to distinguish between the role of chef/seeker and that of advocate for some health-conscious agrarian future. He seems to be saying that raw food can be a cool thing—but it's not necessarily the *only* thing. One gets the impression he is attracted more to the challenge than any underlying philosophy. Commendably, Klein urges similar caution, saying, "I think it's presumptuous for anyone to tell others how they should live their lives."

Nice words. Nice book. Without question, it's an answered prayer for anyone whom religion or personal circumstances has pushed into veganism.

My prejudices against vegetarianism and veganism are well known and deeply held, but looking at the gorgeous pictures, I thought surely any exploration of ways to make food—any food—better is a positive thing. As intellectual exercise, as gastronomy, as "another path," this weird corner of the culinary spectrum might, I thought, be as worthy of respect as any other.

Then I read the opening anecdote of Klein's introduction, an account of the inspiring moment that led to her immersion into the mysteries of raw food. She describes a fateful meeting in Thailand with former *Cheers* star and hemp activist Woody Harrelson.

"Every evening, our group would sit down to a fantastic feast of Thai vegetarian curries, noodles, and rice dishes. Woody, however, would always order a bowl of fruit or a green papaya salad. We *tried to get him to sample the wonderful cooked dishes we were eating, but he always declined* [italics mine]. After more prodding, he explained the reasons why he maintained a diet of raw fruits and vegetables. Michael [Klein's husband] and I found the philosophy interesting and decided to delve more deeply into it."

This story is horrifying on so many levels that my enzyme-starved, toxin-laden, mucus-clogged body shook when I read it.

First of all, *why* would anyone listen to Woody Harrelson about *anything* more important than how to be a working Hollywood actor or how to make a bong out of a toilet-paper roll and tinfoil?

And who would listen to anyone who can visit *Thailand*—a country with one of the most vibrant, varied, exciting culinary cultures on the planet (including a rich tradition of tasty vegetarian fare)—and *refuse* to sample its proudly served and absolutely incredible bounty? What kind of cramped, narrow, and arrogant worldview could excuse shutting oneself off totally from the greater part of an ancient and beautiful culture?

To my mind, there's no difference between Woody, the New Age gourmet, ensuring a clean colon by eating the same thing every day, and the classic worst-case, xenophobic tourist—the one who whether in Singapore, Rome, Hanoi, or Mexico City insists on eating every meal in the hotel restaurant. One fears "dirty" water, "unsafe" vegetables, "ooky," "weird," and unrecognizable local specialties. The other fears "toxins" and "impurities."

It's bad enough when you bump into a curmudgeonly fellow countryman while on vacation in a foreign land. But to bring his tao home with you is another thing. Especially when the curmudgeon's worldview has been shaped in that crossroads of enlightenment, Hollywood.

In striking contrast, Trotter's curiosity is a saving grace. And Trotter and Klein's creativity with a self-imposed restrictive form is something to be celebrated—I guess. *Raw* struggles mightily to convince the reader that "cheese" made from cashew can be a satisfactory substitute, and that "lasagne" made from zucchini "noodles" wouldn't be a hell of a lot better with the inclusion of some real pasta, but even the book's full-color food porn photos seem painfully lacking in some vital aspect. (Pork, perhaps.)

Raw is a quantum leap in the realm of what's possible with fruits and vegetables. But by offering comfort, sustenance, and encouragement to Woody Harrelson and would-be Woodys everywhere, Trotter and Klein have opened a Pandora's box of fissionable material. At a time in history when Americans, to an ever greater extent, have reasons to turn inward, away from this fabulously diverse and marvelous planet and the millions of proud cooks who live on it; at a time when people are afraid of just about everything, the authors have made willful avoidance and abstinence an ever-more attractive option.

I admire their skills. I really do.

But I fear for the planet.

IS ANYBODY HOME?

IT WAS LATE AT night in New Orleans. The liquor was flowing and the large and unruly group of chefs, managers, and cooks, freshly released from their restaurants, was in a truth-telling mode. Among them, a contingent of professionals from one of Emeril Lagasse's better restaurants was particularly disgruntled. Not with Chef Lagasse, about whom they had nothing but nice things to say; and not with the general state of affairs in their restaurant, of which they were quite proud. It was those damn customers again.

"They come in in their ugly shorts, with their cameras. And they ask, 'Is Emeril in the kitchen? Can you get him to come out and say *"Bam!"*?'" moaned one of them. "Dude! We're a fine dining restaurant!"

It's an inevitable effect of the celebrity chef phenomenon that people are as interested now in "who" is making their food as "what" they're eating. While on one hand, the advent of the celebrity chef has been good for America in that it has raised the level of pride and prestige in the profession and inspired people to eat better, cook better, and expect more of their restaurants, it has also created a cult of personality completely divorced from the realities of the business.

There should be little expectation that Emeril himself will be hunched over the stove when you eat at NOLA or Emeril's in New Orleans. The man has an empire to run. He's got restaurants all over the country, a product line, television shows,

171

endorsements to make, books to write. Do you really think he's cooking your chicken? He's put in his time. After all those years on the hot line, all that time building a "brand" and a business, doesn't he deserve to kick back in an office, have a cocktail, spend a little quality time with friends and family, and let others do the heavy lifting?

Of course he does.

And while it's completely understandable that some nitwits who know him only as loveable TV Emeril—and who have no understanding or appreciation of what it took for him to get there—might expect him to come by their table for a photo op in between dunking their squid into the fryer, it's inexcusable that professional food writers knowingly continue to perpetuate the myth that The Famous Chef Is In The Kitchen. They know it not to be true. Yet they continue. It makes, one can only assume, better copy.

An Important Food Writer who knows better recently penned a column in which he snarkily suggested that if he were paying one hundred thirty dollars for a meal at a Famous Chef's restaurant, he had every right to expect the Famous Chef to be in attendance, at least to swing by the table (presumably to pay homage to The Important Writer). Ridiculous! Most times when you see a legitimate restaurant review in which sentences appear like "Chef Flay has a delicate hand with the chipotles . . ." or "Ducasse's feeling for the flavors of Provence inform every course . . ." and you find yourself conjuring an image of the Famous Chef leaning over each of the reviewer's plates, nervously correcting seasoning or adjusting the garnish, you are complicit in a myth. If the chef is famous enough for you to know his or her name, chances are, he or she is currently Not In.

Important Food Writer, of course, knows full well that Chef Ducasse has reportedly barely *touched* a plate of food in nearly twenty years. Chef Ducasse is likely sitting in the first-class cabin of a flight to Hong Kong, or Paris, or Las Vegas. Chef Ducasse personally tossing your salad is about as likely to happen as Wolfang Puck popping up to serve you pizza at the airport.

Important Food Writer knows that Mario Batali is opening his twelfth restaurant in the last six months, and can hardly be expected to be personally making their gnocchi. Yet he persists. Worse, he gets angry. As responsible as anyone for building the legend and career of the Famous Chef, Important Food Writer now feels . . . strangely . . . jilted. Where *is* the Famous Chef he's written so adoringly about all these years, about whose "light touch" and "instinctive way with *oursin*" he's dedicated so many column inches? Why isn't he here, *now*, to kiss the ring of his creator?

"If you're not in your kitchen because you're doing a dinner for one of their charities, then it's okay," says one Famous Chef—who still actually works in his four-star kitchen as much as he can. "If it's not for them [the food writers], though, then it's not okay . . . They're either shaking you down for free meals for events, panel discussions, or symposiums—or crying you are not in your kitchen.

"There are blue-collar chefs—and white-collar chefs. This business is all about mentoring," Famous Chef goes on to say. "Tom Colicchio, Joël Robuchon, the guys who run their kitchens . . . they've been with them twenty *years*!"

"The menus?" he laughs, imitating one Michelin-starred icon. "Show eet to me when eet's done."

"Look at it this way," suggests Another Famous Chef. "You can't be a great chef if the food is not consistent. You need a day off—and the food must, *must* be exactly the same when you are not there as it is when you are there. This is fundamental to the business. Even if you have only one restaurant. You are a leader. You create a team who executes your style. Your vision. It's the same when you start opening more places."

"What about Wylie Dufresne [of New York City's WD-50] and Scott-Bryan [of Veritas]?" I ask, referring to two excellent and celebrated chefs who still seem chained to their kitchens.

"Blue-collar chefs," say both Famous and Another Famous Chef. "And they are terrible on television."

A celebrity chef who's worked particularly hard to maintain a publicly honest and realistic balance is Mario Batali. From the very inception of each of his new restaurants, he partners with—and gives credit to—a chef who has his own unique (yet similarly heartfelt) vision. Fish guru Dave Pasternack is fundamental to Esca, Mark Ladner to Lupa. Each restaurant was created around the strengths and passions of the chef partner as much as any concept. Yet Batali is the frequent target of embittered snarkologists like the *Los Angeles Times*'s Regina Schrambling, whose loathing for Batali seems to increase in direct proportion to his success. That every single one of Batali's restaurants is not only solidly *good* (at least), but even more remarkably—given the fiercely competitive nature of the New York restaurant business—profitable, should, one would think, deserve admiration. Life with Mario for New York foodies is surely better than it was before he arrived on the scene. Each new restaurant concept he's brought us has been, on balance, not only beneficial, but *daring*. Who knew we needed a place specializing in raw Italian seafood (Esca), or Sardinian pizza (Otto), or hoof and snout Italian (Babbo), or offal-centric Spanish tapas (Casa Mono)? Apparently we did. So who cares if you don't like the clogs or the TV show?

Mario, of course, regularly cooks in none of the restaurants. You'll see him hovering by the pass for the first few weeks of operations, as at the recent opening of Bistro du Vent, or swilling wine on the stoop across from Babbo. But cut the guy a break. He's *not* making your pasta.

Even Saint Thomas of Napa, probably America's greatest and most revered chef—Thomas Keller of the French Laundry, that is—now also runs two Bouchons (one in Napa, one in Vegas) and the four-starred Per Se in New York. Hasn't the man done enough? Do you really want him to die behind the range?

The answer to that is probably "yes, you do."

"You create a style," explains Famous Chef. "You work all those years, all those hours. No family life, no free time. All the sacrifice. Around thirty-eight, thirty-nine, you look around and you see the new guys, with their own vision, their own styles—

and it doesn't speak to you. You see it. You respect it. But you can't do it. It's not *you*. You've said what you had to say. It's time to get out. To move on. Expand. Create something for your old age."

It's not just about you, he goes on to explain. "When your chef de cuisine has been with you ten years, they want their own thing. They deserve it. You want to keep them in the company, all these people who have been with you. They want to move up. So you open up another place. Then another. You make room for the next generation."

Judging from the strident opinions on this subject in magazines and newspapers and foodie Web sites, it would be easy to conclude that it's a class thing: The dining classes, who have always been different (at least until recently) from the cooking class, simply hate to see the backstairs help coming up in the world. In England, Gordon Ramsay and Marco Pierre White, in particular, were singled out as "climbers," stepping up from their "class" in a way that seemed to offend. The speed with which some hurried to declare them "over" as soon as they opened another restaurant was breathtaking.

The Famous Chef has no obligation to you, or anyone else, to be present in the restaurant. And you should not expect him or her to be.

"You should expect it to be *good*," says Famous Chef.

That's the bottom line.

BOTTOMING OUT

THERE IS NO ONE less sympathetic to the trials, tribulations, and humiliations of the addict than an ex-junkie. No emergency room triage is more immediate and unforgiving than the way an ex-junkie sizes up a still-in-the grip former colleague. I hear that familiar, whiny tone of voice, I see the pinned, cartoon eyes of the smack user, or the jumpy, twitchy, molar-grinding, gibberish-spewing face of the coke-fiend, and I see a dead man. I'm not listening anymore. If I pay attention at all, it's to make sure they're not rifling through my coat. Cold? Yes. But then, junkies are used to stone-cold logic. Life, for someone whose body, brain, nerves, and cell tissue require (rather than desire) their drug of choice in order to get out of bed in the morning, is actually a very simple matter. You have one job: To get drugs. There's only one thing you *have* to do each day: Get drugs. One's priorities are always straight. Simply put: Nothing else matters. Those of us who've been addicted to heroin and/or cocaine (and I've been addicted to both) understand that better than anybody. You *know*, without question, that your best friend in the world *will*, given the opportunity, steal your drugs or your money or snitch you off to the cops. You *know*, without question, exactly how low you would be willing to go to get what you need. Chances are, you've been there already. More than once.

Stories about drugs and rehabilitation are boring, particularly when it's some Hollywood actor, grinning out from the cover of *People* magazine, yammering about Clean and Sober and their new project. We've heard it all before. Some people live. Others die. Who survives and who doesn't seems most often to have been determined long before the subject enters treatment—when the junkie in question looks in the mirror one morning and decides that he really, truly wants to live. If there's any question in your mind, before you even walk through the doors of the methadone clinic or rehab facility, about *how* badly you want to turn things around, and *what you're willing to do to accomplish that*, then lose my number.

The memory of the bitter taste of heroin in the back of my throat, the smell of burning candles, the taste of paint chips mistaken for a pebble of dropped crack, a whiff of urine and stale air from long-ago tenement drug superstores on the Lower East Side all came back when I watched Robert Downey Jr. being hauled off again in handcuffs. And this time, I actually cared a little. "This guy must *really* hate himself," I thought, reading of cocaine and speed allegedly found in his room. That he is, to my mind, one of the finest actors working in Hollywood, matters not at all. That he's spent some time in jail was, if anything, a recommendation. I'd hoped he'd be cast in one of the film versions of my books, as he seemed to have the perfect résumé for the job. My first thought, though, was, "Cocaine and *speed*!!?" That's not comfortable oblivion! That's pedal to the metal, headed straight into the wall. If there are two faster routes to the dung heap I don't know of them. They can't even be *fun* anymore. After years of having as much cocaine as you want, you find yourself just chasing that first pleasurable hit, looking to recapture that first pleasant rush.

Ally McBeal can't have helped. If I were an actor of Downey's caliber, I can't say I'd be too happy with myself, mugging and lip-locking on that silly, faux-heart-warming exercise in cynicism. I wondered immediately: "The guy's right out of the joint! Who let him work a job where he's going to have damn *good* reason to hate himself?"

People are fragile, very fragile, when they leave rehab. For the first year, it seems like the pleasure centers of the brain have shut down for good, like one's oldest and best love has died. This is not a time to acquire new reasons for shame, fear, regret; you've had plenty of that already. It's time to get away. Far away from old friends, old haunts, old temptations.

In the jargon of rehab, "bottoming out" is mentioned frequently and annoyingly—often as a prerequisite to treatment. When life is at least as unbearable with drugs as without, when the thought of a fat stack of glassine envelopes or an eight-ball promises only more misery, some people make that hard choice to tally up the betrayals and the wreckage and keep living. It's not easy. Many—if not most—fail. Most times, you really have to do something terribly shameful, experience awfulness in previously unimagined degrees, before you see a life without drugs as a preferred, even necessary option. Jail, in Mr. Downey's case, doesn't seem to have been enough. Maybe *Ally McBeal* will be.

FOOD TERRORISTS

RIGHT NOW, IN THE streets of Phnom Penh, in the favelas of Rio de Janeiro, in scores of Caribbean shantytowns, wherever people are poor and struggling and living with little hope of better lives, you'll also find stray dogs, starved, spavined, limping, and covered with mange. In Southeast Asia, sun bears are hooked up to kidney drips, like living ketchup dispensers, and their bile is drained and collected for traditional Eastern medicine. Rhino horn, bear claw, shark fin—the still living parts of every variety of creature are sought after for their supposedly restorative powers, or as holistic alternatives to Viagra. Thousands upon thousands of unwanted cats and dogs are exterminated every month in American cities, victims of the laziness, irresponsibility, and caprice of a wealthy nation.

Yet in San Francisco, our heroic eco-warriors have found a more compelling front line in the struggle against animal cruelty. A supposedly underground group of fanatical animal rights activists has apparently decided that Chef Laurent Manrique's pint-size specialty store, Sonoma Saveurs, must be restrained— by any means necessary—from selling foie gras. To this end, they broke in to the historical adobe structure, spray-painted walls and equipment, destroyed the plumbing with cement, pumped water throughout—thereby damaging two neighboring busi- nesses as well—vandalized Manrique's home, doused his car with acid, and threatened him in phone calls and letters.

Most unforgivably, they have sent Manrique a videotape,

surreptitiously filmed from his yard, of his wife and two-year-old child in their home, with a letter warning that they were being watched.

This is a tactic unworthy of the Mafia. Even the Gambino crime family, to my knowledge, rarely if ever stooped to this. This is the kind of activity favored by Central American death squads and Colombian drug gangs, and it's surprising—no, it's goddamn horrifying—to see it in the touchy-feely heartland of political correctness.

But on the other hand, it's illustrative of the utter gutlessness and self-delusion of these yuppified, trustafarian true believers. Arguably complicit—as we all are—in their comfortable T-shirts and leather-free footwear (surely subsidized by the underpaid labor of some faraway dictatorship) they toodle over in their sensibly fuel-efficient cars to Sonoma (not too far from their expensive homes) and destroy the small businesses of victims completely uninvolved in their argument. They terrorize a mother and infant child.

I have always felt a strange mix of revulsion and gratitude toward the folks at PETA (who insist that while they support the aims of the supposed splinter faction responsible, they are not comfortable with the means). Personally, I would never buy or wear fur—while other material is available. I choose not to hunt for sport. I find it ugly and pointless. While I have shot rabbits for food, it was not an experience I enjoyed, and I would not do it again. The idea of testing cosmetics on animals seems appallingly, extravagantly cruel and unnecessary. (As opposed to medical testing, which I reluctantly, very reluctantly, accept.) I own and utterly adore a mean, six-pound runt of a cat who I adopted from a shelter, and who essentially runs my household. However annoying or offensive or tone-deaf or silly the PETA folks look at times, I've always been glad they're there, to remind all of us the cost in life and in pain of the luxuries we enjoy. If they choose to picket, to advertise, to educate, to harangue, to use every interpretation of the first amendment to embarrass fashion designers, alter public perception, and change behavior, then God bless them. This is, presumably, a free country. And if they want to put up posters and billboards mocking Rudy Giuliani's cancer (GOT CANCER?), however grotesque that might be, he's a big boy. And it makes them look far worse than even the most uncharitable view of our former mayor.

But terrorizing a chef and his family? Using what is essentially racketeering and extortion to frighten chefs into changing menus—in Manrique's case, walking away from a centuries-old Gascogne tradition? This is indefensible, atrocious, and portentous of bad things to come. Already, chefs Traci Des Jardins of Jardinière and Charlie Trotter have made the craven and all-too expedient decision to remove foie gras from their menus, not only knuckling under at the first whiff of opposition, but turning their backs on their peers and their profession when their support is needed most.

I have seen foie gras being produced, the ducks and geese fed in identical fashion to the way that Manrique's suppliers do it. The animals are *not* bolted to a board. At mealtime, they are summoned or gently prodded, by the same feeder each day, and held between his legs. Their heads are tilted back and a long funnel is introduced into their mouths and down their throats. About a handful of feed is ground in a mill and poured into their stomachs. They do not generally struggle. Often, free of any physical encouragement, they come when summoned. Certainly it is not pretty. Watching the process causes an instinctive awareness of the gag reflex. But then any number of adult film stars cheerfully inspire the same reaction. It *is*, no doubt, cruelty of a sort. If any time discomfort is inflicted on another living thing defines the word, then that's what it is. But in the full spectrum of cruelty and horror in this wide world—and even in our own neighborhoods—there is far, far worse.

There is cruelty and neglect and murder readily at hand on Bay Area streets. But it happens to people, creatures of little concern to our clandestine warriors. There is also dog fighting and cockfighting. But the people who run those businesses tend to carry guns, and one thing we can be sure of is that the perpetrators of the Manrique extortion don't want any holes shot in their comfortable clothing. They don't want to miss a shift at the health food store. They don't want to do anything that their supporters or daddy's lawyer can't bail them out of later. Rather than risk harm or inconvenience to themselves on the *real* front lines—in Burma, China, Africa, or even the streets of Oakland—they have chosen to commit the relatively easy crime of extorting a chef and his family. If these people, assured Hezbollah-like of the righteousness of their cause, were capable of shame, then they surely should be ashamed.

Burglary, destruction of property, and extortion are all felonies. Acting as a group, in concert, in an ongoing criminal enterprise—as these hateful and hating people inarguably have—amounts to racketeering. I dearly hope, *pour décourager les autres,* that when they are caught, they are tried and convicted under federal RICO conspiracy statutes and spend the rest of their lives eating prison turkey loaf. And I offer my support and my sympathy to Laurent Manrique, a great chef, a good man, and a proud Gascon.

SLEAZE GONE BY

"NEW YORK MUTHAFUCKIN' CITY."

One used to be able to say that with pride, usually in conjunction with a challenge to whatever tourist had wandered into your orbit, something welcoming and friendly like "Whaddayou lookin' at?!" or, "Gimme a dollar!" With the advent of a strong economy, however, and a crime-busting mayor, more stringent "quality of life" laws, and a number of major corporations eager to pour billions of dollars into redevelopment, New York is becoming a destination resort, offering the same nonthreatening, family entertainment districts as Southern Florida or the "new" Vegas. The way things are going, the city I love will soon present one unbroken vista of theme restaurants, chain stores, Starbucks, and merchandising outlets for the film studios—a smoke-free Disney Zone and amusement park for every flabby-assed, no-necked fanny-packer and rube who thinks waiting on line outside the Hard Rock Café is a thrill ride. Survival of the fittest has been replaced, judging from the docile herds waddling through our streets in search of T-shirts and theater tickets, by survival of the fattest.

Now I know how the aging gunmen of the Old West—Doc Holliday, Wild Bill Hickock, Wyatt Earp, and their peers—must have felt, watching the first waves of homesteaders arrive in Tombstone: the creeping Jesuses and Temperance Leaguers, demanding schools, churches, public parks where once thrived whorehouses, gambling halls, saloons. No more whoring and

183

boozing and eye-gouging, cried the new arrivals. An end to the unrestricted discharge of firearms! Well, look at the American West now, friends. One long strip mall.

No single structure personifies what has happened to my city more forcefully than Show World, a one-time temple of sleaze at the corner of Forty-second Street and Eighth Avenue: three stories of sin, where one could shoot up in the privacy of a peep booth, watch bruised women with tattoos spread their crenulated thighs on a revolting shag-carpeted platform in the "theater," or attend the hourly Live Sex show, where dead-eyed junkie couples would bang bony hips together lifelessly, six shows a day. Now? It's a comedy club.

What happened? Times Square was, particularly for a young man with a criminal bent and a few bucks in his pocket, a wonderland of urban exotica. Not too long ago, you could buy a couple of loose joints on the street, then watch a triple bill of *Lightning Swords of Death*, *Three the Hard Way*, and *Get Carter* from the balcony/smoking section of one of a half dozen cavernous, moldering grind house movie theaters, the film's soundtrack accompanied by the hoots and shouts of the other patrons, for whom the theater was not a diversion but a place of business. All those theaters are gone, replaced by the Disney-owned New Victory and, across the street, the *Lion King* in apparent permanent residence. Where feral young men with butterfly knives tucked in their waistbands used to play video games and pinball among the chicken hawks, selling beat drugs and planning felonies, it's now stores selling Warner Brothers action figures and stuffed animals. Where Matty "The Horse" Ianello once ran an empire of clip joints and peep shows and hustler bars, it's Mickey and Bugs who are the baddest dudes on the block.

Up the street on Broadway, where a midget doorman used to escort you up the dusty plaster waterfall into the gargantuan and half-empty Hawaii Kai for flaming drinks to chill you out from all the bad cocaine, and movie marquees once sported titles like *Anal Rampage III* and *The Sperminator,* there's the All-Star

Café, a hellacious Terrordome of banality: Tourists and their spotty children chaw haplessly at frozen hamburgers, waiting listlessly for a glimpse of Michael Jordan on one of the gigantic video screens. World Wrestling Entertainment has a store. There's a Gap—unthinkable a few years back, when the shelves would have been quickly emptied by enterprising sneak-thieves and shoplifters. The MTV studios look down on the Square, attracting doughy teenage girls hoping for a glimpse of one of their nonthreatening hosts. Wasn't rock and roll dangerous once? The hideous Mars 2112 restaurant offers "Martian cuisine" and a virtual reality trip through a "wormhole in space" to thousands of children and their bored-looking parents where junkies and johns once frolicked unfettered.

On Eighth Avenue, once called "The Minnesota Strip" as it was prime recruiting for pimps who'd catch impressionable young victims fresh off the bus at Port Authority, the blight continues: The Haymarket Bar, a vicious hustler hotspot where young male entrepreneurs would pick up older johns—so they could rob them at knifepoint—is gone. Lady Anne's Full Moon Saloon, called by *Paper* magazine's well-traveled bar reporter "The Worst Bar in the World," where the smell of Lysol and vomit distracted one from the recently released convict population playing pool on a warped table in the rear, is now the Collins Bar, with a smart Art Deco façade. You can walk from Fiftieth Street to Forty-second without once hearing the comforting refrain of "Smoke, smoke" or "Crack it up, got it good . . ." The legendary Terminal Café, across from the bus station, where at eight a.m. you could enjoy a shot of rye and a draft beer, pulling it to your mouth with a dirty bar towel, is now a parking lot. The Hollywood Twin Cinema, immortalized in *Taxi Driver,* is now the home to Big Apple Tours, and the terrifying peep show/bookstore downstairs is now a Burger King. In the convenience stores and shops where once were rows of dildos, crack pipes, bongs, and nunchuks, there are only rows of Pringles.

The Lower East Side is worse. At one time a superstore of

heroin and cocaine, where customers would line up in the streets for admission to a vast underground empire of abandoned, burned-out tenements converted into fortified rabbit warrens of booby-trapped passageways (the dark, candlelit peepholes manned by gun-toting guards)—it's now a neighborhood for the Starbucks generation. And an *expensive* one. Once the air smelled of burning candles, piss, and desperation. Now it smells of CK1. The old name brands (of heroin) proudly shouted out over the ever-present salsa music—Toilet, Laredo, Try-It-Again, Check-Mate, 357—have been replaced by Prada, Comme des Garçons, and Tommy Hilfiger.

The meat district? Crisco Disco, the Anvil, the Mineshaft—a former world of unsafe sex, amyl nitrite, Quaaludes, and leather, sandwiched between meat wholesalers—is now the hottest restaurant district in town.

Tribeca? A former no-man's-land of warehouses where mob-run after-hours clubs thrived, and you could pass out on a stack of empty beer crates in a rear "VIP" room and wake up near a nodding Johnny Thunders or a gibbering Belushi, greet the cold gray dawn with a shot of Wolfschmidts vodka poured from a Stoli bottle. Robert DeNiro seems to own it all now. You'd think that that might make it interesting. It doesn't. One swank restaurant after another, offices for the cell-phone set. Conversation at bars tends to lean toward back-end points and development deals rather than hijacked loads and who's got the bag.

Upper Amsterdam Avenue? You'd think the former Crack Boulevard would retain a vestige of its glories. Now it's a cluster-fuck of frat-boy bars, serving girl drinks and Jello shots to a bunch of towheaded projectile-vomiting college boys for whom Ecstasy is a dangerous drug.

New York used to be a tough town. It demanded of its visitors a certain vigilance, a certain attitude. If you didn't walk the walk and talk the talk you could end up naked and walletless in a hot-sheet motel, wondering how the hell you got there. The wrong look at the wrong person and you could be looking at the business end of a Saturday Night Special (a cheap .38). Buying drugs without getting beat or cut up was an accomplishment, visiting some neighborhoods an adventure. Everyone was always admitted—but not everyone could stay. Survival required speed, flexibility, volume, aggression. If you stopped to look up at the skyscrapers or decided to linger over a friendly game of three-card-monte the locals would be all over you like carnivorous beetles. I saw a New York comedian a while back, talking about the Boston subway system—how they had, to his amazement, cash machines right there on the train platforms. "Of course, we have cash machines on our subway platforms too," he said knowingly, "only we call them 'tourists.'"

Now the tourists are scarier than the locals. They don't even look worried, consulting their maps and adjusting their lederhosen without fear of discovery. Who's gonna stop them? You can't even spray-paint your name on the subways anymore. Subway cars used to be an exciting showcase for dedicated artists, a place where they could create masterworks two and three hundred feet long that would rocket across the boroughs, write their names in the sky, every wild style "piece" more outlandish and distinctive than the one that came before. Now, every subway car, like every American city, looks the same— another soulless space, filled with slack-jawed, sleepwalking bodies, unconnected to anything, running from nothing, to nowhere.

Giuliani's right, of course. That increased "quality of life" enforcement leads to a lower violent crime rate. Let's face it— you get rousted every time you crack a can of beer on a particular corner, you're less likely to shank a visiting tourist there. But with the diminishing threat of violence comes a deadening torpor, an end to life. Movement and thought become optional.

It's been a while since I felt that adrenaline-juiced exaltation, that "I can't *believe* I'm *still* alive!!" feeling that made me proud to be a New Yorker. A half-decaf mochaccino is a pretty poor substitute. I'm not alone. I can see it sometimes—the vestigial memory of sleaze past—in the faces of my fellow smokers, huddled in the cold outside their glass and steel office buildings, stoking up on nicotine before reentering their antiseptic, climate-controlled towers. I can see it in the disappointed faces of kids from Jersey, scouring Hell's Kitchen for a thirty-dollar whore and finding only Tweety and Goofy. "What happened?" they seem to say, their innocent expressions sagging as they put Dad's car back into gear, going home empty. What they came for is no longer there.

UMAMI

PURE AND UNCUT LUXURY

AS MUCH AS I love to espouse the "luxuriousness" of simple, often inexpensive things, the idea that a fifty-cent bowl of pho in Vietnam or a properly made bagel in New York can often be more satisfying than a fourteen-course tasting menu at Ducasse, sometimes you've just got to spend money. Lots of money.

Sometimes, if you want the very best, you really *do* have to be the sort of person who can shrug off five hundred bucks for your dinner. Sometimes, a very high price tag *does indeed* translate directly into quality. Masa Takayama's tiny, thirteen-seat sushi bar–restaurant on the fourth floor of the unimpressive-looking shopping arcade at New York City's new Time Warner building is perhaps the best example of this principle. It's widely referred to as the most expensive dinner in the country. At Masa (as opposed to the less pricey Bar Masa next door) if you want to play, you've got to pay.

And it's worth every dime.

I'll go further. At three hundred fifty dollars per person as a starting point (that's before tax, tip, beverages, and any extras), it's a *steal*. It's the deal of the century. It's a completely over-the-top exercise in pure self-indulgence, like having sex with two five-thousand-dollar-a-night escorts at the same time—while driving an Aston Martin.

Imagine if you will: You are one of only thirteen customers sitting at a long, wide, blond hinoki wood counter of such warm, inviting loveliness that you want to curl up on it and go to sleep.

You want to spend the rest of your life rubbing your cheek—if not your nether regions—against it. The nation's most highly regarded sushi master is standing directly in front of you with a knife, a plane grater, a hunk of fresh wasabi root. On both sides of him are casually deposited heaps of the sexiest looking fish you've ever conjured up in your wildest, soy-spattered dreams of sushi heaven. You catch your breath and gape in wonder at the thick hunks of pale, fat-rippled otoro tuna, flown in that morning from Tokyo. Two silent assistants with shaved heads help the chef, moving among the austere trunks of green bamboo and a simple Stone-Age grill. There's no menu and you don't order, so you have no idea what's coming. But already, as you sit there, blood rushing to your head, lips engorged, hands trembling slightly, saliva thickening, semitumescent, you are absolutely certain that *no one,* anywhere on the planet, is going to be eating better than you tonight. You are alone, in the nose cone of a rocket headed straight to the epicenter of gastro-culinary pleasure. And there's nowhere you'd rather be.

Not to rub it in or anything, but on my most recent visit to Masa, I had it even *better* than that. Sometimes it's good to be a chef.

I rolled into Masa with Le Bernardin's four-starred chef, Eric Ripert, on one flank and the well-known author of such professional foodie classics as *Soul of a Chef,* Michael Ruhlman, on the other. Michael had just emerged from a long day observing the kitchen operations at Per Se, down the hall. In case you didn't know, that's Thomas Keller's breathlessly anticipated, just-opened temple of haute cuisine. Michael co-authored *The French Laundry Cookbook* with Keller, and I guess that experience left a reservoir of goodwill because on entering Masa, we were immediately followed by Per Se's sommelier, who for the full span of the evening kept us lubricated with a progression of jaw-droppingly good wines. I'm talking wines that never in my life will I be either smart enough, or wealthy enough, to order again.

As always, there was nothing on the bar but napkins and

chopsticks. A glass of wine for each of us—and for chef Takayama—and in the hushed, reverential silence, it began.

First, some raw crayfish tossed with cucumber, served, like all the courses to follow, in simple earthenware vessels designed by the chef. Next, a lovely lighter-than-air softshell crab tempura. Wine. Then more wine. A thick, nearly puréed disk of raw toro tuna, heaped with a giggle-inducing pile of osetra caviar, followed by bonito rolled around radish sprouts—I think (the wine beginning to kick in now). Then a simmering stoneware hotpot, a bowl of *combu* broth in which we were invited to dip slices of fresh foie gras and lobster, before shoveling them greedily into our faces. The broth, now beaded with tiny golden pearls of foie gras fat, was then served in soup bowls. Keller's sommelier was pouring heavily, each wine, each course leading beautifully to the next unbelievable thing . . . and then the next. (I'm relying increasingly on Ruhlman's notes here, as I was by this point pleasurably drunk.)

Masa put a dark gray slate square down in front of each of us and my favorite part of the meal began: sushi. One piece at a time. Don't even *think* about soy or dipping sauce or that hideous, electric-green wasabi paste you see in most sushi bars. Each warm, ethereal pillow of rice and fish came preseasoned, with yuzu or sea salt or soy or freshly grated wasabi, as the chef felt appropriate. Fresh water eel . . . then sea eel . . . screamingly fresh mackerel . . . buttery, unctuous otoro tuna that seemed to sigh as it relaxed onto the rice in front of me.

The three of us were eating with our hands now, eyes glazed, begging for seconds. All caution, logic, and reason were long gone as our brains spit out endorphins overtime.

More wine . . . more sushi.

Ruhlman tells me that by now I was moaning audibly, muttering things under my breath like, 'Oh yeahhh, ohhh baby . . . mmmmm." I don't apologize. Watching Masa run his scary sharp knife through that pale, pornographic-looking tuna, separating and peeling back one layer after another before slicing and applying it to your piece—the piece you know is going to be in your mouth in just a few more seconds—is like sex. In fact it's better than most sex. There is no risk of disappointment. Watching Masa pack about eighty dollars (wholesale!) of that incredible once-in-a-lifetime tuna into a single nori roll makes you want to faint.

There was grilled toro . . . a grilled shiitake mushroom wrapped around rice that fabulously mimicked fish . . . sea urchin roe so sublime it should probably be illegal . . . scallop, tenderized by Masa's delicate crosshatching . . . sweet clam (had more than a few of those) . . . squid . . . shrimp . . . eel brushed with home-brewed soy . . . finally, there was kobe beef that with each bite squirted its pampered, oft-massaged fat between the teeth.

If the preceding account sounds like it was ripped from the pages of a cheesily written stroke book, don't let that slow you down. Go to Masa. Go now. Book late and show up on time. Sit down, shut up—and relax. He'll take it from there. Give yourself over to the experience. And enjoy.

Cooking professionally is a dominant act, at all times about control.

Eating well, on the other hand, is about submission. It's about giving up all vestiges of control, about entrusting your fate entirely to someone else. It's about turning off the mean, manipulative, calculating, and shrewd person inside you, and slipping heedlessly into a new experience as if it were a warm bath. It's about shutting down the radar and letting good things happen. When that happens to a professional chef, it's a rare and beautiful thing.

Let it happen to you.

THE HUNGRY AMERICAN

NEARLY FIVE WEEKS OF hotel rooms, airport lounges, mammoth meals, and equally mammoth amounts of drink, and yet, only thirty minutes out of Hanoi's Noi Bai Airport, I'm nearly levitating off the ground, absolutely giddy with excitement and pleasure. I'm no longer jet-lagged, burned out, or jaded. I'm alive. I'm hungry. And back in Vietnam.

I start grinning idiotically right away, beginning with the warm welcome from Linh, waiting for me by customs, and continue on the ride into town. Out the window are rice paddies, narrow two-story homes decorated with rows of drying corn, gray skies, and bright red banners everywhere, most bearing the Tet (lunar new years) greeting: Chuc Mung Nam Moi; others are flags, yellow star on bright red field, anticipating Monday's anniversary of the founding of the Vietnamese Communist Party. (Though it's sometimes easy to forget it, this is still a communist country.) The road into town is crowded on both sides with motorbikes, bicycles, and scooters, most overloaded with passengers dressed in their Tet best: jackets and ties, children swaddled in blankets or netting, women with scarves and face masks covering everything below the eyes. Everyone is smiling and loaded down with holiday goodies. They carry fruit, flowers, traditional *chung* cakes still wrapped in artfully tied leaves, shimmering gold paper trees, bundles of bright red joss sticks. The center of the road is for four-wheeled vehicles, meaning that cars and trucks barrel at full speed, headlong into each other's paths down the center line, beeping maniacally, pulling out only at the last second.

I am supposed to head straight to the Sofitel Metropole Hotel to check in, but Linh is a Hanoi native, anxious to show me the best of his hometown, and as soon as we pass the long, Russian-built Dragon Bridge over the Red River in the inner city, we pull over to an open *bia hoi* joint.

Eight or nine people sit at low tables on tiny plastic chairs outside what looks like an out-of-business garage. A large square keg of *bia hoi*, the legendary, fresh draft "bubble beer" of Hanoi, is situated prominently out front by the curb. You won't find this stuff in Saigon. The beer is made fresh daily, trucked or hauled to area shops—and quickly consumed. Most places serving it run out by four p.m., and what's trucked outside the city seems not to make it too far south. I haven't even taken a seat yet and the proprietor hurries to fill two glasses, challenges me to a chug-a-lug. I drain my glass and we repeat the process two more times before I've even settled into my little chair. The man's wife wants to show me her child, dressed up in his holiday best. An ancient Vietnamese gentleman in a weathered tweed jacket and jaunty beret, smoking from a bamboo pipe at the next table, offers me a puff and another beer.

"*Je suis un cinéaste*," he says. "*Nous sommes tout cinéastes.*" He indicates a few other smiling septuagenarians around him. Soon the beer is coming fast and furious. The owner insists on changing to a fresh keg.

"How did you know this place would be open?" I ask Linh. Because of the holiday, most businesses are closed.

He smiles, and points across the tamarind–tree lined street to an old, unpainted building.

"That's the oldest brewery in Hanoi," he tells me, ordering another round of foamy, fresh, and delicious beer.

I love Vietnam. Maybe it's a pheromonic thing. Like when you meet the love of your life for the first time, and she just, somehow, inexplicably *smells* and *feels* right. You sense that given the opportunity, this is the woman you want to spend the rest of your life with. I'm in town an hour, and I'm already tipsy, delighted, giggly, and elated. In the gray afternoon, beyond the curb, passing vignettes of beauty and color, the usual mad patterns of two-wheeled traffic miraculously weaving through crowded yet fast-moving streets. It's a gray city, Hanoi, old French Colonial architecture, grim socialist monoliths, ornate pagodas, the ultra-narrow multistory and at times wackily ornate new homes of the new not-so-underground economy. The infamous *crachin* of February, a constant spitting mist, has not officially begun, but it is chilly and drizzling ever so slightly. "Good luck for Tet," Linh assures me. The rain and the mono-chrome of the old city seem only to highlight the supersaturated colors of the flags, banners, clothes, and packages everywhere.

Tomorrow, I'm to be the guest of Linh and family at their New Year's celebration, but today, I'm anxious to get out there and eat. The show I'm in town to shoot is all about Linh, his family food, his local haunts, his favorite places. So after dropping off my luggage at the Metropole, I soon find myself sitting in Hanoi's Old Quarter, hungrily slurping down a bowl of *bun cha*.

"I eat here every day," says Linh with pride. "Sometimes twice a day."

An old man grills morsels of pork and pork meatballs over a small, homemade charcoal grill (the *cha*) on the sidewalk, turning the meat with bamboo splints, small plumes of smoke issuing from the glowing coals as juice from the meat strikes them. Just inside an open-to-the-street storefront, his wife ladles out bowls of a room-temperature mixture of vinegar, *nuoc mam*, green papaya juice, sugar, pepper, garlic, and chili, with sliced cucumber at the bottom. The still-sizzling meat hits the table with a bowl of the "soup," accompanied by a plate of lettuces, sweet basil, mint, cilantro, and raw vegetables; side plates of sliced red chilies, salt, pepper, and lime; and a big plate of cold rice noodles. First you drop some pork into the soup, the meat issuing a thin slick of juice into the liquid; then, grabbing a bit of green and herb and a healthy ball of cold noodles, you dunk and slurp.

The place is dark and grim, the floor streaked with charcoal and littered with the detritus of Vietnamese post-lunch-rush papers, cigarette butts, empty beer bottles. (Vietnamese litter with abandon, but then clean up scrupulously afterward.) The cooking equipment is rudimentary, the chopsticks look decades old, but the *bun cha* is an amazement: sweet, sour, meaty, crunchy, forceful yet clean-tasting and fresh, with just the right amount of caramelization and flavor from the low-temperature grilling. The cold rice noodles separate perfectly when dipped in the liquid, as they should in any good *bun cha*, I'm told. The proprietor puts down two more plates, fried spring rolls and puffy fried shrimp cakes, also good to dip when the pork runs out.

I begin to understand Linh's passion for the place and why, on his lunch hour, he travels across town to eat here.

By Hanoi's West Lake, families pull up on their scooters and crowd into the temple of Chau Quoc on a spit of land extending out into the water. They are here to make offerings to their gods and ancestors, burn incense, reflect, and hope for good luck, good health, and prosperity for the coming year. I'm here to eat *bun oc*, and I've got my eye on a long, low table under a tarpaulin by the water's edge, where an old woman is carefully arranging two kinds of freshwater snails, crabmeat, noodles, and tomatoes in bowls before covering them with steaming hot pork broth. The smell coming off the simmering broth is maddeningly good, and she's doing land-office business with the crowd returning from the pagoda, so even though this is an unscheduled stop, I quickly duck under the tarp, walk bent over at the waist to the table, and scrunch down and try to find someplace for my knees among a large extended family of Vietnamese. Linh, a fellow foodie, just smiles and shakes his head. I catch the old woman's eye, point to the person next to me, already happily slurping down the last of his noodles, and smile. She beams back at me.

When a proprietor or a server smiles proudly at you like that, when locals are clamoring to get at what they're selling, when your fellow diners' expressions mirror your own, you know that good food is on the way. They do fast food right here. The glorious tradition of "one cook, one dish" continues: one lone artisan, or a family of artisans, making the same wonderful dish—and no other—year after year, frequently generation after generation. That kind of close identification with a particular dish—that continuity—is nearly always a guarantee that one can expect something fresh and tasty.

Case in point: A few days later, Linh pulls the car over unexpectedly on the side of a major artery. We head down an embankment to a shabby, litter-strewn neighborhood and proceed down a forlorn-looking alleyway to the smoky back entrance of Luon Nong Ong Tre, the Eel Shop. An open kitchen is heaped with dirty dishes. Two big pots steam on an outdoor charcoal grill. A few hard-drinking Vietnamese men are way over their limit inside, singing and shouting. On worn, brown bamboo matting outside, facing an unpaved intersection of narrow alleyways and disused heavy machinery, are a few low plastic chairs, a ratty umbrella or two, a few wobbly wooden tables. Neighborhood kids, squealing with delight, pick unripe oranges off an anemic-looking tree and hurl them at each other. Linh is rubbing his hands with anticipation.

"What do you eat here?" I inquire.

"Eel," he replies. "This is the Eel Shop. Only eel."

"How did you find this place?" I ask.

"A friend took me here. He knows I like eel—and he heard about it from a friend."

I explain to Linh what the word "foodie" means and he seems very pleased. "Yes," he agrees. "Often, you must go off the road. You must investigate."

As we wait for the food, we watch the comings and goings of the neighborhood, a small, rural village existing in the midst of a major city. A trash collector (a woman, naturally), in peaked round hat, face mask, and gloves, picks up trash bags and piles them onto an overloaded handcart. Bicycles containing improbably balanced display racks of housewares are pedaled slowly by. Women carry yokes of fresh vegetables and fruit, men sell lottery tickets, a man pulls up on a motorbike to collect spent cooking oil from the eel shop, another takes away edible waste for sale to pig farmers. Aluminum cans are whisked away to makeshift recycling operations, where they are heated in works and stamped on by sandaled feet. The impurities are sold for paint, the metal, of course, reshaped, reformed, reused. Apparently, a number of *viet kieu* (overseas Vietnamese) and their partners are becoming rather wealthy on the unofficial recycling of trash and garbage, prompting, it is said, one Central Committee member to muse chidingly, "We—all of us—always ask only the big questions. It took just one foreigner to ask a small question: 'Where does the garbage go?'"

In the kitchen, live eels are quickly divested of their bones, sauced lightly, and stuffed into lengths of hollow bamboo with garlic. Both ends are plugged with blanched morning glory leaves and the bamboo is charred slowly over the outdoor charcoal grill. The bamboo is then split open lengthwise and served. Ever had *unagi,* the cooked, glazed freshwater eel, at sushi bars? This is better. Tender, flavorful, smoky, sweet, and hearty. We picked the delicate chunks right out of the blackened halves of bamboo, washing it down, of course, with plenty of warm Hanoi beer.

A few days later, I'm back in the Old Quarter. I have to duck my head to get through the low concrete passageway to the home and kitchen of Madame Anh Tuyet and family. Up a steep flight of steps, off with the shoes, and I'm ushered into a typical old Hanoi residence: a living area facing the street, with a small balcony, dining table, vanity mirror in the corner, raised platform in front of the family shrine, which is crowded with photographs of departed loved ones, offerings of flowers, fruit, figurines. Overhead, a sleeping loft, and upstairs, a large, covered but open-to-the-street kitchen where Madame Tuyet and daughters prepare her famous *ca qua quon thit,* snakehead fish stuffed with pork, and *ga nuong mat ong,* a honey-roasted, hacked chicken that has local patrons lining up and down the street when she's open. Madame Tuyet has won numerous gold medals in countrywide culinary competitions, and she proudly shows me her certificates before hurrying to her upstairs kitchen. She fillets the snakehead fish, deep-fries the carcass and head for garnish in a wok full of simmering oil, then sets it aside. She slices the fillets paper thin on the bias, fills them with a ground pork and mushroom mixture as for *paupiettes*, then dips them in batter and deep-fries them before arranging around the now leaping, curved fish body—as if reassembling the creature. Her chicken, which she has butterflied up the breast bone and splayed flat, she slowly roasts in one of a row of small, carbon- and grease-blackened old electric ovens, removing them constantly to shellac with a secret honey–sugar–syrup mixture and covering them periodically with bits of lined white index cards strategically placed to prevent scorching. A daughter effortlessly fills spring rolls with shrimp and pork; fills condiment bowls with chili sauce, *nuoc mam*, vinegar and green papaya, salt, pepper, lime, and chilies. Suddenly there's stir-fried shrimp and vegetables, and spicy beef too, and I'm seated with Linh and the whole family at the dinner table. It being Tet, a *chung* cake is placed center table. No one touches it. Apparently, the *chung* cake is the fruitcake or panettone of Vietnam: gotta have it—but no one really eats it.

We all know by now that Vietnamese food can be great. And I could describe that sensational meal at Madame Tuyet's using all the words you hear so often from travelers returning from Vietnam: fresh, flavorful, vibrant, crunchy, supernaturally bright looking and tasting. But I won't.

Vietnamese food can be great in Texas, or Minneapolis. But Vietnamese food in Vietnam, when outside the window it's Hanoi—a slice of an apartment building with faded, peeling façade just visible across the street; women hanging out laundry; the chatter of noodle and fruit vendors coming from one flight down; the high, throaty vibrations of countless motorbikes; Madame's two daughters giggling upstairs, perhaps laughing about the freakishly tall, unbelievably hungry American who sits downstairs, ineptly struggling to eat Mom's still-bone-in chicken with chopsticks—at such times, Vietnamese food tastes even better.

Linh is happy. We're getting into shots of *nep moi* now, the vicious, delicious Hanoi rice vodka, and everybody at the table is in a festive holiday mood. Chris and Lydia finally put down their cameras and join us hungrily at the table. When we are finished with this, there will be tea, and Madame's award-winning blend of fresh roasted coffee, and 555 cigarettes, and Madame's lighter-than-air, crunchy coconut macaroons.

Tonight, as the camera crew and I sit in comfortable rattan chairs at the Bamboo Bar of the drenched-in-history Metropole Hotel, drinking vermouth cassis and reviewing the day's events, we will all smile, and nod silently to one another—maybe uttering an occasional "Oh yeah!" to commemorate the day's events. We know we've got it good. We're happy to be alive. And still in Vietnam.

DECODING FERRÁN ADRIÀ

EVERYBODY WANTS IT.

"It's the most magnificent book you can find—anywhere in the world," says Eric Ripert, chef of Le Bernardin in Manhattan. He's talking about Spanish chef Ferrán Adrià's mammoth cookbook *El Bulli 1998–2002,* the first of three volumes that will track backward the development of recipes and procedures at the famed Spanish three-star restaurant. Currently available only in Spanish and Catalan, costing about one hundred seventy-five euros and weighing in at nearly ten pounds (with its accompanying guidebook and CD-ROM), it seems more the mysterious black monolith in *2001: A Space Odyssey* than a cookbook. It is also the most talked-about, sought-after, wildly impressive and intimidating collectible in the world of professional chefs and cookbook wonks. If you're a hotshot chef, even if you can't read it, every minute without it is misery.

Science-fiction and space-travel metaphors come up frequently when discussing it. "There's no cookbook like it. I love the fact that it's like *Star Wars,*" says Wylie Dufresne, an unabashed fan of Adrià whose WD-50 menu in New York was unapologetically created under the controversial Catalonian chef's influence. "He's going *backward!*" (The next book will cover the years 1994 to 1997.) "We're all looking at Spain. And Adrià's ground zero."

For years now, I'd been hearing from chef friends about their experiences at El Bulli. Some, like Sydney's Tetsuya Wakuda, had clearly had life-changing experiences. (He immediately set about designing an upstairs "laboratory/workshop" along the lines of Adrià's.) Others, like Scott Bryan of Veritas, were dazzled but confused by the experience.

"It was . . . like . . . *shock value*. I had *seawater sorbet*!" I'd been gaping with a mixture of fear and longing at The Book for some months when I finally decided I was way past due. There was a massive, shameful, and gaping hole in my culinary education. There were things I needed to know. It was time to investigate the matter.

Ferrán Adrià sat at a small table in the closet-size back room of Jamonisimo, an Ibérico ham shop in Barcelona. He was nearly vibrating with enthusiasm as he held a thin slice of Salamanca ham in his hands and rubbed it slowly on his lips. At exactly blood temperature, the wide layer of white fat around the lean turned translucent, then melted to liquid. "See! See!" he exclaimed. We had already polished off a bottle of Cava, several glasses of sherry, a plate of tiny, unbelievably good tinned Galician clams, some buttery also-straight-from-the-can toro-quality tuna from Basque country, some anchovies—and numerous tastings of hand-cut Extremadura and Salamanca ham. The man generally thought of as the most innovative and influential chef in the world was not turning out to be the detached, clinical, mad scientist I'd expected. This guy liked food. He liked to eat. And he neatly linked the "scientific" approach of some of his cooking to simple pleasure: "What's wrong with science?" he asked. "What's wrong with transforming food?" He held up another slice of ham between his fingers. "The making of ham is a 'process.' You 'transform' pork. Iberico ham is better than pork. Good sherry is better than the grapes it's made with."

At El Bulli Taller, Adrià's laboratory/workshop in a restored Gothic palace in Barcelona's old quarter, metal shutters rolled up to the touch of a button to reveal a panoply of gadgets and utensils. A worktable slid back to uncover an induction stovetop. Cabinets opened, displaying an impressive hyperorganized array of backlit ingredients, each in identical, clear glass jars. The place looked more like Dr. No's sanctum sanctorum than a kitchen. But the subject here was always food.

"What is 'better?'" asked Adrià, holding up a small, lovely looking pear. "A pear? Or a white truffle? Is a white truffle 'better' because it's more expensive? Because it's rare?" He doesn't know, he said. But he wanted to find out. The *taller,* or studio, is a place where questions are constantly asked, about the physical properties of food ("Can we do this? Can we do that? Can we make a caramel that doesn't break down in humid conditions? Can we make a cappuccino froth that tastes of the essence of carrot? Can we make a hot jellied consommé?"), about dining, about the fundamental nature of cuisine and gastronomy. For six months out of every year, Adrià closes his restaurant, and along with his brother Alberto, chemist Pere Castells, industrial designer Luki Huber, and his chef, Oriol Castro, he works here, experimenting, scrupulously document-ing everything, and asking questions—some of which are clearly threatening, even heretical to the status quo.

What is a meal?

What is dinner?

What is a chef?

One can't help but ask oneself these things, even as Adrià and crew turn their attention to smaller, less metaphysical questions. On this day, as I watched, they were asking if a thick slab of ripe peach could be caramelized to mimic the appearance and con-sistency of pan-seared foie gras. (Apparently yes.) Can a beauti-ful fresh anchovy be cooked, yet still appear raw, leaving the attractive outer skin as untouched-looking as it appears in nature? (Seems like it.) Can one make "caviar" from fresh mango purée? (Again, yes.) Of five or six experiments—each conducted in various ways—during the course of the day, generally positive results were recorded in the accompanying charts and notebooks.

"If I can come up with two or three important ideas a year, that's a very good year," said Adrià. Many of you have no doubt seen the ripple effects of some earlier successfully executed ideas on menus near you: foam (which he no longer does), hot jellied consommé, pasta made of squid, jellied cheese, frozen foie gras "powder." Say what you will about Adrià. Many of the same chefs who've been sneering at the very idea of him now shamelessly crib his ideas, peeling off the more applicable concepts to use in their more conventional menus.

They may ask questions at the *taller,* but a high-risk, high-wire act like El Bulli demands questions of its diners as well. Big questions. Is it food? Or is it novelty? And is it "good"—in the traditional sense of that word (whatever that might be)? At El Bulli, the constantly evolving thirty-course meal seems to gleefully invite furious debate.

The restaurant sits by a remote Mediterranean beach, about seven miles of twisting, clifftop road outside of the town of Roses on Spain's Costa Brava. Invited to join Adrià for dinner in the El Bulli kitchen, I sat down and ate what was by turns a shattering, wondrous, confusing, delightful, strangely comforting, constantly surprising, and always marvelous meal.

About thirty different plates appeared in the course of the four-hour experience. The kitchen itself defies convention: cool, quiet, elegant, and modern, with large picture windows and works of sculpture placed throughout. A crew of thirty-five to fifty-five cooks serve one seating per night to an equal number of customers. It is a serious, relatively serene environment, light years away from the fiery mosh pits and sweaty submarinelike spaces most cooks are familiar with.

Voices are seldom raised. There are no shouts or curses, no clatter of pots, no oven doors being kicked closed. The chef and I ate at a plain, white-covered table devoid of elaborate setups or floral arrangement. Whether it was more "experience" or "dinner" I will probably spend the rest of my life figuring out. The evening was a long gastro-thrill ride ranging from the farthest reaches of chemistry class (a single raw egg yolk shellacked in caramel and encased in gold leaf) to the stunningly simple (two pristine, fresh prawns cooked in their own sauce—no other ingredient). Mr. Adrià, who insists he can tell everything important about people by watching them eat, set the pace, eating every course along with me (and in some cases ahead of me), explaining which striking-looking objects to eat first, which second, and how. "Eat in one bite! Quickly!" Pace and rhythm are important, he insisted. "One musn't eat too slowly or one gets sluggish and tired."

"Snacks" arrived first. A green "pine frappé cocktail," artichoke chips, an austere black plate with toasts, sea salt, finely chopped peanuts, and a white toothpaste tube of homemade peanut butter hit the table at the same time as "raspberry lily pads," hazelnut in "textures," lemon tempura with licorice, rhubarb with black pepper, a terrifically tasty row of salty sea cucumber "cracklings" arranged on a tiny black rack, and large puffs of pork scratchings with a yogurt dipping sauce.

"*Jamón de toro*" arived next. A pun on the word *toro* (bull), it was in fact fatty tuna belly cured like Ibérico ham, served with silver pincers to pick up the ethereally thin slices without bunching or tearing them. The pincers looked (intentionally) like a surgical implement.

Adrià watched me eat each course as it appeared, his face lighting up again and again as my expression registered surprise. "Cherries with ham" looked like fondant-covered cherries but were in fact cherries glazed entirely in ham fat. The "golden egg," a tiny golden pillow of egg yolk wrapped in caramel and gold leaf, confronted the palate with flavors in distinct sequence: shock, disorientation, then comforting reassurance. A tiny "Parmesan ice cream sandwich" was an extreme example of a play on comfort food: a salty–sweet remembrance of a childhood that never happened, one of many throughly delicious practical jokes. Apple "caviar"—tiny globules of unearthly apple essence—were served in a faux Petrossian tin. Two crepe courses, one made with chicken skin and the next made, improbably, entirely of *milk* (!), were a pleasure to eat. Pea "ravioli" was a seemingly impossible concoction in which the bright green, liquidy essence of baby peas was wrapped only in itself with no pasta or outer shell to contain it: a ravioli filling miraculously suspended in space. Carrot "air" was an intensely flavored, truly lighter-than-air froth of carrot and tangerine served in a cut-glass bowl. I accidentally inhaled while bringing the spoon to my mouth—aspirating some into my lungs—and struggled to maintain composure as I coughed and turned red. The inconceivable-sounding iced powder of foie gras with foie gras consommé was one of those revelatory concepts for which Adrià is famous. A hot, perfectly clear consommé of foie shared a bowl with a just-fallen snow of foie gras "powder." Instructed to eat from one side of the dish then the other, alternating between hot and cold, I was awestruck by the fact that the frozen, finely ground powder somehow maintained its structural integrity in a bowl of hot broth. It defied all known physical properties of the universe. And it was as good as anything cooked anywhere—a direct rebuke to centuries of classical cooking, miles out in front of all the "foie gras cappuccinos" and stacks of "pan-seared foie gras with chutney and microgreens" one sees everywhere these days. I thought it the strongest, best argument for what Adrià says he's trying to do. "Every night is like opening night," he says. "It has to be . . . magic."

"Oysters with oysters and yogurt, rolled with macadamia nut" was another astonishing success. Two perfect oysters, in an essence of liquefied smaller oysters, a dot of lemon relish, and then a macadamia yogurt cream, when eaten precisely in sequence, took the tongue on a wild yet strangely familiar ride around the world—and then right back to my very first oyster. A shimmering, translucent globe of raw tuna marrow topped with a few beads of caviar was so good that Adrià says, "I won't serve it to my Japanese customers. If the Japanese find out about this the price for tuna bones will go up!" He had a point. The ultralight, unearthly substance tasted like top-quality Edo-style sushi—from another planet. Like nearly everything I tried that night, it had a carefully calibrated progression of clean, precise flavors and a pleasurable aftertaste that didn't intrude on the course to follow.

Cuttlefish and coconut "ravioli" was two tight pillows of cuttlefish that exploded unexpectedly (and disturbingly) in the mouth, flooding it with liquid. When I recovered from the surprise, I looked up to see Adrià laughing delightedly. Summer truffle "cannelloni" with veal bone marrow and rabbit brains was rich, over the top, sumptuous and buttery flavored, and the most traditional "entrée" of many.

"Two meters of Parmesan cheese spaghetti" was one six-foot-long strand of cheese-flavored consommé suspended with agar-agar. Coiled in a bowl like a small portion of spaghetti carbonara, with a dot of black pepper, it is to be slurped into the mouth (Mr. Adrià demonstrated noisily) in one long sucking movement. A single rack of fried anchovy rack—just crispy head and bones—arrived in a funereal cloud of cotton-candy-looking substance and once again tasted wonderful despite its scary appearance.

The unconventional, even horrifying-looking, "chocolate soil," which resembled a bowl full of playground dirt and pebbles, was in fact a conventional tasting chocolate and hazelnut dessert. A "morphing" course of "English bread"—a loaf with the appearance of Wonder Bread that virtually disappeared once placed on the tongue—leaving no trace of ever having been there was followed by a freebie take-home "surprise." A bag with what seemed to be a baguette protruding from it was placed in front of me. Mr. Adrià suddenly reached across the table and brought a fist down on it. It shattered into brittle shards of fennel-scented pastry.

Was dinner good? I don't know if that's a word one can use when describing the El Bulli experience. It can be more comfortably described as "great"—meaning hugely enjoyable, challenging to the world order, innovative, revolutionary. It was an uncomfortably revelatory experience for an old-school cook like me who had always thought food was about *terroir* and tradition, the familiar ways in which chefs have always sought to please their customers. Everything about the meal was clear evidence that the world has changed in bold, new, and uncontrollable ways.

Perhaps no one says it better than Juan Mari Arzak, the more traditional chef-owner of the Michelin three-star restaurant Arzak in San Sebastián and Adrià's staunchest supporter. "What Ferrán does is very *important*," he said, sitting down to join us for coffee and cigarettes at the end of the meal. The two men— Arzak, the passionate Basque, and Adrià, the driven, inquisitive Catalonian—have become best friends. "We call each other at four in the morning all the time," Arzak says. " 'I have an idea!' one of us will say. He is moving cooking *forward*."

Back in New York, Mr. Ripert is a little more equivocal. "He's a phenomenon. We need *one* Ferrán Adrià, *not* five. Not even three. I don't see anyone succeeding in emulating him."

In the final analysis, it was while Mr. Adrià ate lunch the next day, at *his* favorite restaurant in the world, Rafa's, a simple twenty-seat eatery in nearby Roses, that his true nature, I like to think, revealed itself. The restaurant serves impeccably fresh seafood, almost always cooked with only a little sea salt and olive oil. Rafa, the proprietor, and his wife serve from a single stovetop and tiny grill behind a glass-front counter displaying the catch of only a few hours earlier. After tucking into a few slices of plain grilled sea cucumber, Mr. Adrià attacked a plate of screamingly fresh local pawns, greedily sucking the brains and juice from the head. His eyes wild, hands flying, he said, "Magic! It's magic! When we make prawns we dream of Rafa's prawns. *This* is what I want. To find my way to this."

In his own strange and transgressive way, that's exactly what he's done.

BRAZILIAN BEACH-BLANKET BINGO

AT THE END OF a long shift, or six long shifts, I tend to look for a nice, soft, horizontal surface where I can slip quickly into a near-coma. Maybe, on the way, I'll stop for some raw fish and some liquor. Feeling, as I often do after work, like I've been beaten from head to toe with a garden hose full of ball bearings, I'm not likely to look for a nightclub. And since I work in a French steakhouse, the last thing I want to see at the end of the day is a skewer loaded with oversized hunks of Argentine beef. (In fact, after some of the things I've written, any waiter heading my way with sharp metal skewers usually has me reaching for my pepper spray.)

I do love sushi, however. And I love caipirinhas, the deadly, delicious drinks made from *cachaça* (sugarcane liquor), sugar, and fresh lime. And I like Brazilian music as long as there's no question of me dancing to it. Whenever I work a double shift, usually on Fridays or Saturdays, I take a break in the middle of the afternoon and walk a few blocks down from my restaurant to Sushi Samba on Park Avenue South. There, sitting at the sushi bar in my reeking whites and food-spattered clogs, I enjoy a nice cocktail, an order of *sawagani* (the tiny, insect-size crabs one sees skittering around in a fishbowl on the Sushi Samba bar), maybe some *uni* and *unagi,* a little toro, and an inside-out roll or two of fried soft-shell crab. For me, there were already many good reasons to like the restaurant and the people behind it, though until my recent Brazilian Expedition, I'd never met them. Not until I'd gotten *the call.*

I was in the back of a taxi on a cold, gray Seattle morning, rain drizzling down, headed out to the airport after a long, grueling swing across the country on a book-flogging tour. My phone rang, and it was the publisher of *Food Arts,* asking me if I wanted to go to Brazil.

Let's see. The beach? Rio? Palm trees? Tanned flesh in tiny little bathing suits? I don't know. I think I can do that. When he told me I'd be accompanying the Sushi Samba crew, chronicling their explorations of the food, music, and culture of São Paulo, Salvador, and Rio de Janeiro, I said something thoughtful and measured, something along the lines of, "Dude, I am there!"

Once back in New York, I threw some cutoff shorts, a few T-shirts, sandals, and a bathing suit into a bag and headed for the rendezvous at the restaurant.

There were seven intrepid adventurers in our party. None of us spoke Portuguese. Shimon Bokovza, one of the Sushi Samba owners, a tough, energetic Israeli, was the only one who'd been to Brazil before. I was introduced to Shimon's partner, Matthew "Matty" Johnson, an ex-cop, legendary ex-nightclub owner, and one of those people who, ten seconds after meeting them, I decide is a compadre, an amigo, a Noo Yawk-talkin' wise-ass ball-buster of the old school. With us also were Eiji Takase, aka Taka, Sushi Samba's Japanese chef; Michael Cressotti, formerly of Patria, who heads up the South American end of the restaurant's menu; Danielle Billera, Shimon's wife, our chief organizer/scoutmaster (responsible for keeping Matty out of jail); and Philadelphia-based food writer and author Aliza Green.

Sushi Samba, I was informed, was about to open a big, new store in the West Village, a two-hundred-seater with rooftop dining room. The idea of our trip was to flesh out and expand the Brazilian elements of the menu and design. We were going to eat "everyday" Brazilian food and investigate the markets, ingredients, lifestyle, and culture of the country. We were going to have a good time.

Matty, I discovered on the first leg of the trip, has an enviable ability to sleep anywhere at any time. One minute conscious, the next? Dead to the world. The bastard slept all the way to São Paulo (and on every subsequent flight). I kidded him it was his police training. It took a nicotine patch, two sleeping pills, and a cocktail for me to get a brief, fitful nap, jammed upright in a center seat. I could hear Matty snoring, six rows away.

São Paulo is *big*. It's the third-largest city in the world, with fifteen million people, many of them living in absolutely abject poverty. The rest seem to spend all their time in cars (the traffic is unbelievable). The largest industrial center in Latin America, São Paulo has skyscrapers, banks, public buildings, monuments, parks, and museums that are offset by mammoth shantytowns called favelas, acres of dirt-floored shacks built out of cardboard, planks, rags, and pilfered construction materials that occupy any open spaces where they are tolerated. The city, as Paulistas will cheerfully tell you, is for the most part ugly as hell: a polluted, run-down, visibly crumbling sprawl where a thriving ultrarich upper class "trickles down" little of its loot. Crime, the guidebooks assured me, is rampant, with an accent on muggings, home invasions, kidnapping, armed robbery, and pickpocketing. According to the guidebooks, while in Brazil you will inevitably be robbed at knife point, be stabbed by murderous transvestite hookers, or have your jewelry snipped off by feral youths who live in the street and emerge from their lairs only to sniff glue and make off with your Rolex.

Anticipating an aggressively larcenous populace and tropical climes, I arrived in Brazil with a ten-dollar watch bought at the airport, cutoffs, T-shirts, and sandals. Unfortunately, São Paulo, particularly in September, is cold. The throngs of knife-wielding miscreants never materialized. Nobody even looked at me cross-eyed, anywhere in Brazil. But I was freezing my ass off.

On the first morning, our party rose early and walked to the

Mercado, the market in the city's center. Shimon can't pass a food stall without trying it out; so within fifty yards of the hotel we were drinking sugarcane juice. The vendor simply takes a whole length of sugarcane, cranks up a loud, menacing-looking contraption of ancient gears, and feeds the cane in, crushing and squeezing the bark until a dribble of the ultrasweet juice trickles into a plastic cup. Breakfast! A few yards down the road, Shimon honed in on a mob of Paulistas clustered around another stall, this time eating *bolinhos* (little fried balls of salt cod or manioc) and *pastels* (delicious meat pies that look like flat *zeppole*), which the locals tear open and douse with hot sauce. We dug in. We soon found that these stalls are everywhere, serving deep-fried meat and vegetable pies, breaded fried balls of who-knows-what, and candied chunks of coconut, just about all of it greasy and delicious. I saw Shimon, Michael, and Taka taking it in as they ate, thinking, no doubt, "Bar menu!"

The Mercado, situated in an old limestone Beaux-Arts palace long gone to seed, was quiet but impressive. Live poultry, Amazonian fruit, mushrooms, dende (palm oil), hearts of palm, okra, sugarcane, ginger, *graviola* (custard apple), *marajuca* (passion fruit), *beterraba* (beet root), all were displayed in neat stacks. We hit a quiet restaurant for a lunch of whole roasted fish and Chilean wine and then headed off to Liberdade, the Japanese district.

Sushi and samba together is not as kooky-sounding a concept as you might think, some awkward hybrid of cuisines that shouldn't have anything to do with each other. Brazil hosts the largest population of Japanese outside of Japan, and has since they started coming over to farm and do business in 1808. Sushi is very popular here, even in traditional *churrascarias*, where a buffet loaded with sushi and sashimi is considered an additional enticement. Liberdade is filled with sushi bars, yaki-tori joints, karaoke bars, shops, pachinko parlors, and Japanese steakhouses. Sad to say, however, the quality and variety of sushi we saw was less than spectacular. When we returned to the area for dinner, we were disappointed to find Sushi Yassu, said to be one of the best in town, closed. We ate instead at Restaurante Suntory, a big, swank Benihana-style steakhouse–sushi bar–nightspot where an inept griddle cook hacked listlessly at some undistinguished meat. Taka and Michael and I (the chef contingent) cringed each time he brought his knife blade down against hard metal, then scraped it across the surface like a spatula. The sushi was decent but unsurprising. I'm only guessing—Taka is a man of few words—that this lame re-creation of Japanese cuisine was excruciating for him.

Late that night, some of our posse went on to a *cachaçaria* where more than two hundred different brands of the potentially lethal cane liquor are offered (I wisely, and uncharacteristically, declined to go along). The next morning, Michael and Taka looked like they'd been dragged through a battlefield by their heels. They still managed to get down an impressive Brazilian breakfast, though: three varieties of fresh fruit juice, great coffee, cold cuts, chorizos, baked goods, and eggs. I ducked out after breakfast and bought a sweater, then did a little sightseeing in the city center. For lunch, I stopped at the *lanchonetes*, little stand-up eateries selling snacks and beer and sodas. To my delight, my inept Mexican-infected kitchen Spanish, while amusing to the Portuguese-speaking locals, was apparently understandable.

The next day, we visited Ibirapuera Park, São Paulo's largest. The weather was beautiful, and the park was mobbed with tens of thousands of school kids and locals. At first look, Brazil seems to be a utopia of race mixing and integration. Black, white, every hue of coffee-colored person, seem to hang out, intermarry, make love, and socialize with little or no distinction. I'm sure it's not all that simple, and there are centuries of backstory, but it looks idyllic, particularly compared to New York.

Lunch was in Bela Vista, São Paulo's Little Italy. The chefs became decidedly more enthusiastic at this meal. Platters of spicy grilled shrimp, *ensopados* (Portuguese-style stews), whole fish, squid stew in a hearty tomato–cumin broth like I've enjoyed in Provincetown and New Bedford, and heaps of good stuff—little of it Italian. Michael and Taka scrawled notes furiously, asking for menu copies and even taking a tour of the kitchen. A late-night trip to another *cachaçaria* lifted everyone's spirits further and the following morning we left for the airport. Next stop: Bahia.

Bahia is a whole different story. We knew it before the plane hit the tarmac. There was sand. There were palm trees. And when we descended from the plane, the balmy, tropical heat was exactly what I'd been hoping for. Bahia is the African heart and soul, the main vein of everything one dreams about when one imagines Brazil. Sensual, spiritual, boasting spicy African-influenced cuisine, colonial architecture, percussion-heavy tropicale music, voodoo, and some of the best beaches in South America, it's everything I like in a place, somewhere one can easily imagine reinventing oneself as a beach bum, mystic, fugitive, or permanent expatriate. You know you're somewhere else in Salvador, Bahia's capital and major city. Favelas climb steep hillsides and bluffs, sleek hotels tower over the Bay of All Saints, and there is music and magic and food everywhere.

Until the late nineteenth century, Salvador was the center of the Portuguese slave trade. Forbidden from practicing their religions, the unwilling transplants simply went underground with their spiritualism and their culture, conducting ceremonies in clandestine groups and folding them into Portuguese-approved Catholic services. Ultimately, as with so many things Brazilian, the natives absorbed the Portuguese and were absorbed by them, intermarrying, mixing in their okra and their spices and their spiritual view of the universe, opening the way for the music, food, and culture of Brazil to become the fabulous gumbo it is today. Animism, superstition, fetishism, and voodoo (*candomblé* being one variety) are as much a part of everyday life there as going to the market. *Capoeira*, a once-outlawed martial art developed by slaves, is now practiced everywhere, by children on the beaches, by street performers, and in well-rehearsed professional shows for the amusement of tourists, with the *berimbau*, a single-string gourd instrument, keeping rhythm.

Our first night in town, we visited Pelourinho, the cobblestoned colonial-era neighborhood that was once home to the slave owners and the center of Portuguese power. Now quaint, unthreatening, and picturesque, the neighborhood that once housed the whipping post is a well-tended, well-policed tourist mecca, high on a hill. It's a place that could drive, and has driven, poets and artists mad with pleasure. Our taxis pulled up the bottom of a steep climb, as night was falling, and we climbed the hill just as a *candomblé* service was winding down. I wish I could adequately convey the heartbreaking beauty of it all: the locals joining hands and holding candles, affixing *lembranças de Bonafini* (little fetishistic ribbons thought to fulfill wishes) to their wrists, singing, and wishing each other well in the failing light of a centuries-old square, with the heady aromas of incense, dende oil, and things cooking everywhere. When the ceremony broke up, the crowds dispersed and we were swept along with them through the narrow cobblestone streets and alleys, passing tantalizing glimpses of food and handicrafts in tiny shops and dimly lit storefronts, kids selling cigarettes and *lembranças* nipping at our heels. Tropicalia issued from distant windows, words were exchanged in many languages, in strangely hushed voices between passing tourists. Even the street hustlers were gentle if persistent. A boy approached and reached down to fondle my rope sandals, curious and completely uninhibited. I slipped him a few reals.

We ate at Sorriso da Dadá, a tiny, much-loved place located on the ground floor of a plain, whitewashed colonial home, decorated with warm, colorful oil paintings. Dadá is an imposing black woman, pictured in a painting on the wall in traditional garb, and considered to be one of the best Bahian cooks in the country. Her other restaurant, Tempero da Dadá, situated in a somewhat rougher neighborhood, attracts the wealthy and powerful in their limousines; bodyguards and security goons are said to line the street, watching after their cars while the rich eat her wonderfully soulful and hearty home-style cooking.

It was easily the best meal of the entire adventure: unpretentious, colorful, jacked with spices and flavor, unrestrainedly African, smelling so good we almost fainted while waiting to eat. The food was served family style, and we blindly ordered just about everything on the menu: *moquecas* (seafood stews cooked in coconut milk and fiery red dende), grilled piranha cooked in banana leaves, *acaraje* (fritters of black-eyed peas filled with dried shrimp), soft-shell crab, spicy shrimp, crawfish, prawns, lobster, all accompanied by the ubiquitous and intoxicating Bahian condiments, *farofa* (a starchy yucca side), cararu (a piquant mix of well-spiced okra, peppers, and dried shrimp), and *vatapa* (a bread and flour porridge with cashews, dried shrimp, and ginger). I don't remember it all; my head was swimming from the caipirinhas (made with fresh cashew fruit) and the tall Antarctica beers, as well as the frenzy of trying to get all that incredible food into my mouth.

Manioc, coconut, chilies, okra, dried shrimp, yucca, cashew fruit, and of course dende oil play significant roles in much Bahian food, but the broad range of textures and flavors, and the surprising array of seafood, can keep you busy exploring indefinitely. This is not boring food. It's assertive, muscular, unafraid. In larger restaurants, Bahian dishes appear side by side with Portuguese and German dishes, faux-French classics, and workaday favorites. The menus can be a mosh pit of clashing flavors and cultures, an international riot of the classic and the extreme. There was a lot of smiling and moaning at the table among our increasingly inebriated number, and once again, the chefs were hatching plans. Taka and Michael discussed where in New York they could buy the necessary ingredients, strategizing about *moqueca* and roasting fish in banana leaves. I was encouraged, as I didn't want to have to fly back to Brazil every time I wanted to relive this incredible experience.

After dinner in Pelourinho, we walked through the dark streets, heels clicking on cobblestones. Around midnight, I broke away from the group to sit in the central square, chatting with street kids in broken English and Spanish, giving out the occasional cigarette and real. Except for the reggae music from the idling taxis and the occasional tourist, it could have been the 1700s.

The Sushi Samba crew had a full day of sightseeing planned, but the following morning I decided I was going off the reservation: no churches, markets, or for-tourists displays of regional/ethnic dancing and native handicrafts. It was a national holiday, Brazil's five-hundredth anniversary, and all of Salvador, I was convinced, would be going to the beach. The sightseeing portion of the week's entertainment was over. No samba lessons. No buffets. The surf was up.

I woke up late, left the hotel, and walked smack into a parade. Now, I hate parades. I'd rather hear the sound of my own teeth being drilled than the music of John Philip Sousa. But this was different. The streets were packed solid. Held in place by the throngs, I got an unexpected look at Bahia's idea of their best foot forward. First came the military, all the branches, one highly motivated unit after another. Each tried to outdo the other with loud, deep-throated chants of "Bra-ZEEL!!" "Ba-HEE-YA!!" "SALVA-DORR!" Army, navy, fire rescue, mountaineer units, sinister-looking folks in black pajamas and balaclavas, it was fascinating to see which groups were popular with the crowds and which weren't. Female cadets, goose-stepping in Cuban heels, got a big hand. The riot police, who paraded with their crowd-control gear, were decidedly unpopular. Representatives of the indigenous culture passed to polite claps and what looked like embarrassment. Indians everywhere, it seems, get the short end of the stick.

When the parade had finally gone by and the streets became passable, I walked down to Barra, a long and imposing strand overlooking a magnificent beach. From the *farol da Barra*, an eighteenth-century lighthouse at one end, all the way to an open-air restaurant on a bluff at the other, the sand was mobbed. Thousands of barely dressed locals were packed around a cluster of thriving *barracas*, basically beach shacks that serve *chopp* (icy-cold draft beer) and food. Oiled up with sun products, they were swaying to music, splashing around in tidal pools, riding body boards in the surf, swimming, socializing, playing soccer, practicing *capoeira* moves, sunbathing, sleeping, making love, flirting, eating. I grabbed a plastic chair, ordered a *chopp*, which came in a helpful insulated sleeve, and dug in for the afternoon.

Food came at me from all directions. Vendors hawked *acaraje*, *bolinhos*, paper cones of dried shrimp, grilled fresh shrimp, paper tubes of shelled nuts, boiled quail eggs, and *pastels*. Others came by with a mozzarellalike cheese on skewers (for a few centavos they'd dredge it in herbs and, fanning the coals in the metal buckets they carried with them, they'd toast the skewers until the outside was brown and crispy and the inside runny delicious).

People cracked open coconuts and served them with long thin straws. Spear fishermen, right out of the water, dropped still-twitching groupers, snappers, crabs, and lobsters right on the tables, offering to have them cooked up at the nearest *barraca*. Sitting only inches from the neighboring tables, I couldn't help but nearly join in with others' meals. People tore at whole grilled fish with their hands, handing out pieces and sharing *chopps*. Now and again, someone would get up to cool off under a running water pipe. Since the music was loud and seductive, and the mood bordering on orgiastic, each visitor to the shower felt compelled to do a little wriggling and dancing under the water for the amusement of the throngs. Women in white skirts and traditional headdress fried up little cakes and poured *cachaça* in coconuts. Couples nuzzled and hugged and kissed. Everyone was friendly, informal, a little drunk, and having a good time while their skin sizzled in the strong midday sun. The music played on. It seemed a paradise.

What can one say about Rio, except that it's all true. Everything you've heard. It's stunningly beautiful. The people are gorgeous. Our hotel was located right on the beachfront in Copacabana. On the way from the airport, Michael and Matty and Taka, noses pressed to the glass, gazed longingly at the white sands and blue-green water, the verdant green rainforests, and high bluffs and clifftops, listening with horror as our unexpectedly swinish Brazilian escort tried to hard-sell us a guided bus tour. We'd barely arrived at our hotel, and Matty was headed across the street like a heat-seeking missile, peeling off his shirt and calling for caipirinhas. There was no question of going anywhere that didn't involve a beach.

You know about the Corcovado, the high mountaintop sculpture of Christ with arms outstretched. You've seen Sugarloaf. I've seen the pictures too. I'm sure that there were beautiful churches, fabulous museums, incredible public parks with unspeakably lovely waterfalls, a rich and fascinating history to be discovered. But I hit the beach. I had, I told myself, solid investigative reasons for this decision. In Brazil, and in Rio in particular, it is said there is no figure more important to the culture, no creature more admired and emulated, than the *carioca*. The *carioca* is a role model and the ideal state of being is his.

What is a *carioca*? Simply put, he's a lovable scamp, a guy who somehow finds a way, always, to avoid legitimate toil in favor of the popular Rio diversions of going to the beach, flirting, making love, dancing, and hanging out. He is a man who survives on charm and what are called *jetinhos*, improvisational, amiable hustler/joker strategies to avoid work and keep doing what he's doing, which is basically nothing. Rio is filled with *cariocas*: crowded around café tables, playing volleyball with their feet on the beaches, surfing, tanning, swaying to music, hanging out at *lanchonetes* and *barracas*, usually with fabulous-looking women feeling them up—in general behaving like aristocratic rogues in Speedos. Whether they go home at night to the walled compounds of the rich, or take the bus to a hillside favela, all *cariocas*—in fact most Brazilians—are shockingly sophisticated about fashion, culture, the events of the world, and stratagems for survival. Everyone, rich or poor, seems to know how to dress stylishly (even on a budget), handle themselves in most social situations, and make the most of their charm, winging it through life. Is there appalling poverty? Are there organized drug gangs, squalid housing, and rampant prostitution? Yes. Do I oversimplify? Yes. Remember, I didn't get too far from the beach.

In fact, I confined my investigations exclusively to the coast, beach-hopping from Copacabana with its tourist hordes, big hotels, nightclubs, and family beaches, to the slightly more segmented Ipanema. In Ipa, there are beaches for surfers, beaches for gays, beaches for aging leftists and artists, a beach with a band shell for live music. The surf is stronger, and the social strata more intricate. A few blocks back from the beach, it's like Sutton Place. Ten blocks beyond? Slums that make the South Bronx of the 1970s look like Club Med. I traveled down the coast, through mountain tunnels to Barra (another one), a Montauk-esque beach community with even wilder waves and a less crowded beach—a sort of dress-down-if-you're-stinking-rich enclave strip of cafés and shops and modest but well-kept homes, a few full-bore pleasure palaces. I ate *caldo verde* (Portuguese kale soup), fried fresh sardines, and grilled chorizos and onions; drank *cachaça* and *chopp*; and looked out for good places to return for dinner.

When the whole group was briefly reconstituted at the hotel, we set out for dinner at a *churrascaria*, a highly recommended place in Copa with an extensive buffet. But the minute we sat down, we knew it was a mistake. The meal was awful, pointless, and touristy. The Argentine beef was bland, chewy, and uninteresting. I felt like a carnival mark watching the bolero-jacketed waiters carving slices off indifferently grilled meat. There was only sirloin, filet, and round—no skirt or hanger or kidneys or interesting bits. I hate all-you-can-eat concepts to start with. Few foodstuffs, in my experience, are actually better festering under heat lamps, or growing oxidized on a buffet. A late-night sushi snack the next night was equally dreary. Taka's face, previously filled with enthusiasm as he discussed the films of Werner Herzog, went slack as he laid eyes on the limp graying tuna, the insipid California rolls. The bastards didn't even have Japanese beer!

What *was* sensational was my first experience of *feijoada*, the national dish of Brazil. *Feijoada* is traditionally eaten on Saturday afternoon, in gargantuan, gut-busting portions, the idea being that after a full experience of this hearty mix of hooves, snouts, tails, and other meats stewed in black beans, one need not eat again for the rest of the weekend. Eager to find the best available, I strolled down the main drag of Copacabana, eyes peeled for locals, until I found a particularly busy café packed with *cariocas* happily digging in.

Major score. My *feijoada* arrived baked in a massive earthenware crock, accompanied by plates of white rice, sautéed kale, and pork cracklins. It was breathtakingly good. Like so many truly great dishes, *feijoada* derives from desperate and humble circumstances. It's said originally to have been thrown together in impromptu fashion by African slaves, with leftovers pilfered or passed along from their cruel masters' plates. Pigs' feet, ears, tongue, shoulder, spicy chorizo sausages, what looked like snout, some tail, all slowly braised in a hearty, heart-clogging mix of black beans and spices. Heaped in increments over rice and sprinkled with cracklins, it can take hours to eat at a leisurely pace. Mine was titanic in size and astonishingly good. The sun was setting over Sugarloaf beyond the dark turquoise water by the time I'd scraped every last morsel and mopped up the beans with a crust of Portuguese-style bread. Samba music was playing faintly in the background; beachgoers covered themselves with simple wraps and waited for the busses that would take them home, or strolled down the boulevard looking for friends and drinks and music. Lovers held each other by the waist wordlessly, friends chatted, hookers posed, food arrived at other tables, disappeared, was replenished. Bossa nova insinuated itself from the café next door, the *chopps* flowed, older couples sipped strong Brazilian coffee and stared blissfully out to sea. I sat for hours, perfectly content for a brief time at the center of the world.

THE OLD, GOOD STUFF

I WAS STANDING ON East Sixtieth Street in front of the uninspiring façade of Le Veau d'Or, one of those places you walk by without a glance (hell, you've already walked by it a million times), where faded, framed reviews from likely long-dead restaurant critics still hang in the window. I was having a last cigarette before going inside to meet a friend for lunch, when a stranger approached me.

"You're going to lunch *here*?" she demanded.

"Uh . . . yes," I replied warily, a little afraid of what she might say next.

"You're going to *love it*!" she squealed. "I *adore* this place! It's so hilariously, *wonderfully* old school!" Then, her face took on a suddenly serious expression as she considered something she hadn't thought of before. "Just don't tell anyone about it, okay?"

A few minutes later, the ancient proprietor–waiter of Le Veau d'Or threw my coat over an unused table and ushered me across a small, mostly empty dining room to join my friend. A couple sat at a corner table, side by side on an aged red banquette. A few lone diners, regulars from the look of them, ate silently by themselves, concentrating on their food. At forty-seven years of age, I was the youngest person in the room.

I was in The Restaurant That Time Forgot, an observation reinforced by one look at the menu, a historical document as untouched by the decades as the dining room. Reading down the

224

list of menu items and the day's specials was like a blast from the past, a dizzying drop into a time warp. Even the typeface and logo looked like a 1940s film prop. As I read, I felt myself repeatedly catching my breath, inhaling sharply with each defiantly out-of-fashion offering: *Céleri rémoulade, saucisson chaud, poireaux vinaigrette, hareng à la crème, vichyssoise, endives roquefort* . . .

"Oh my *god*!" I spluttered idiotically, my face breaking into a big grin. "I can't believe this!"

Trout *meunière, navarin d'agneau*, sautéed chicken tarragon, *poussin en cocotte "Bonne Femme," rognons de veau Dijonnaise, coq au vin, tripes à la mode de Caen* . . . one forgotten French bistro classic after another. And the desserts! The *desserts!* Okay, crème caramel and tarte aux pommes—still obligatory. One would expect to see those two here. But *oeufs à la neige? Pêche Melba!?* These were preparations you had to go digging for in old copies of *Le Répertoire de la Cuisine* or *Larousse* to find. This was madness! This was insane! This was absolutely fantastic!

One might think—considering the sight of me giggling at Le Veau d'Or—that perhaps I was appreciating this dino-era menu in a modern, post-ironic way. That I was somehow snickering at the proprietor and his improbable, almost irrationally unsellable choice of menu items, that there was something funny about how out of touch, days-gone-by, stubbornly incongruous and *French* Le Veau d'Or's menu was—the height of unfashionable, only a few feet from Bloomingdale's and Madison Avenue.

But one would be wrong.

My eyes filled with real tears. My heart sang. And as I ate my *céleri rémoulade* and my proudly ungarnished *rognons de veau*, and later, my *îles flottantes*, I was bursting with admiration for the place. This was the good old stuff. This was roots cooking, the kind of French food I first came to know and love, the wellspring from which I—and many cooks like me—came. And I know that I am not alone in my affection.

In Paris, of course, they continue to serve this kind of fare sans irony. On a recent trip, I found myself walking in the Saint-Germain-des-Prés with my editor, who'd grown up in the neighborhood. Every few blocks, she'd stop and excitedly point out a forlorn-looking storefront and say, "Oh! That place there makes the *best rognons de veau flambée*!" or "the *boeuf aux carottes* there is superb!" This is akin to walking through suburban New Jersey with an American and having them passionately expound on the glories of diner meatloaf, or coffee-shop tuna salad. I love the French. Their maniacal obsession with the simple act of lunch has, I think, made the world a better place.

But what about us? What's left of the once common, even de rigeur, yet now forgotten cuisine bourgoise, and the more upscale "continental" classics that seem to have gone down with the *Titanic*? Who still loves them? Who continues to uphold the glorious tradition, against the forces of time and trend and simple good sense?

Riffing on old-school classics is something well-known American chefs have been doing for some time. It's been decades since you could find a "napoleon" in a restaurant that in any way resembles the original pastry. Thomas Keller serves a faux "blanquette" (of lobster), and Eric Ripert serves a "croque monsieur" (of caviar and smoked salmon), and other hotshot modernists both here and abroad have been freely pilfering the kernels of forgotten classics for ages. They're not serving the "real deal." But they're not laughing, either.

They'd serve *rognons de veau Bercy* if they could. I just know it.

It can be a hard thing for a chef to do "forgotten" classics the old way, the way they're supposed to be done. Making a "real" *blanquette de veau,* for instance. Tradition dictates that you simmer veal neck or shoulder in plain water—no jacking with stock or medley of herbs; that the mushrooms be uncaramelized; that you serve it with plain white rice. In short, that there be *no* color. No garnish. And no fancy black plates, either. This goes against every modern chef's first instincts, conventional wisdom, and all our training. The natural urge, of course, is to always seek color contrast, that presentation be bold and eye-catching, that chefs at the very least "tweak" all that passes through their kitchens, no matter how classic the dish, essentially making it, with the addition or subtraction of the odd ingredient, somehow their own. But *blanquette de veau* should be *all white*. Not even a single shred of chopped parsley or tuft of chervil to set off its uninterrupted monochrome. To change anything is to not make a blanquette. Not really.

This can be tough for a chef. To do it "right" can be a bold, almost reactionary move. Or, it can be a bald, thoroughly guileless expression of earnest and undying love.

Or, as is thankfully still the case in isolated pockets in America, it can be the still-offered fare of an institution that for whatever reason has chosen to stay stuck in time and space, a fly in amber, unchanging—unaware, perhaps, or else afraid to change, or simply clinging to the old ways for the sake of an original clientele, one very likely dying of attrition.

Look at Louis XVI in New Orleans, where they still serve such Cunard Line–era monsters as oysters Rockefeller, *feuillantine de crustaces* (vol-au-vent of shellfish in Nantua sauce!), canard Montmorency (duck in cherry sauce), filet au poivre prepared *tableside*, and, most remarkably, the unthinkably retro, perennial ruler of the elephant graveyard, filet de boeuf Wellington! Think about that: A filet of beef slathered with foie gras and mushroom duxelle, wrapped in pastry, baked, and served with a truffled bordelaise (*Périgordine*). When was the last time you saw the words *duxelle, truffle, foie gras,* and *pastry* all in the same sentence? This heavy, labor-intensive, difficult to hold and reheat cliché of a dish has endured nouvelle cuisine, cuisine minceur, the single slice of kiwi—with fanned skinless poussin breast—on large plate, pink peppercorns, Asian fusion, New American, quick grills, Atkins-mania, molecular gastronomy—and plain old good sense. And you've got to admire the folks at Louis XVI for it. They're like the Robert Mitchum, the Johnny Cash, the Keith Richards of restaurants: too old, too mean, and too *cool* to change. Louis? I salute you.

La Chaumière in Washington, D.C., continues to feature *quenelles de brochet* (pike dumplings in Nantua sauce), a dish maybe one chef among thousands remembers, much less knows how to prepare. They also feature cassoulet Toulousain, *boudin blanc*, tripes, and calves' brains. The tripe and calves' brains can hardly be flying out of the kitchen—especially in these fearful, troubled times—but kudos for sticking with them. It's a decision that borders on the heroic.

La Petite Auberge in New York City still sells coquilles Saint-Jacques, served in scallop shells, just like my mom did back in the sixties. Frogs' legs with garlic, chasseur sauce, and bordelaise sauce still take their place on the menu. It's been a long time since I've seen bordelaise on a menu—it's usually been long supplanted by the healthier-sounding "demi-glace" or "reduction."

New York's Pierre au Tunnel wins the Biggest Balls award for keeping the unthinkably scary-ass *tête de veau* (essentially calf's face, rolled up and tied with its tongue and thymus gland and slowly stewed in court bouillon) on their menu. They must get a lot of old Frenchmen as customers, because even in Paris these days, you pretty much have to point a gun at someone's head before you can motivate them to eat a calf's face. Pierre? Good on you. I wish I could serve *tête*. Really I do.

For sheer number and frequency of lumbering, old-style, unapologetically French dishes, you've just got to give it up to (again New York's) Chez Napoleon. A trip down memory lane into inspired lunacy: *rillettes de porc*, veal *forestière* (Remember that one from school? Anybody?), tripes, kidneys, liver, brains, *boudin noir*, coq au vin, bouillabaisse, hot souflées—and cherries freaking *jubilee*! The mind reels.

At Boston's Ritz-Carlton Hotel, their Dining Room continues to prove the existence of the old-style professional waiter, serving Dover sole *meunière* tableside. One wonders where one can find a server these days who knows how to fillet a whole sole with fork and spoon in front of an audience, or prepare the Dining Room's crepes Suzettes flambées without igniting themselves or their customers. It's inspiring to know they're there, and doing what they do.

Chefs, many of whom grew up with these dishes, are often passionate about them. But are their customers? It's interesting to see how resolute and determined modern chefs try and slip in the occasional oldie through guile and seduction. At Vincent in Minneapolis, they have had to make concessions to the marketplace, dutifully offering up a hamburger and a "carpaccio" of beets along with the steak tartare and escargots. The *escargots de Bourgogne*, tellingly, are helpfully described on the menu as "a traditional bistro dish"—as if to take the sting away from the more straightforward "snails." The "blanquette" is a compromise between urges and generations, a "braised veal shank . . . with cauliflower, wild rice, and green onions." "Les haricots persillades" sit next to "creamy yellow grits" on the list of side dishes. But, under the regularly changing header of "Something Strange But Good," they have managed to sneak in that beloved old warhorse, "Normandy-Style Braised Tripe"—incredible.

The central irony of a subject already overloaded with ironies is that the market is, perhaps, beginning to come around full circle. Cult hero-to-chefs Fergus Henderson of London's offal-centric St. John just rolled out a widely touted new edition of his classic *Whole Beast: Nose to Tail Eating* cookbook, and was feted by Alice Waters in San Francisco, Charlie Trotter in Chicago, and Mario Batali in New York. A posse of chefs, including Eric Ripert, Marcus Samuelsson, Mark Ladner, Gabrielle Hamilton, Patti Jackson, Mary Sue Milliken, Maurice Hurley, and Kerry Heffernan (as diverse a mix of modernists, traditionalists, Francophiles, and Francophobes as one can imagine) gathered to eat tripe and cassoulet and talk about a shared love of the old school with Henderson. Pork belly is now a "hot" menu item on both coasts. Duck confit has permeated menus across the nation and "house-made" charcuterie is everywhere.

Does this mean that Le Veau d'Or will suddenly find itself "hot" again, after all these years? Will air-kissing trendoids in little black dresses and loud-talking yuppies with beeping cell phones flock to their doors, looking to experience calves' brains in *beurre noir*?

I kind of hope not.

They might have to hire another waiter.

DIE, DIE MUST TRY

MY FIRST TIME IN Singapore, I hated it.

The heat punched me in the chest every time I stepped outside, a thick, penetrating humidity made worse by relentlessly broiling sun. Three-shower-a-day, change-your-clothes-at-noon kind of heat; yet, whenever I ducked inside for a beer, the bars were refrigerated, with locals happily sipping Tiger beers in their T-shirts in the bone-chilling, meat-locker cold. R.W. Apple Jr. has referred to Singapore as "Disneyland with the death penalty," and for good reason. The list of things you *can't* do (spitting, littering, gum chewing, jaywalking) is as endless as it is hard to believe, and the government's mania for relentless social engineering and development has left much of what you and I would find charming replaced by ultramodern rabbit warrens of interlocking shopping malls. They censor the Internet, you do *not* want to get caught with drugs within its borders, and yes, technically, even blow jobs are illegal (though thankfully, readily available.)

But now I love it. And I go back whenever I can.

Because Singapore is probably the most food-crazed, lunatic-eater's paradise on the planet. We're not talking about "gourmets" here. Singapore's "foodies" are nothing like the annoying, nerdy, status-conscious variety one finds in New York, chattering about Jean-Georges's new place, or how such and such a restaurant lost a star. Singaporeans do not collect dining experiences like stamps, to be discussed or bragged about later.

Singaporeans are not gastronomes. They simply *eat*. And living in a country where Chinese, Malay, and Indian cuisines are equally (and proudly) represented, they are accustomed to eating well. When they talk about food they tend to know what they're talking about. They are not snobs and are far more likely to gush about a bowl of noodles at a Mom-and-Pop hawker stand than to be concerned with the new "hot" place.

I learned this the hard way, when addressing a black-tie gathering of well-heeled Singaporeans in a swank hotel's ball-room. There was a question from the floor, a fan wanting to know my preferred spot for the local specialty, chicken rice. When I sheepishly admitted that I had not yet tried it, the entire room of five hundred people erupted in loud (if good-natured) boos. This was followed by near anarchy, as the crowd then began arguing passionately among themselves over which of the hundreds of chicken-rice places they should recommend to the pathetically ignorant American chef–author. Chicken rice, by the way, in case you didn't know, is, basically, boiled chicken and white rice. It is to Singaporeans what chopped liver, pastrami, or pizza is to New Yorkers. Everyone has their favorite. Discussing the subject, people tend to get enthusiastic, even contentious. The question of who's got the best could very easily lead to a fistfight—were fighting not illegal (and therefore unthinkable) in Singapore.

The next morning, I called my friend K. F. Seetoh, the "guru" behind the *Makansutra Guide*, a sort of better-than-*Zagat* guide to Singapore's hawker stands, eating houses, and street food. Eateries are graded not with stars or numbers, but by rice bowls signifying "good," "very good," "excellent"—and the Singlish "Don't try, regret ah!" and the ultimate accolade, "Die, die must try!" Seetoh pointed me to Tian Tian Hainanese Chicken Rice, a closet-size food stall in the bustling Maxwell Road Food Centre, generally accepted as serving one of the very best versions.

I ordered a plate from the tiny one-room stall with the head-on chickens hanging from hooks in the window and settled down to eat a heap of soft, pillowy white rice with pale, juicy chunks of chicken piled in the center. A little cucumber, some supersticky spicy hoisin-style sauce, a little grated ginger, and a garlic pepper sauce are served on the side. You mix it all together to fit personal preferences—and they are as varied as the imagination. Looking around at other tables in the long hallway between rows of brightly lit hawker stands, I watched locals eagerly drizzling, dipping, and mixing the basic elements into personalized concoctions, no two plates the same. The dish is remarkable for such a simple thing, almost baby food for adults, a bone-deep comfort food for locals, a reassuring trip down memory lane with every mouthful. And at Tian Tian it was, as advertised, wonderful. Next time I'm asked the question, I'll be ready with a very respectable answer.

From Tian Tian, I wandered down to stall number five, an establishment called, appropriately enough, simply "Oyster Cake." The woman proprietor proudly told me she's been serving the same dish, and only that dish, for *forty-five years*. I figured, correctly, that after all that time she had to be pretty good at it. A throng of local customers, lining up for the deep-fried, Foochow–style beignet of oysters, minced pork, prawns, and batter, seemed to support this conclusion. I sat down at a center table (all the businesses share and jointly maintain the bare, bolted-down center tables), poked a squeeze bottle of spicy pepper sauce into the center of my cake, and gave it a good squirt. Pure goodness, washed down with a tall cup of sugarcane juice from an adjoining stall.

Once I got started, it was hard to stop. At a business advertising "Pig Organ Soup," a brightly colored sign offered the appetizing-looking Malay specialty, *ba ku the*. I sat down once again and was presented with a brightly colored bowl of tender boiled pork ribs in a bowl lined with greens and clear, piping-hot broth. I ordered a freshly made mango juice and happily gnawed bones and slurped broth until full.

It was tough to leave. Left untried were dozens of specialties, including an entire halal section set apart from the other stands; fried *mee suah*, sporting a tempting-sounding combination of mussels, pig's stomach, prawns, chicken gizzards, liver, and squid; and *nasi lemak*, a spicy broth of seafood, noodles, and coconut milk. There was an enormous line of people waiting for a congee-style porridge—as in Taiwan and Thailand—and everywhere I looked, there seemed to be good, fresh, brightly colored stuff, brimming from crowded stalls with proud-looking proprietors. The place was clean, organized, friendly, and informal. Each business prominently displayed its grade from the health department. At the end of the day, in keeping with Singapore's stringent food-handling requirements, all leftovers would be disposed of—every business starting the next day from scratch with all new ingredients.

This is what a food court should be, I thought, as I waddled toward the door. Imagine if there were a food court near you, at the mall, for instance, where instead of the soul-destroying mediocrity and sameness of American fast food, a wide spectrum of ethnically diverse lone proprietors—all of whom had been perfecting their craft for decades—offered up their very best. Imagine independently owned and operated businesses next door to each other, each serving one specialty as far from and different from the adjacent offering as each individual culture. Imagine—if fast food could be good food. That there were quick, cheap, delicious offerings that tasted unique to their locale, all across America. That people smiled and laughed as they ate at their brightly colored tables—as they do in Singapore—that they talked and argued about food while they ate, taking pleasure in even this small, simple, everyday thing . . . instead of joylessly chomping at paper-wrapped disks of graying beef-flavor-sprayed meat before lumbering unquestioning toward cardiac apocalypse. Wouldn't that be something?

Flush with my experience at the food court, I called Seetoh the next day and put myself entirely in his hands. "Feed me," I said, "the very best."

The first place he took me was Sin Huat Eating House at the junction of Geylang Road and Lorong 35, a tired, dumpy-looking joint (one could barely call it a restaurant) in the red-light district. The dining room—such as it is—had been taken over by a mean-faced server–prep cook who was busily peeling garlic and shallots, rarely bothering to look up. A glass-front refrigerator contained bottles of Tiger beer, and little else. We served ourselves—as the server didn't bother to offer. A few bare, unstable round tables sat outside, a perfect vantage point from which to observe the parade of lumpy and forlorn-looking prostitutes, and the arcadelike space was filled almost entirely with fish tanks, cases of beer, and Styrofoam and wood crates jam-packed with shellfish. All seafood, in fact, is kept alive and happy at Sin Huat until ordered by customers

The overlit ambiance, dirty-T-shirted staff, and stray cats who patrol near the tables were not impediments to a truly great meal. This came as no surprise to me. As I have found in my travels, a certain degree of dirtiness, lack of refrigeration, and close proximity to livestock is often a near-guarantee of something really good to eat. If you see a crowd of locals lined up to eat at a filthy-looking little dunghole on the edge of town, it is often a sign of good things to come.

Referring to chef Danny Lee, who swung by the table to say hello in white T-shirt, shorts, and knee-high rubber boots, Seetoh volunteered that, "This guy is like a lotus flower. A lotus flower cannot bloom unless it sits in a swamp. It's about extracting heaven from hell."

I don't recall actually ordering anything. I certainly never saw a menu. But what followed were seven courses of the tastiest, most screamingly fresh goddamned seafood I have ever put in my mouth—a miracle of wild, passionate, rule-breaking brilliance. I never saw a single vegetable, save a lone, half-hearted garnish of flowered scallion bulb. No rice. No sides. Every course arrived heaped with garlic, swimming in garlic, studded with garlic, or perched atop a Himalaya of garlic. Yet, each and every dish tasted distinctively, magnificently different, devoid of *any* garlic-related unpleasantness. Always, the principle ingredient (the fish) spoke loudest and most freely.

Gong-Gong, which translates, Seetoh said, to "stupid-stupid," was a stainless-steel serving platter of fresh whelks, steamed and sautéed in garlic. We twisted the tender, buttery-light meat out of the shells with toothpicks. Next came garlic prawns heaped with garlic stuffing and quick roasted; again, the sweet flavor of the prawns (only a few minutes ago skittering at the bottom of a fish tank) shone through, somehow beating the garlic into gentle submission. Scallops with roe, still in their shells, arrived glazed in black-bean sauce, by which time I was eating with my hands and slurping every clinging streak or drop. A steamed spotted grouper arrived—on the bone, of course. The highly prized one-and-a-half-pound fish costs about a hundred bucks a pop. I tunneled directly into a cheek, which pleased Seetoh no end. We ate frogs in "chicken essence" and a single stingray steamed with scallion, which inspired my mentor to exclaim "Shiok!" and "Steam!" meaning, I gather, "fucking *good*!" in Singlish. (He explained the local dialect as "think in Chinese, speak in English" before commenting on the next course, Sin Huat's famous crab *bee hoon*: "Good-ah! Hot-Hot!")

The massive Sri Lankan hard-shell she-crab had been hacked into hunks of roe-studded goodness, crisped in hot oil, and simmered with a magical mystery sauce of home-brewed soy and stock and tossed with rice noodles, chilies, and garlic. "You eat the noodles first," Seetoh advised, his eyes getting a glazed, faraway look. By now the table was a wrecking yard of prawn shells, emptied scallops, frog femurs, fish bones, and empty Tiger bottles. Blissed out on food, beer, and what had now become a warm and welcoming environment, I became suddenly nonconversational as I sucked, slurped, and dug at my crab.

"Seetoh, old buddy," I slurred, absolutely sincere, "I have eaten all over this earth. I've eaten fish most have only dreamed of. I come from a long line of French oyster fishermen. I've been to Tsukiji market in Tokyo. I've eaten two-hundred-dollar-a-pound otoro tuna off the still-quivering fish. I've had the full-press treatment at Le Bernardin for Chrissakes! But this, *this* is the best seafood meal I've *ever* had!"

Seetoh smiled, sucked a little crab fat out of a shell, and looked up at me indulgently. "Why you wanna talk when there's good food-ah?"

A TASTE OF FICTION

A CHEF'S CHRISTMAS

IT WAS ABOUT A week before Christmas and all through the restaurant, not an employee was stirring, not even the usually hyperactive busboy, Mahmoud, who sat bolt-upright at the end of an empty banquette, staring into space. The decorations (six hundred forty-nine dollars worth, Marvin recalled with dismay) had been hung in the foyer and front picture window with care (five hundred dollars to some overpaid drapery queen) in the hopes that if not Santa, then at least a few walk-in customers would materialize. A tree (another three hundred smackers to the sorriest-ass, coverall-wearing, Pine Barren–dwelling, inbred motherfucker Marvin had ever seen) had arrived yesterday by truck and now twinkled and glittered with muted white and silver lights by the host stand, where Laurie, who was working tonight because she'd swapped shifts with Alexandra, the good hostess, slouched over the reservation book and covertly prodded a zit.

Marvin had, at the last minute, decided against Christmas music. That would have been too much: happy sleighbells and songs about sugarplum fairies and reindeers and shit. A week ago, when business had been better, he'd briefly considered budgeting for music, then abandoned the idea, sensing the potential for truly painful irony. Things were bad enough, thought Marvin. He didn't need excruciating background music. Bing Crosby walks in the door right now, he mused, starts in with that "I'm dreaming of a white Christmas" shit? He'd never get to finish the line. The whole floor staff of the beleaguered Restaurant Saint Germain would race each other to beat him to death with the nearest bar stool. Instead of carols, French "lounge" music oozed out of the bar's recessed speakers as always. Innocuous enough and what people liked these days, according to Rob.

Marvin sat by the service end of the bar, glumly observing— but not really—the three regular customers drinking Chimays at the other end, and the deuce on table number seven who were already looking furtively around Saint Germain's empty dining room and whispering to each other. They were going to lose the table. Marvin knew it without having to look over at them. They hadn't ordered food yet and were clearly reconsidering their options over drinks, planning an exit strategy. The body language: purse repositioned on lap, the male half of the equation looking around for a waiter while he balled up his napkin, said they were ready to bolt, ready to blurt out some ridiculous lie like "We weren't really as hungry as we thought," or "my wife is having an allergy attack" or "I left the gas on" before they were out the door and in the wind. Gone. Like Marvin's entire stake. Twenty-two years of sweat and toil, warehouses full of mufflers and brake pads, trailer loads—container loads even—of radial tires and retreads, blown up and away, two turns around Madison Square Park and into the void like a lonely, wind-buffeted snowflake. A thing of no consequence. Never existed.

Marvin drank his second scotch and water of the evening and tried to avoid thinking about numbers. He didn't want to think about the loan he'd personally guaranteed so that the busboy, three waiters, and the twelve—count 'em, *twelve*—cooks Rob had insisted they absolutely had to have, could all sit around the kitchen doing jack-shit. The half-million-dollar kitchen with the brand spanking new Jade ranges and All-Clad pots and pans and induction burners and Pacojet machine and marble counter for the pâtissier and the custom-made rolling racks and reach-ins and the tandoori oven that Rob had used once and never again as far as Marvin knew, all of which it had been insisted they absolutely *had* to have.

And where was Rob, anyway? Where was "America's Sexiest Chef"? Why wasn't he here to share the pain, the humiliation, the death—in increments—of all their dreams?

This is what he got for wanting to play the Bogie part. This is what he got for all those gin-soaked evenings in the Hamptons, still flush with the accumulated liquid assets of years in the auto parts biz, those sweet, lazy afternoons by the pool, dreaming of a white dinner jacket, a smoldering cigarette, of signing checks for favored customers in his very own place. "Okay, Rick." Or, "Okay, Marvin" in this case, swanning around the dining room of his very own place, the hottest place in town, his favorite songs playing in the background. Ingrid Bergman, or someone very much like her, waiting for him in an upstairs apartment. It had seemed so serendipitous at the time, meeting the young Rob Holland just down from Boston, weekending with the Haver-meyers, who had taken a place at the beach. "The hottest chef in the Northeast," Ellie Havermeyer had confided in whispered tones, beaming like she was showing off a prize Pekingese. "And the sexiest fucking thing in checked pants," added her sister Cissy in a slightly more strident aside, coloring as she said it. This had impressed Marvin, as Cissy liked to use the word *fuck* a lot, and never blushed for anything.

Chet the bartender, a long-in-the-tooth ex-model who'd long ago resigned himself to slinging drinks for the rest of his life, wiped the bar and, from the corners of his eyes, glanced pityingly at Marvin (as much as bartenders can feel pity). Chet looked worried, thought Marvin with some satisfaction. Probably be-cause the place was so damn slow the miserable, thieving son of a bitch couldn't even steal like he used to. About a hundred bucks a night he'd been taking down, Marvin figured, back when things were good. Those were acceptable losses for a busy house with a good bartender, like back in the days when the dining room had been full of wine drinkers and hurrying, upselling waiters moving Calvados and magnums of expensive burgundies and twenty-year-old ports, the bar packed three deep with giggly, well-dressed women wondering "Is Rob here tonight? Is the chef around?" Now Marvin wished he could have all that money back. A hundred dollars a night, four shifts a week, times the year and a half Chet had been with Saint Germain—that was enough to pay down the D'Artagnan bill. D'Artagnan, who quite sensibly wouldn't even take COD anymore because the restaurant was so far in arrears, requiring Rob to buy even-more-expensive French foie gras from the dairy and provisions company (who were also, of course, on COD, and likely to suspend deliveries any day now).

He was going to lose the house, Marvin just knew, the certain knowledge sitting like an indigestible, malignant lump, halfway down his esophagus. When the house went, his wife would go too. He hadn't let on how deeply in trouble he really was. Things were bad enough, he'd thought, without having to hear about it at home too. She'd divorce him—go for full custody, of course—and the no-doubt wildly expensive lawyer she'd hire off the society pages would get it for her too. Easily. (On the basis of the regrettable "hostess incident" a while back.) She'd get half of what was left, *after* everybody else piled on. After the banks, the vendors, the credit card companies, the lawyers, accountants, the IRS, state, city, and marshals had finished stripping away what assets they could. And what about Christmas? It was torture coming to work every morning. The decorations, the lights, the Santas on Fifth Avenue were an affront, a reminder of obligations and impossibilities. His kids for instance. Melissa, the eldest, had been agitating for a pony. James, his son, wanted a wide-screen plasma TV and an Xbox. The bottle of Cutty and the gift box of promo goodies from the meat company definitely were not going to be enough for the wife.

And where was Rob?

Things hadn't turned out too badly for Rob, Marvin thought. He'd parlayed his 60-percent food cost and 40-percent labor cost into that most desirable state of affairs (for a working-class kid from Revere, Mass., anyway): He was now, truly and certifiably, a "celebrity chef." Rob Holland: The name was never mentioned anymore without being preceded by the two other words, *celebrity* and *chef*. Two words that, as far as Marvin was concerned, should never go together. Young Rob, always in the news now, on the covers of the trade mags, in the glossy foodie journals, and, increasingly, in the lifestyle–fashion rags. He had a pose, a way he always held his head for the photographers, that Marvin was coming to hate. It was that look with cheeks sucked in, chin tilted slightly, head shading to the left, that was starting to drive Marvin crazy. Of course, behind the pancake makeup Rob wasn't looking so hot either. His various business ventures weren't going so well. The places in Boston and Philly (with other partners) weren't working out with the locals and Marvin had just heard that the partners were suing him. The airport deals had been a disaster. I mean, who wants a cassoulet of fucking monkfish before they get on a shuttle to fucking Washington? Marvin had further heard that Rob's wife—his second—was leaving him. No surprise there. Rob's social life needed a flow chart to fully comprehend it. Marvin had seen Rob's cookbook on the remainder pile at Barnes & Noble on sale for nine ninety-five right next to a mountain of poor-me memoirs, inspirationals from disgraced CEOs, and picture books of Gus the polar bear. And as badly as he seemed to want it, as hard as he tried, they still wouldn't let Rob on television. Not with his own show, anyway.

The thing was, the restaurant business was very forgiving of *chefs* who walk away from a high-profile failure but not so forgiving of owners. A chef's place goes under and he can just walk across the street and there will be a whole gaggle of knuckleheads waiting to give him more money. As a chef, Marvin was beginning to suspect, it was not only possible to fail upward, but maybe even desirable. No doubt, in a year's time the same companies who now refused to ship to Saint Germain would be cheerfully extending Rob thirty-day credit—bygones be bygones—while banks and lawyers and government agencies would still be bending Marvin over a sawhorse and probing rudely for assets.

In a terrible moment of paranoia, Marvin wondered if this was what Rob had planned all along. A big, expensive flop. A loss leader for Rob Holland Incorporated? All those cooks, the 60-percent food cost; maybe the prick had never had any intention of making the nut at Saint Germain. Maybe the whole enterprise, Marvin's investment, his house, his fortune, had all been an offering to the restaurant gods, a springboard to bigger and better things. Maybe the whole idea had been for Saint Germain to fail slowly, a glorious failure—but a failure—while Rob rose in the world, stepping adroitly over Marvin's eviscerated corpse on the way to greater glory. That would explain a lot.

While Marvin was in the front of the house nursing his drink, back in the kitchen at Saint Germain, the mood was even uglier. Paul Kelly, Rob's chef de cuisine, had just broken the bad news to the crew, all of whom sat on the cutting boards of their work stations, looking very unhappy.

"What the fuck you mean—no Christmas bonuses?! That's bullshit, man! That's totally fucked up!" said Kevin, the *saucier*. He pounded his fist against the stainless-steel worktable and shook his head back and forth.

"No *way!*" insisted Thierry, the highly paid pâtissier who Rob had lured away from an uptown four-star. "Zees is boolsheet!"

Michelle didn't say anything. She just hopped off her board and began wiping down her station. That really worried Paul as he suspected that Michelle, being not only the best of the cooks but also the smartest, knew that any wailing and whining was useless and that there was truly nothing to be done. He tried to make eye contact, read her expression. They were close, after all. They'd even slept together once, and stayed friends afterward. But Michelle avoided his gaze. The cat was on the roof, Paul decided. She'd already made up her mind. A week, two weeks from now and she'd be giving notice. You can't bullshit her. She knew about this business.

Manuel, Juan, Omar, Jaime, and Rigoberto—the Puebla Posse—said nothing. They weren't going anywhere. They'd been with Rob since the beginning, were well paid and well appreciated, and, most importantly, had been fucked over so many other times at so many other places they were used to it, and probably saw it all as inevitable. God love them, thought Paul. When I die, I want to come back as a Mexican, a Poblano, a fucking grown-up. As the familiar smell of Terminal Restaurant Syndrome gathered about the room, who better deserved to go home to their families with fat bonus checks than these guys? Paul hated himself for the dishonesty of the situation. He would have loved to have just said, "Okay, vatos! El restaurante esta finite. Grab a stove! Grab a freezer! Manuel? You get the Pacojet—let's sell this shit off before the consultants and the marshals get here! Vamanos! I recommend the crystal. Don't waste your time on the pinchay camarones!" But he couldn't do that. Once again the skipper of a sinking ship, he had to keep the crew at their stations.

So he gave the standard inspirational "don't worry, things will turn around" speech, complete with general hints and expressions of future goodwill. He did the best he could to look like he believed it, then slunk off to Rob's office to sulk with a cocktail.

"Chef de Cuisine: Paul Kelly" was what it said on the bottom of every menu—right below the words "Executive Chef: Rob Holland." Rob, he knew, had put that there as a way of acknowledging that it was Paul who did all the work, that it was Paul who was likely to be there should a customer ask to see the chef, Paul who did the ordering, the expediting, the scheduling, the setting of specials, and, increasingly, the dirty work of screwing people over when circumstances required. He lied to purveyors, telling them that the check was on its way; lied to customers who asked if Rob was around, replying "He just stepped out a few minutes ago" when, of course, he hadn't seen Rob in days. He lied to the food mags and VIPs, loyally insisting that "the chef designs every facet of the menu" and that he "supervises every detail"; and, increasingly, he lied to the cooks. He lied every time he told them that things were okay, that they were "just having a few slow weeks." This was what a chef de cuisine did, after all, wasn't it?

When he found himself bridling at the prospect of committing some new outrage on behalf of Rob Holland Incorporated, Paul liked to picture himself as loyal underboss, with Rob as capo. You did what you had to do. Once in, never out. Semper fi, Cosa Nostra forever. Someday, he'd have his own chef de cuisine and would leave the scrounging, the hustling, the lying, the blood-letting, and the bulk of the cooking, to him. That was the way it was. That was the way it would always be.

He didn't mind toiling in obscurity. That wasn't the hard part. He didn't need his name on the damn menu. When he and Rob had started out at Red House, a thirty-five-seat storefront with no liquor license on the Lower East Side, it had been just the two of them and a dishwasher. Rob had worked sauté, Paul was at the grill. When things got jammed, the dishwasher would step in and help plate the veggies. The kitchen had been cramped, swelteringly hot, and caked with ancient dirt. Roaches had streamed through every crack in the grease-browned walls and the floor behind the ranges, and the dishwasher hadn't been cleaned in thirty years. But Paul had never felt so pure.

Merry Motherfucking Christmas, thought Paul, squeezing his temples between thumb and forefinger. Poor bastards, he thought. Poor me. Poor Rob, even. Rob, who only wanted to be loved. Paul didn't—just couldn't—hold Rob's rather meteoric rise against him. Okay, maybe he wasn't the greatest chef in the world. But he was a good cook. And to Paul, that was what mattered. As silly and as sad as all Rob's social climbing, star-fucking, and ass-crawling might be: the TV Boot Camp where Rob had assiduously studied the fine art of simultaneously cooking and being telegenically charming, the dermabrasion to remove the evidence of an adolescent bout with acne, the ever-changing hair styles, one day straight, one day spiky, and suspiciously fuller these days at the crown (Jesus! Was he getting plugs?), the voice coach, the elocution lessons, the personal trainer, the constant sucking up to those miserable fucking shakedown artists at the Institute for Fine Food. Where were they now?

Paul winced, thinking of all the whoring they'd done together, all the times Rob had put on his smile and floated and sucked up to Mortimer Hitchcock, the egotistical reviewer-slash-professional extortionist who published the ubiquitous *Hitchcock Guide to Restaurants*. More free food. More command performances at ridiculous charity events designed to do nothing more charitable than pump more gaseous air into Hitchcock's already bloated ego. An eight-cylinder hoodlum in the guise of an erudite diner, his face absolutely wriggling with corruption—he could probably teach the Genovese crime family something about coercion. Taste of Tribeca. Taste of Times Square. Taste of Gramercy Park. The ludicrous and thankfully short-lived "Restaurantgoer's Manifesto," an attempt by the loathsome author publisher to elevate his status to more Jeffersonian heights. And Food Week! More bite-size portions of free food, more freebies. Chefs all around the city had to dumb down their menus, discount chicken or salmon for a bunch of cheap, useless shut-ins in cat-hair-covered skirts and basketball sneakers who'd just as soon be sucking down the early-bird special. What was that line in *Taxi Driver*? "Someday a big red tide is gonna come and wash them all away"? Paul hoped so.

Jesus it was hard. It was probably hard being Rob Holland, who'd had to figuratively (or literally) French kiss all of them. Paul, though he'd been working without a day off, sixteen or seventeen hours a day, for three months while Rob worked the room, took day trips to the Hamptons and Aspen and Paris, wouldn't have traded places with him for any amount of money or fame. He just couldn't summon any animosity. Because Rob could cook. Because even now there was something of a little boy in Rob, so desperate for affection and respect, a yearning, Paul thought, for the day when the kid from Revere could look at himself in the mirror and be happy and proud of what he saw there.

He did, however, resent that it had been left to him to break the news about the bonus situation. It made him feel even more complicit in all the madness and stupidity. And Christmas. It had to be Christmas. He sat there, holding his head, feeling like a Vichy French shopkeeper—in bed with the enemy. Where *was* Rob? He wished he were here now to reassure the crew, to inspire the troops at this particularly desperate moment, to send them home proud, still eager to return tomorrow. Rob could make them feel that they were doing God's work, that things would turn out okay. Rob could have talked to them all and it would have been better somehow.

Where was Rob? Right now? Where was America's sexiest chef?

In the filthy, fetid locker room where the cooks and waiters changed at the end of their shifts, the kitchen crew lingered uncharacteristically long. Usually they performed what minimal ablutions they thought necessary before rejoining the civilian population: a quick washing of hands, a perfunctory scrubbing of armpits, a heavy application of deodorant or patchouli, a little foot powder into the socks, maybe some gel in the hair—then away with the food-encrusted clogs and the knife rolls and the pilfered stacks of side towels stuffed into the bin with the checked pants, aprons, chef coats, and they were gone. They did not drink at the Saint Germain bar. No employees at the bar was the rule, even on days off. As Rob had pointed out many times and in typical style, "Who wants a bunch of smelly cooks talking loudly and indiscreetly a few stools down from them? Who among even the most foodie of foodies *really* wants to rub shoulders with the people who actually cook their fucking meal? Nobody. That would destroy the illusion! Motherfuckers wanna picture a bunch of smiling industrious movie Frenchmen back there. Charles Aznavour, Yves Montand, Charles Freaking Boyer in a motherfuckin' apron. They want to think that I, the chef, am back there laying hands on every damn meal, personally—every damn side of veg. Believe me, they do *not* want to see your debauched, butt-ugly, cholo, white-trash faces associated in even the most subliminal way with anything they put in their mouths. It's like the bathroom, right? I'm an owner. I could piss in the dining room if I wanted to, roll right up on table twelve and take a nice long leak right into the potted plant there, but you notice? I sit in that hotbox downstairs and do my business under the petrified snotballs and the graffiti just like you. Why? It's not some kind of democratic solidarity shit or anything, me demonstrating I'm still like some kind of man of the people. It's because the very last thing the customer wants to see is the chef coming out of the john. In the customer's mind, I never take a dump. That's the way they want it, brothers and sisters. Don't matter I come out of that door with my hands glowing pink and dripping from a vigorous washing, they do not want to think about that. They see me and they see a bathroom? The illusion is destroyed. Reality intrudes. First rule? Cooks don't exist except in the mind. Rule two? The chef may *be* an asshole—but he does not *own* one."

That was Classic Rob.

Tonight, the cooks were not running out the door like they were escaping from a burning building as they usually did. Tonight, most remained. The Poblanos left at their usual pace, wry smiles and knowing looks for those staying as they disappeared off to Queens en masse. They'd been through this before. Let the silly *gabachos* fret over the inevitable. Shift was over. Not another minute to be wasted here. Let the foolish *norteamericano* youths spend their hard-earned money on overpriced drinks, while surrounded by unlistenable music, talking all the while about *trabajo, putas,* the bosses, *los pilotes.* Time was precious and they'd spent absolutely enough of it already in the Saint Germain kitchen thank you very much.

Michelle, in sweat-stained sports bra and checked work pants, recognized the look the Poblanos gave them as they passed through in single file as nothing less than pity.

"Zees is an abomination," complained Thierry—for about the tenth time in ten minutes.

"How long you been with the company, Thierry?" asked Michelle, annoyed. "Four fucking months? Only a communist cheese monkey like you would expect full bennies after four months. What? They're not paying you enough? Are your checks bouncing or something? Suck it up, bitch. You got no rights."

"Eet is not right," muttered Thierry, who was already planning on calling his mother in France from the kitchen phone to complain about this latest injustice, this latest outrage from the detestable Americans. "I don" care what you say. In France—"

Michelle cut him off, "In France, you'd be working a split shift at some shithole pâtisserie in some shithole little village in the fucking mountains, making lopsided motherfucking tarte au pomme and sweeping the floor after your mom, okay? Suck my dick with that 'een France' shit."

"Man's correct for a change. It's not right," said Kevin. He'd worked at Saint Germain from the beginning, wrestling ranges and equipment in the front door, struggling through the near disaster of the "soft" opening, working loyally, tirelessly at the sauté end, his attention to every tiny brunoise of carrot or leek the same as if he'd been defusing a live nuke, and this, *this* was the thanks he got. The previous year the standard bonus had been a week's pay. He had counted on the same this year. He had bills to pay. The overpriced apartment in Dumbo, the money he owed to his X dealer, the cable TV, the high-speed Internet connection, credit card payments for the presents he'd bought for his little brother back in Cleveland, his girlfriend, his mom and dad. He'd overspent, counting on that bonus, wanting to impress, and now he was in the shit. It was fucking Christmas, man! What was he supposed to do now? "This blows," was all he could muster. He sat there shirtless and forlorn, tugging on the fuzzy little soul patch on his chin and chewing nervously on the filbert-size silver tongue stud that deformed his speech slightly, then finally added, "Fucked *up*. Thass all I gotta say. This is fuuucked up."

Billy, the *commis–saucier*, said nothing. His situation was somewhat more desperate than that of his colleagues, he guessed, as he was already two months behind on his rent and the Christian-rock band he shared a Hoboken apartment with had been making some very un-Christian noises of late, labeling their containers of yogurt in the refrigerator and even suggesting they might throw him out on the street if he didn't come up with rent, and soon. He looked around the room, trying to discern who might be most sympathetic to his plight. Who might be inclined to lend him money, maybe let him crash on their couch for a while. Thierry? Forgetabout it. He was French. Kevin? Maybe, though he didn't look too sympathetic now, tossing a spinning boning knife into the air again and again and catching it by the handle. Michelle? She'd turn him down cold. He was out of his league there and he knew it. He barely felt equal to the task of talking to her. Jimbo the garde-manger was a possibility, but Billy suspected he was gay. (There was no other explanation—in Billy's mind—for the music he liked to listen to in the kitchen. No, no way. He'd rather move back to Minneapolis than have to wake up to that music.)

"We got a pretty desperate situation here, *carnales*," said Leon, the pastry assistant. He liked to think he spoke Spanish, though the Mexicans nearly pissed themselves laughing every time he tried. "This puppy is closing, man. Finita la fucking musica. Stick in a fork, *papi chulo*, turn us over 'cause we are done. This place is going down."

"What do you think?" asked Kevin quietly, turning to Michelle. "How long do you think we have? I mean, we're on COD already. The dining room is fucking dead. How long till the checks start bouncing? How long till I gotta find a new job?"

All Michelle said was, "you do what you gotta do," then she kicked off her pants and struggled into her jeans. She'd been faxing out résumés for a month already, and with January coming up fast, when every cook in New York who'd been burned out by the holiday season or become pissed at the size of their Christmas bonus or other perceived slight would be looking for work at the same time and at the same places, most of which would already be laying off seasonal help. Situation not good. Closing imminent. The only places that had responded to her fax either wouldn't come up with the kind of money she wanted or, on further examination, were themselves already fast-approaching death. There was no point jumping from one sinking ship to another. She looked over at Leon and wondered if he could be trusted to keep the engine of a getaway car running long enough to get in and out with the take at a mom-and-pop liquor store, something she'd done briefly with some success with her old boyfriend back in her junkie days (she still had the jerk's chrome-plated Airweight .38 in her underwear drawer). She quickly banished such idle foolishness from her shrinking list of possibilities. The old boyfriend was in an upstate prison for exactly that kind of nonsense and Leon, sweet kid that he was, was too dumb to get out of his own way much less participate in an armed robbery.

Kevin finished dressing, sprayed himself in a cloud of musk, and headed for the door, muttering, as he passed Michelle, "God bless us—every fucking one."

Where was *Rob*? Michelle wondered if he had a Plan B. There had to be a Plan B, right? He wouldn't, couldn't just be taking this lying down. Rob was an ambitious young man and a smart one, smarter, she thought, than his abjectly needy, neurotic behavior would lead one to believe. She'd gone home with him once. Michelle remembered the incongruous details: the wall of books and old jazz records, prints on the wall that betrayed a somewhat more complex character than one would have expected solely from seeing his mug in the magazines or listening to him at the bar. It was too bad he was so awful on television, when television seemed to be what he really wanted.

And he *was* awful. Nothing helped. Not the hair, not the voice coaches, the media training, format changes, nothing. The TV people had even conducted focus groups, dragooning unemployed loners from every demographic into dark screening rooms, trying to solve the problem of Why America's Sexiest Chef Sucked On TV. When the cameras turned on, Rob stood there like a hapless lox, swallowing his words, moping uncomfortably like a downbeat Eddie Haskell, exuding nothing of the charm or the ability he conveyed in the kitchen, the dining room, or face to face over a shot of tequila and a beer. That he was a brilliant cook meant, of course, nothing on television. The focus groups deemed him adequately "likeable," but he scored low in the "sincere" category. He had no schtick to speak of. No catch phrase. He refused to have a sidekick or to submit to a band or some cranked-up hyperactive studio audience or even a funny sock puppet. The last thing the television audience of Bible thumpers, widows, spinsters, and horny divorcees (deemed likely to tune in by the pollsters) cared about, really, was how to make a lemongrass-infused grilled octopus salad with Thai basil vinaigrette and pancetta lardons. Hell, most of them lived a few hundred miles from the nearest pancetta and would probably rather toss off a rabid jackelope bare-handed than let octopus anywhere near their mouths.

So *where was he*??

It was no longer unusual for Rob to not be around, to have gone off on "research" trips to the Napa Valley or France, a book tour, a foodie symposium, golf weekends, or just to hole up in some fuck-shack with whoever he was doing lately. But it *was* unlike him to stay away for so long, especially when the situation was so desperate. Michelle finished dressing and poked her head in the office, where she found Paul at the desk, staring blankly at a spreading water stain on the acoustic tile on the ceiling.

"Paul," she said, "has he called? Does he know what's going on?"

"He knows," said Paul.

"What does he say about all this?"

"I haven't heard from him in a couple of days," admitted Paul. "Two days ago, he said he was coming in. He said he had to talk to me. Since then? I ain't heard shit. He doesn't answer the phone. There's nobody at his house and his cell phone goes right to voice mail. I just don't know—"

"Where could he be?"

Paul just shrugged. "Lissen, okay?" he said, lowering his voice, "it's not just here, all right? The whole fucking empire is going down. He's got bigger problems than just this place." Paul turned his gaze to the bulletin board on the office wall. Between price quotes from produce companies, a calendar with a wine company's logo, cooks' schedules, and a fuzzy faxed photo of the *New York Times* food critic, was an old snapshot of Rob and Paul, standing out front of Red House: two young men, looking cocky and triumphant in snap-front dishwasher shirts, brandishing their knives and grimacing for the camera. Red House had been the place chefs ate after work! All twelve tables were constantly booked! They had been the toast of the town . . .

Things were different now, he thought. Turning slowly to Michelle, he asked her for a cigarette, lit it, took a deep draw, and sat back in his chair. "I know where he's going to be tomorrow," he said. "Get somebody to cover for you until nine. We'll go and get him."

The Hitchcock Annual Christmas Party was in full swing at the Turgeson Galleries in Chelsea. An entire floor of industrial space had been set aside for the event. In the center of the room, an enormous ice carving of a letter H kindly provided by Tavern on the Green melted slowly into a bed of crushed ice and seaweed. Behind it, two uniformed oyster shuckers from the Grand Central Oyster Bar, dispatched at the last minute after a late-night request heavy with implicit threat and promise, opened littleneck clams, Wellfleet oysters, and sea urchins from a not-characteristically-so-generous seafood company. Cooks from a cross-section of New York restaurants struggled to keep up with the hungry partygoers, arranging tiny sculpted portions of intricately garnished food on paper plates and decorating them with squeeze bottles, tiny heaps of frizzled vegetables, and truffle chips, while their chefs looked nervously on in their best embroidered finery with pained rictuses of smiles stitched across their faces. A charcuterie and provisions company had come through with twin towers of Armagnac-soaked foie gras–stuffed prunes, pâté assortments, galantines, and sausages, and a cook seared tiny packages of *feuille de bric* pastry filled with duck rillettes on a hot plate.

Rob Holland, dressed as Santa Claus (though without wig or beard), posed for photographs with giggly female Hitchcock staffers and their mothers. He was drunk and smelled of old lady.

"And what do *you* want, little girl?" he managed to say, as yet another blushing assistant from the ad sales department squirmed sweatily on his lap. Jesus, she had her legs apart on his thigh, was rubbing herself on his red polyester-clad upper leg while her pink-blotched mom snapped a photo. This was the final straw, Rob was thinking. Free food, fine. Reservations at the last second, sure. Sending over some hors d'oeuvres for his cocktail parties, kiss the ring. Reasonable. Hook him up with a Viking range or a Sub-Zero at cost (or better), all right, why not? It sucked, but this is the business we chose. And he is the all-powerful one who must be pleased at all costs. How this latest outrage would forestall what was clearly shaping up to be the inevitable, however, Rob didn't know. He'd agreed to do it when the despotic entrepreneur had last been in Saint Germain for dinner. Hovering cheerfully at the table after the last course had been served, fussing and flattering Hitchcock for the benefit of his guests (two future victims, no doubt), Rob had been too surprised, too horrified, too pressed against the wall to give what should have been a flat "no" followed probably by two kicks in the groin. He'd found himself saying, to his surprise, that yes, yes he'd be delighted to play Santa at the annual Hitchcock Christmas party. Of course he would.

It had taken a half bottle of vodka to get him past his bathroom mirror in the Santa suit: floppy peaked cap with white pom-pom, oversize red coat with fluffy white trim, red pants with black synthetic boots that were made of the same material as a child's Halloween costume. This was it, thought Rob, as a cruiserweight-size assistant editor took her place on his lap and a gaggle of girlfriends snapped her photo. The wait between pressing the button and the blinding flash seemed always to take forever. Rob was already drunk. Spots swarmed around in his eyes, making it even harder to focus on what was happening in the rest of the room. The other chefs were no doubt snickering up their sleeves at his sorry predicament. Oh Jesus, oh God, please make it stop, he was thinking. Where is *my* fucking Santa Claus? Who will save *my* pitiable restaurant? How will I escape this headlong rush to shame, embarrassment, disappointment, and ruin? Is *this* the bottom of the barrel? How much lower can I go? Rob pictured himself flogging Ronco garlic presses at mall openings, doing infomercials for fat-free grills, print ads for Lomotil and Kaopectate. No. It could not possibly get worse than this.

"Fuck it!" he said suddenly, unsure if it was he who had said it. He stood up, nearly upending an approaching office manager, and lurched toward the bar. He saw a worried Hitchcock shoot him a look, but he ignored it, making straight for the bar, where two well-built young men in tight-fitting black T-shirts and elf hats served martinis donated by a liquor company.

"Give Santa a fucking vodka mart," he snarled, pushing between two representatives of a suburban shopper newspaper. "Santa needs a drink—or he'll put a cluster bomb up your chimney." When the drink arrived, he knocked over a bowl of taro chips but managed to negotiate the thin-stemmed glass, draining the drink in one gulp and quickly demanding another.

At some point someone, he wasn't sure who, put a hand on his shoulder, suggesting in the kind of tones you use with a recalcitrant child that he once more take his place in Santa's North Pole workshop. He responded by balling up his fist inside the black polyurethane Santa glove and slamming it as hard as he could into somebody's face.

After that, there had been some jostling and struggling. He would later recall that he might have reacted badly, responding with some additional moves of his own, possibly a kick or two here and there and maybe a few blows, before he was wrestled to the ground and beaten and kicked by headset-wearing security goons who were most definitely not in the spirit of the season as they frog-marched him to the door and shoved him onto the freight elevator. That he vomited on himself at some point was without dispute, as the evidence was now spread across his red and white coat and wide black belt. As career moves go, thought Rob, sagging inexorably to the floor as the freight elevator began its descent, this had not been a good night.

"Dude! Wake up!" came the voice. Rob opened his eye, the one that *did* open (the other had swollen shut after contact with an elbow), and saw Paul and Michelle, looking down at him. "What the fuck happened to you, bro?" The two grabbed him under his arms and managed to haul him to his feet before half dragging him to the street.

"Rob!" said Michelle. "For Chrissakes. Wipe your mouth! You're drooling!"

It was snowing hard outside, the large flakes burning cold when they landed on his skin. They were big and fat and slow-moving and they were everywhere, swirling and drifting slowly around him, collecting in heaps as the plows made their first forays down the streets and the shop owners cleared their sidewalks. The black plastic boots had no traction at all. Rob's feet slipped out from under him again and again, finally forcing Paul and Michelle to sit him up as best they could in the service entrance of a clothing store. As he slipped into unconsciousness again, Rob heard the distorted tones of "Jingle Bells" playing from a damaged speaker and glimpsed an unhappy-looking Pakistani, also in a Santa suit, handing out flyers for the clothing store's Christmas sale at the corner. The two locked eyes in a brief second, a shared moment of misery.

"So, genius," said Paul. "What now?"

Michelle had never in her life been an optimist. Her faith in her fellow man had generally, up to this point, extended only to what she could see with her own eyes. Given inadequate scrutiny and half a chance she'd found, after years in professional kitchens, and more than enough unhappy relationships with men, that people will inevitably disappoint you. She had, she thought, comfortably reconciled herself to this, careful at all times to have low expectations. But looking down at Rob's unconscious face, his eyes closed and without expression or care, blissfully snoring as "Jingle Bells" played on and on, the snowflakes beginning to collect on his lashes, she found herself thinking how sweet he looked, how strangely innocent he'd once been. She remembered the first time she'd met him. Just a quick hello between orders at Red House, where she'd had to poke her head into the kitchen to greet the people who'd prepared what had been a spectacular meal. He'd been distracted. His eyes had swept right across her face without registering. He'd managed a "Nice to meet you" before hurrying back behind the single six-burner range to rescue an order of skate grenobloise. It had been all about the food then. She'd recognized that look.

They could leave him like this. It might serve him right. Could be a much-deserved wake-up call, coming to in a doorway in a puke-stained Santa suit. But he looked so abjectly helpless, didn't he, so fucking adorable lying there in that ridiculous outfit, snow collecting on his chest and legs like something out of Dickens. She could take him home. Drop him in a hot tub. Feed him hot cocoa with marshmallows. Or she could draw the word *asshole* on his forehead with red lipstick and leave him to possible hypothermia and a "Page Six" item. She looked at Paul, saw the fatigue, the worry, the disgust in his face—the look she'd seen in so many good cooks' faces over the years when faith and hope had begun to ebb. And then she had an idea.

"I know what to do," she said. "Hail a cab and help me pick his sorry ass up. America's sexiest chef is gonna work the line tonight."

When they arrived at Saint Germain, Michelle and Paul hauled Rob down the service stairs and hosed him off. Michelle then helped peel off the sodden Santa suit and they managed to dress him in a snap-front dishwasher shirt and some ill-fitting checks borrowed from Manuel. After several large mugs of coffee and threats and numerous stomach-emptying trips to the bathroom, Paul announced to the crew that Rob would be working the sauté station for the rest of the shift.

"I can't do it," Rob had protested, as he was half carried, half pushed onto the line. Kevin, eyes gaping, stepped aside after a final wipe of his cutting board, and Michelle moved in to take over at grill. Paul took his place at the expediting station. "You can do it, chef," he said. "Remember? Out all night snorting blow and doing Jäger shots, puking on the line into the trash bins? Cold sweats and shakes? We *cooked*, man. We got *three* fucking stars working like that, bro. You can do it. Think of the good old days."

"Oh God . . . Please . . . kill me now," said Rob, leaning down instinctively to check his mise en place in the lowboy refrigerator. "Just come now, tear my head off, empty out this rotten husk of a body and leave the pitiable empty shell right here. Oh God . . ."

"That's it, chef," said Michelle. "Nice and morbid, that's the spirit."

Suddenly, the printer began to click out its taktaktak tune, spitting a curl of three-layered paper into Paul's hand.

"Oh fuck *me*. Oh God, oh Jesus . . . a motherfuckin' *order*!"

"Relax. It's for Marvin," said Paul. "And the missus. They're having dinner together tonight." He adopted his best, most impersonal expeditor tone, the fighter-pilot drone he favored, and began to read: "Ordering: One Dueling Foie . . . one sweetbread . . . followed by a lamb MR and a Dover sole!"

Rob snapped into motion, reaching down for a trimmed, boned-out loin of lamb and a whole Dover sole, laying them out in separate sizzle platters and then preheating two pans.

"It's Robo-Chef," said Michelle.

Out in the empty dining room, Marvin nearly choked on his lamb when he heard that Rob had actually cooked the thing himself. What was going on? He looked around the dining room, trying to gauge from the expressions on his staff's faces what might be happening. Was there something he should know? There did seem to be something, a collective smirk, a slightly cheered look of amusement or something that he couldn't put his finger on.

"Is something wrong?" asked his wife.

"No," said Marvin. "Everything's fine. Little slow tonight. They're probably coming late."

Maybe there are Christmas miracles. And maybe there are special angels for chefs and cooks and for all the people who toil and scheme in the vast underworld of the restaurant business. Maybe once in a very great while, everybody who deserves a break gets a big fat one. All at the same time and on the same night. Because that's what happened on that night before Christmas at Restaurant Saint Germain. The doors opened, an icy draft blew in a few flakes of snow, and with it came Roland Schutz, the poodle-coiffed multimillionaire developer, with two girlfriends and a bald-headed security guard. Alexandra, the good hostess, greeted them warmly and helped them with their coats.

"I guess we don't need reservations," quipped Schutz as Alexandra pulled his camel-hair coat over his thick, stubby, but well-manicured fingers. "Wow!" he said, momentarily concerned as he looked around the empty dining room. "Did I come on a bad night? What the hell *happened*?"

Marvin, hearing this from his table, did his very best to look like six or seven very happy customers instead of one very worried owner and wife, bursting forth with a forced "ha ha ha" of faux holiday mirth. His wife looked at him like he was out of his mind.

"Are you all right?" she asked, her eyes narrowing as she searched his expression for any signs of incipient insanity, stroke, or Tourette's.

"Fine! Fine!" insisted Marvin, beads of sweat erupting on his brow. "Best meal I've had in *ages* . . . ho ho ho. Waiter!" he commanded. "Some dessert, please!"

Of course, Alexandra adroitly rescued the situation, smiling warmly at the two women guests, patting one on the hand and confiding, "Actually tonight's a very *good* night to be here. A *very special* night. The chef is cooking everything *himself*. You know he can't do that very often anymore. Tonight is a very *special* night. You're in luck." She whisked them to a four-top in the center of the dining room and seated them with menus. Ricardo, the restaurant's best waiter, was at their elbows in a second, while Paul, in a moment of possibly divine inspiration, pretending to visit the service bar for a consultation, whispered an order to extinguish the lights out front and draw the curtains. "Lock the door," he said. "No more customers." There was a brief exchange with Ricardo.

"Mr. Schutz," said Ricardo in hushed tones meant to convey solemn, yet breathlessly concealed, delight, "the chef has instructed me to close the restaurant to all other customers. It would be his honor and pleasure to prepare a special menu for the four of you. If it's all right with you he'd like you to just relax and enjoy. He has something really extraordinary in mind for your party. Would that be satisfactory to you and your guests?"

The two girls, already thrilled that America's Sexiest Chef would be personally preparing their meals, were exuberant, particularly as the two of them had, until their recent move to New York, experienced nothing more extravagant than Shoney's and Olive Garden. Here they were now—with Roland Schutz! Being fed *personally* by Rob *Holland*. And *look*! Look at *this*! A magnum of champagne, gratis! Headed their way was Ricardo, at his most graceful with the white napkin as he peeled the foil, removed the wire stay, and gently released the cork with a muffled pop. Schutz, who at this early stage of the evening was concerned with nothing more substantial than getting the two girls to go tag-team in his heart-shaped bed later, was happy to go along. They were happy? He was happy. Fuck the food. He'd just as soon be sitting on his couch in his silk boxer shorts, eating his usual peanut butter and bacon sandwich (no crusts) and watching *American Gladiators* with his chin-strap on. But chicks didn't dig that. The girls looked pleased. They looked impressed.

And that was what was important. Cleveland, his security guard, ate, as far as he could tell, only energy bars and Grape Nuts.

"Yes, of course. That would be delightful," he said. "Please thank Rob for me." His use of the chef's first name implied familiarity, though he had never once eaten Rob Holland's food or even met the man, to be honest. "Tell him I'd be very pleased to eat whatever he'd care to send us."

Back in the kitchen, Rob had been, of course, immediately apprised of the situation.

"C'mon, chef," said Paul, grinning horribly, with a death's-head who-gives-a-fuck smile you generally saw in war movies just before the last suicide charge up a machine-gun–infested hill. "This could be the last damn meal we ever cook in this dump. Let's make it a keeper."

"Show me some fucking moves, chef," said Michelle snapping Rob's ass with a side towel. "Victory or death!"

There was a lot of unused food in the Saint Germain stores. Most of it would probably never be eaten. Rob pillaged his refrigerators and shelves for the best of everything. Working quickly, he whipped up a batter for cornmeal blinis, browned them in a nonstick pan, teased them with a few shavings of homemade gravlax, carefully applied dollops of crème fraîche, and heaped them with beluga caviar until they threatened to topple over. He applied near microscopic dots of bright green chive oil—in gradually descending size around wide white plates, and sprinkled a tiny, tiny brunoise of hard-cooked egg yolk over and around. His hands flew. They did not shake.

There was a *torchon* of foie gras, which Rob sliced and cut and stacked into artful submission between paper-thin slices of toasted brioche and quince chutney, a thin drizzle of balsamic reduction issuing from his spoon with a precision Paul and Michelle had thought long gone. He worked silently, saying absolutely nothing, other than when he issued faint commands to his left and to his right. He didn't just work the sauté station, he worked *every* station, moving from sauté to grill to garde-manger like he'd lived there every waking hour, the other cooks serving as *commis*. Michelle even found herself wiping his brow at one point when a drop of sweat threatened to fall onto a plate of "mosaic of copperhead salmon and fluke carpaccio with citrus jus," surprisingly, not minding at all. Those cooks not helping—Billy, Jimbo, Leon, and the rest—simply stood by and watched as Rob moved efficiently, as if to some internal rhythm, back and forth from station to station, from one plate to anther, course after incredible course. They were silent, as if by speaking, they might break the spell. There was a total hush in the kitchen. The back waiters and busboys tiptoed in to do their work and then tiptoed out. It was as if Rob were a pitcher working on a no-hitter, and a dropped fork, a plate set down too loudly, might destroy what might well turn out to be a perfect game.

While Ricardo cracked open the very best wines from the Saint Germain cellar, knowledgeably describing the domain, vintage, grape variety, and history of each without belaboring the point, Rob cooked, and kept cooking. Six two-bite courses, then seven, eight, nine, and they were still on appetizers! Nothing was from the menu. Each dish seemed to drop fully formed from Rob's mind in a direct route to his hands, then the plate.

Oyster "stew" with a panacotta of cauliflower and lobster essence, ravioli of white truffles with a sauce of morels and confited woodcock (Paul and Michelle had never seen ravioli made so quickly from scratch), "linguine" of baby eels—not linguine at all, but quickly marinated baby eels from Portugal, translucent and tender, tossed with fresh herbs and olive oil from a tiny estate in Italy, the bottle hand-numbered and signed by its creator. Fricassee of sweetbreads, dusted with spice and crisped in a pan with rendered duck fat before being propped up under wide, thin disks of black truffle. It went on and on. Nikki began to wonder if they would be able to eat it all.

She need not have worried. The girls, who hadn't eaten in weeks in anticipation of an imminent shoot for Victoria's Secret (in this they had been misled), ate like hungry longshoremen, devouring everything on their plates and mopping sauce with their bread. Schutz, after the fifth or sixth glass of wine, had begun to enjoy himself with abandon, licking his woefully stumpy fingers with a tiny pink tongue, drops of sauce falling on the napkin fastened under his chins. When the Trio of Bellwether Farms Lamb arrived—a single medallion of perfectly seared and roasted loin, a glazed kidney, and a tiny scoop of braised shoulder, along with lovingly caramelized shallots and glazed cubes of turnip stuffed artfully into a hollowed-out courgette—there were oohs and aahs and even Cleveland, Schutz noticed, seemed uncharacteristically inspired, attacking his food with fervent dedication.

"Extraordinary," said Cleveland. "Absolutely ethereal. Intoxicatingly good. This man is brilliant. This man is a genius. I've eaten a lot of good food in my life, Mr. Schutz. A lot of very good food. I used to drive for that guy from Vivendi, the French dude? He knew how to eat, man. In France. Used to take me with him everywhere. And I've never experienced anything like this. This man doing the cooking? This Rob Holland guy? This man's a genius."

Schutz had never heard Cleveland speak so extensively on any subject. He was dismayed to hear of his prior experience with haute cuisine. He felt suddenly embarrassed about the napkin under his chin, and his own efforts with a fork, as Cleveland worked a veal cheek with lemon and saffron risotto like an aristocrat, doing the fork–knife cross-over with effortless grace, dabbing occasionally at the corners of his mouth as he savored the latest wine with the glass held elegantly by the stem, swirling it almost imperceptibly in his cheek before swallowing.

"You are absolutely right," he said, hurrying to agree. "This is something truly remarkable. I've eaten around a bit too, you know. We have some of the best, the very best chefs in the world at my casinos—but *this*—this *is* something else, isn't it?"

Schutz downed another glass of wine and looked across at the two girls golden in the flower of their youth, imagining they'd taste of strawberry ice cream. But how could anything taste better than this? He felt, in a rush of heat that seemed to rise from his toes to the crown of his overly coiffed head, elated, near giddy with delight. He'd have to pay more attention to what he ate in the future. He'd clearly been missing something.

Marvin lingered over his third cup of coffee and pretended to listen to his wife. He hoped, of course, that Schutz would enjoy himself. That he'd tell his friends. Maybe book a Christmas party or two at Saint Germain, provide a little last-minute cash flow to keep the doors open a few more days or weeks. But who was he kidding? The prick could bail out this business with what he spends on carpet cleaning each week. But why would he?

Chet, the bartender, had more measured hopes for the evening. He wished for nothing beyond a very fat tip, which the floor would carve up and of which he'd get one fifth. Signs were favorable in this department. One rich guy, bodyguard, and two good-looking women usually translated into a heavy tip meant to impress the broads as much as anything else. Chet calculated in his head the likely total, what with all the wine and the multiple courses and the likelihood of port or cognac to follow. He was thinking big. A few rounds of Louis Treize, now *that* would be nice.

In the kitchen, Paul, Kevin, Michelle, and the rest hoped for nothing beyond what they had right now, the pure pleasure of seeing Rob Holland cook again. He was in the zone now, oblivious to the outside world, cooking and cutting and arranging and moving about in some wonderful culinary fugue state, cooking—as all the best cooks do—solely for himself now, climbing the mountain for what might well be one last, best time.

It was okay now, thought Michelle, knowing that Paul was thinking the same thing. All would be okay if they closed the doors to Saint Germain forever after this evening. They had seen Rob Holland at his very best. They could always tell this story and it would all be true. That they were there the night Rob Holland kicked ass like no one else they'd ever seen; that he'd shown them what a cook could be.

As it turned out, they needn't have worried. Roland Schutz liked to own the things he admired. Even more, he liked to own the things other people admired. And when, after the four rounds of Louis Treize and a chocolate soufflé dusted with a few grains of sea salt and the petit-fours and a single spoonful of Meyer lemon sorbet, Rob emerged from the kitchen to dazzle the girls (who were now so drunk as to be nearly unable to speak) and receive sincere thanks from Cleveland, Roland Schutz sat Rob Holland down and did what *he* did so well. He made a multiunit, multiyear, multimillion-dollar deal, acquiring (after the lawyers and accountants had looked things over and cleared the way of any obstacles) a 65-percent share in the soon-to-be-formed Rob Holland Group International.

The Boston and Philly partners would be bought out and the restaurants closed. The airport operations would be sold (at a tidy profit) to Wolfgang Puck, who needed more locations to sell pizzas. New Rob Holland restaurants would open in Schutz-owned casinos in Las Vegas and Atlantic City, and in hotels in Miami, London, and Dubai. Trusted Holland associates Paul, Kevin, and Michelle would each head up a unit. Other loyalists would be similarly rewarded with positions suiting their skills. Even Thierry scored a position as chief of operations at the retail baking and pastry wing in the soon-to-be-erected Schutz Plaza in midtown Manhattan. Marvin accepted a very generous offer of two million five for his stake in Saint Germain, which would allow him to return to the more secure prospects of the auto body business. (Which, he had to admit these days, he'd always loved and never should have left. He'd be able to quickly open up five new stores across Long Island and become wealthier than his wildest dreams—a rare survivor of the New York restaurant industry. There was the added perk that Marvin would still be able to eat and entertain for free at Saint Germain whenever he wished.)

Saint Germain, as the flagship of the new Schutz–Holland Axis, was allowed to retain its 60-percent food cost and to run even higher labor percentages as it was the showcase (and loss leader) for the whole empire. Schutz and eventually the repugnant Hitchcock were favored with regular tables of their choosing. Hitchcock was additionally favored with the offering of a free renovation of his kitchens in Bucks County, South Hampton, and Manhattan (supposedly from Rob but actually from a Schutz-controlled contractor). The restaurant was saved. The Puebla Posse soon ran the kitchen—even hiring additional friends and family members from their hometown of Atlixco. Though Rob continued to retain the title of chef, Manuel was given the day-to-day responsibility of running the kitchen and the title of chef de cuisine and a sizable raise to go with it.

Needless to say, everyone got a generous Christmas bonus. No one got kicked out of their apartment. Credit card payments were made. Thousands of miles away, new satellite dishes appeared on rooftops in tiny Mexican towns.

Best of all, Rob continued to cook now and again. On slow Sunday or Monday nights, his black Town Car would pull up outside and he'd walk briskly through the dining room as voices hushed and people pointed out that "the chef is here." He no longer ventured into the dining room. He never schmoozed. With his future secure, he gave up his dreams of television. Though he worked relatively little at Saint Germain—or anywhere else for that matter—content to golf and read and dream much of the time, to settle things with old wives and current girlfriends, he did drop by now and again. He'd put on a snap-front dishwasher shirt, some faded checks, his old clogs, and an apron. He'd tell Segundo, or whoever was working sauté that night, to knock off early and he'd cook. He'd cook every order off his station, and off others besides. He'd stay till the very end, until the last order was gone. Then he'd dutifully clean and wipe down his station like he'd done when he'd been young and coming up. Afterward, he'd sit at the bar with his crew, who were now allowed to drink at Saint Germain, and they'd review the evening and tell stories and bust each other's balls.

They'd tell stories, like the night of the Christmas Miracle, when the restaurant was saved. When they'd stayed, the whole crew, to drink the remainders of all those magnificent wines left over from their new benefactor's table and to congratulate themselves on their good fortune.

A few days or weeks later, he'd return. And do it again. He'd cook.

He'd cook like an angel.

COMMENTARY

SYSTEM D

I wrote this piece shortly after *Kitchen Confidential* came out and was clearly feeling nostalgic for my kitchen and my cooks. I still felt like a punk, guilty even, for not working as a chef anymore, for doing something as relatively easy as writing about myself and talking about myself—and getting paid for it. And I think the piece reflects that feeling of homesickness. Leaving day-to-day operations at Les Halles, I felt like a traitor; and by celebrating my old friends, my old life—and some of the less lovely practices of that life—I was revisiting it in my mind, seeking some kind of vicarious absolution. Non-cooks might not understand that when describing a steak caught "on the bounce" or finishing sliced gigot under a salamander, for instance, I was never "exposing" or looking to shock or inform. I recall all that nonsense now with warmth and affection. It makes me kind of sad rereading this piece. The yearning for something that even then I suspected I'd never get back, coupled with the growing realization that I would probably have a very hard time hacking it at this point, make me feel a million years older and many lifetimes removed from the person who put this on paper.

THE EVILDOERS

Damn, was I angry! This is one mean-spirited rant. I was spitting mad, having just endured a four-hour flight, economy class, on American Airlines where I'd found myself seated between two gigantic specimens of humanity. One of them, a woman of Jabba the Hutt proportions, literally took up half my seat in addition to her own, leaving me balanced on one butt cheek, leaning forward and against the seat back in front of me. I couldn't sleep. I couldn't sit back. I couldn't do anything but fume silently. Neither she nor the flight attendants ever acknowledged my obvious distress. For the duration of the flight, I tried to lull myself into a state of calm by focusing on the in-flight telephone against which my face was mashed, imagining what would happen if I wrapped the cord around my neck, leaned forward with my full body weight, and ended my life. That thought was what got me through.

The notion that eating yourself up to five-hundred-pound weight class, requiring assistance to even drag yourself out of bed, is an "alternate lifestyle choice" deserving of respect and accommodation always struck me as disingenuous. And in the uncertain times during which the piece was written, it even seemed "wrong" to be so unapologetically huge, when (it appeared at the time) we might at any moment be called upon to flee a building or make our way quickly to an exit.

Equating morbid obesity with a lack of patriotism was, I grant you, a bit of a stretch. But I'd just (along with Eric Schlosser) debated a duo of professional apologists for the fast-food industry—in front of the Multi-unit Foodservice Operators Association in Houston, no less—and when statistics and good sense failed to make an impression, the low-blow argument that "you bastards are hurting the war against terror" landed squarely in the groin.

A COMMENCEMENT ADDRESS NOBODY ASKED FOR

I actually used the substance of this overtestosteroned primal scream as the basis for a later commencement address to a graduating class at the Culinary Institute of America. The tone, I think, reflects my general sense of growing wussification after deserting my old job at Les Halles. Like an aging guy worried about his penis who suddenly and uncharacteristically buys a too-fast-for-him sports car, I think I was overcompensating. The piece was written for a British magazine—I was pondering the subject of Gordon Ramsay, annoyed at the bad press he was getting for being a "bully." I knew well of his loyalty to his chefs, and had recently seen a lot of his interacting with cooks after hours. The way some journalists were "shocked" by his bad language and "harsh" treatment of staff seemed fundamentally ignorant and dishonest—as anyone who knows Gordon knows him to be a complete cupcake.

FOOD AND LOATHING IN LAS VEGAS

This is what happens when a major food magazine is foolish enough to assign me to write about Las Vegas. I'd never been there, but I hated the place in principle. And I was scheduled to do a television show about that tortured relationship. All I really wanted to do was rent a big red classic Cadillac like Hunter Thompson and pretty much reenact *Fear and Loathing in Las Vegas*. And have somebody else pay for it.

At the end of the day, it was a pretty hard place to hate. Unsurprisingly, I had a lot of fun (most of it not described in the article). And despite serious doubts and suspicions, I was encouraged by what some of the chefs I admired were doing there. The first draft/original version appears here, with my friend Michael Ruhlman mentioned by name. My editors at *Gourmet*—sensibly—gutted much of the piece for publication. The shameless duping of Thompson's masterwork is, of course, no accident. *Fear and Loathing in Las Vegas* changed my life when it first appeared in serial form in the pages of *Rolling Stone*, and here I was, at forty-nine, finally able to live it. Homage or cheesy imitation? You decide. I had a helluva time.

And if you've never jumped out of an airplane with a flying Elvis? I highly recommend it.

ARE YOU A CRIP OR A BLOOD?

More and more frequently in my travels, I find out that everything I know is wrong, or at least very much in question. After sneering relentlessly at "fusion"—having experienced so much of the worst of it—I'd started coming across some more interesting and virtuous expressions. In Sydney, I'd been dazzled by Tetsuya Wakuda's Australian/Japanese. In Miami, Norman Van Aken had astonished me with a menu consisting of ingredients that were almost entirely unfamiliar. I recognized the dogma in my own relentless sneering about the evils of fusion, and didn't like the feeling of repeatedly finding myself in rooms filled with people who agreed with me. As much as I admired and appreciated the slow-food movement and the increased interest in better, more seasonal ingredients, there was a whiff of orthodoxy about it all that I felt contradicted the chef's basic mission: to give pleasure. I'd met a lot of very hungry people in recent years, and I doubted very much whether they cared if their next meal came from the next village over or a greenhouse in Tacoma. The notion of "terroir" and "organic" started to seem like the kind of thinking you'd expect of the privileged—or isolationist. The very discussion of "organic" vs. "nonorganic," I knew, was a luxury. I've since come to believe that any overriding philosophy or worldview is the enemy of good eating. This was an early slap back at a perfectly respectable point of view.

VIVA MEXICO! VIVA ECUADOR!

I'd regrettably agreed to be a presenter at the annual James Beard Foundation Awards ceremony just a few weeks before writing this piece. There I was, at the Oscars of the food world. I stood up on that stage, reading from the teleprompter and looking out at a huge audience of America's foodie and restaurant-industry elite. I'd never seen so many white people assembled in one room in my life. It looked like a rally for George Wallace or David Duke. Hundreds and hundreds of smug, self-satisfied white people in tuxedos and evening wear, waiting around to congratulate each other before hitting the buffet. And I felt sickened by the experience. Here we all were at an event celebrating cooking—and presumably the people who do the job of cooking—and barely a Latino in sight. This when as much as 65 percent of the workforce in our industry is, in fact, Mexican, Ecuadoran, and otherwise of Spanish-speaking origin. Where the hell were they? How come they weren't here? Who honors them? While we were all swanning around patting ourselves on the back, the people who keep us in business were still hiding out from the Immigration and Naturalization Service, paying dodgy lawyers for services barely, if ever, actually rendered, and sending money home to families they rarely saw.

The awfulness of that moment made me very angry, and as unattractive as it might be to admit, I can tell you that when it was finally revealed how little money raised by the Beard House was actually going to "scholarships"—and when the foundation's president found himself facing jail time and its board of schnorrers, grifters, and marginal dipshits had to step down, I was overjoyed.

After the scandal broke, a journalist asked me what I thought should be done with the Beard House, the author's former West Village home, restored and maintained as a shrine to a man who, by many accounts, was a complete (if talented and important) bastard. I suggested they convert the property into something useful, like a methadone clinic. I wasn't entirely kidding.

COUNTER CULTURE

I remember reading a food critic's complaint about all the fancy meals he'd had to "endure" over the years, his sense of burn-out—and felt no sympathy whatsoever at the time. How could anyone be expected to feel sorry for a person who was regularly fed the finest wines, the best ingredients, in the most expensive places? This is a fairly recent piece, illustrating, I think, my own growing sense of "fine dining fatigue." On book tours and on trips to promote the shows, and back in New York, again and again, I'd found myself eating much better—and fancier—than I would have liked. Though I usually craved nothing more extravagant than a simple bowl of noodles, or a meatloaf sandwich, my proud and generous hosts of the moment would insist on bringing me to the "best restaurant in town." And whether this was Chicago, Reykjavík, Frankfurt, or Stockholm, there was a growing sameness to the offerings. Quality was up everywhere as the ambitions and abilities of chefs rose, but so was the sense of seriousness and self-importance. I turned some kind of corner when, at Alain Ducasse New York, I was offered a painfully extensive discourse on the water selections—a lengthy distraction which bled out any possibility of joy from what was already a dark, stiff, and humorless exercise in pomposity. My meal at Joel Robuchon's new concept operation in Paris, L'Atelier, was a welcome relief, and seemed to light the way for other chefs to serve high-style food in more comfortable, less stuffy surroundings. And Martin Picard's outrageously over the top Au Pied de Cochon in Montreal was an answered prayer, a loud, defiant, and joyous "fuck you!" to convention for which I was (obviously) very grateful. When I find a chef or a restaurant I love, I tend to make a cause of it—to get hyperbolic. But I feel a real sense of relief, a return to sanity and reason, when I eat at St. John in London, or at Martin's Au Pied, or at Avec in Chicago. When it's finally and only about the food, and all the nonsense and artifice are stripped away. When I can be certain the words "truffle oil" will never issue from a waiter's mouth, and no sauce shall be foamed, and nothing will be served in a shot glass except tequila.

A LIFE OF CRIME

Writing incessantly about food is like writing porn. How many adjectives can there be before you repeat yourself? How many times can you write variations on the tale of the lonely house-wife, temporarily short of funds, and the horny but hunky delivery boy who's not averse to negotiating for that pizza? How many times can you describe a fucking salad without using the word "crisp"? So it's always a pleasure when I'm given the opportunity to write about something that doesn't involve food or chefs. I do have other interests. Crime is one of them.

ADVANCED COURSES

I think all the international travel began to make it easier for me to see and appreciate my own country, and I stopped sneering and started looking at the flyover and the red states not as the enemy but as strange and potentially wonderful foreign lands. It certainly helps that it's usually the chefs and cooks I meet first, but after sitting down to eat with ex–Khmer Rouge, for instance, or being hosted with incredible generosity by former VC cadre leaders—and a lot of other Very Nice People who've done some Very Bad Things—I began to be (I like to think) less judgmental about my own country. I mean, if I can get drunk with a bunch of probably murderous Russian gangsters and have a good time, why can't I get along with an Evangelical Republican from Texas? This was an early grope at being comfortable with that vast space between the coasts, a coming to terms with my own snobbery.

NAME DROPPING DOWN UNDER

Written for a British magazine, and dripping with Britishisms. I'd spent so much time in the UK by this point, I was starting to sound like Madonna. "Where's the loo?" "I have to stop and buy some fags." "Brilliant!" "I have to go have a slash . . ."

MY MANHATTAN

Years later, this piece still stands as a decent visitor's guide to New York. I'd add the restaurants Masa and Per Se in the Time Warner Center on the high end, and maybe Corner Bistro for burgers on the low. Siberia still reigns supreme among dives, though some weekend nights lately are reserved for an all-male leather crowd. Better phone ahead.

HARD-CORE

This is an unabashed blow job of an article. Like everybody I've introduced to her, I'm hopelessly, gushily a fan of Gabrielle Hamilton. I neglected to mention in this article exactly how good a writer she is. Two subsequent pieces she wrote for the *New Yorker* and for the *New York Times Magazine* were genius. Not too long after this article was written, she got a monster-size advance from a major publishing house to write what will presumably be a memoir. It will no doubt be better and more interesting than *Kitchen Confidential*. Every day that Gabrielle Hamilton likes me? It's reason to live.

WHEN THE COOKING'S OVER

I'm sure Ruth Reichl got a lot of angry mail from *Gourmet* readers about this piece. It's something of a departure from their once traditional territory of bundt cake recipes and restaurant roundups. There's a dark, perverse streak to Ms. Reichl I'm very grateful for. I mean, the scuzzball strip club, the Clermont Lounge, in the pages of *Gourmet*? I think that's a first.

THE COOK'S COMPANIONS

Some of my favorite books on The Life. To which I'd now add Ludwig Bemelmans's *Hotel Bemelmans*. When I finally became aware of it, it was both delightful and dismaying to discover that

I'd done nothing new when I wrote *Kitchen Confidential*—that Bemelmans had been there before me, and done it better and with more authority.

CHINA SYNDROME

China is great. China is BIG. China is FUN. And it's hugely frustrating to know that even if I dedicated the rest of my life to the project, I'd never see all of it. There's little question in my mind that as China continues to emerge as an economic super-power, and as we find ourselves increasingly dependent on its manufacturing—and its credit line—that it will eventually pretty much rule the world. To which I say, "Welcome to our future masters!" With China as our landlord, we will, at least, be eating a hell of a lot better.

NO SHOES

Also written for a Brit magazine, hence the reference to the loathsome and inexplicably popular Michael Winner—a shit film director turned shittier food columnist—and the Gordon Ramsay references and the egregious use of Britspeak. I stand by my Sans Footwear Theory, though. Food indeed does taste better with sand between your toes.

THE LOVE BOAT

Happier times . . . Written a while back, this was my first assignment for *Gourmet*. They send me on the coolest jobs. This one was a real punisher.

IS CELEBRITY KILLING THE GREAT CHEFS?

I think I was perhaps being a little disingenuous in this piece. I'd myself, by this point, become quite accustomed to nice hotels and flying business class. And I was a little harsh on poor Rocco, who now hosts a local radio show in New York where he answers telephone calls from old ladies who want to know where to buy the best kosher chicken. Remembering how talented a cook Rocco once was, and no small amount of self-loathing, infused this piece with a little too much bitterness—and bullshit. Looking at Rocco's painful progress, I have to admit that I see—if not for the grace of God and all that—myself . . . minus the cooking talent.

Let's face it. I'm pushing fifty. If I had to go back to the kitchen now? It would break me. This *vida loca* better last—or I'm fucked.

WHAT YOU DIDN'T WANT TO KNOW ABOUT MAKING FOOD TELEVISION

This was a much more honest piece than previous ones, when I was still representing myself as some kind of outraged working class hero. It's far more descriptive of what my life was really like (and still is) most of the time. Since the piece was written, I've left New York Times Television and ended relations with the Food Network. But I'm still together with Chris and Lydia, and many of the same shooters and editors who produced and made the first TV show. Only now, it's the Travel and Discovery Channels that are enabling my swinging new lifestyle.

These days, we've got a bigger budget, more freedom, and more indulgent masters, but the day-to-day is the same. It's like traveling with a band, on constant international tour. I sold my soul to the television gods so that I might see the world and live out my childhood fantasies of faraway places. This is the way things are. I've become a character in *Spinal Tap*.

WARNING SIGNS

Anyone who's ever spent any amount of time in London knows exactly which chain I'm talking about here. Incredibly, they're still in business.

MADNESS IN CRESCENT CITY

I have no idea which of these places still exists after New Orleans was nearly wiped out by hurricane and flooding. I suspect many of the places mentioned are still trying to get back on their feet—if they can. I dearly hope that Snake and Jake's in particular returns, as there are few nobler establishments. This piece is a classic example of the kind of "triple dipping" I do these days. Here's how it works:

First: Visit city on book tour. Inevitably, end up eating, bar-hopping, and getting trashed with all the local chefs.

Second: Using all the valuable "insider" information accumulated during earlier book tour debauch, return to the same location to make a television show.

Third: Using one's experiences during filming—and the handy production notes and videotape—write an article about the place for a magazine and get paid TWICE!

A VIEW FROM THE FRIDGE

Something of an apology here, to all the waiters I've been curt with or abusive to over the years. There really is nothing more loathsome or shameful than some miserable prick who walks into a restaurant determined to have a bad time, ready to lord over a relatively powerless server. Behaving like a mean, sarcastic, superior, and dismissive "boss" to your waiter should be a flayable offense. It really is in your interest—most of the time—to be nice to your waiter. It's also the decent thing to do. It's pretty much a relationship ender for me when a new friend behaves imperiously with a server, or makes ludicrous and unreasonable demands. I find it mortifying—and never repeat the experience. If you can't behave in a restaurant you can't be my friend. It's that simple. Bad behavior is for bars. They're used to assholes—and know how to deal with them.

NOTES FROM THE ROAD

God, I hated Singapore the first time I visited it (the experience described here). The heat, and the transition to the freezing cold bars, then back out into the heat again—it nearly killed me. As did the sheer volume of food and my general state of exhaustion. After many return trips, I've since come to love the place with a passion. (See "Die, Die Must Try," page 231). But back then, I was having a real problem adjusting. I've since become better at airplanes, airports, book tours, hotels, and so on, and whine about it a lot less. It's always amusing to me to see some twerp musician on *Behind the Music* complaining about "life on the road," or to hear some first-time novelist griping about the rigors of a book tour. Two years ago they were sitting in Mom's cellar noodling away on a guitar, or clacking away on a word processor, and now they're griping about the agony of fine hotel rooms and world travel and a fat publicity budget? That barely qualifies as work. I know what work is—or once knew. I still remember it, however faintly at times. Standing in a busy kitchen twelve hours a day is work. The rest is a privilege. I read this piece now and want to say, "Shut the fuck up, you spoiled, whining bitch! You're lucky anybody gives a shit about you at all in Singapore! Now sit down and eat the turtle fat, you lazy, bloated gasbag."

THE DIVE

Ahhh, yes. This piece.

Written originally as an e-mail (never sent). At the time, I was heartbroken, in love, and feeling really sorry for myself. As self-serving as the piece may be, I was being truthful about one thing: When I jumped from that rock? I really didn't give a fuck.

A DRINKING PROBLEM

Another piece for the Brits. And who was I kidding? What's wrong with good food in a pub? There's a reverse snobbery to my position that's hard to defend. After an initial frenzy of overenthusiasm, many of the so-called "gastro-pubs" seem to have settled down to serve pretty simple, honest, and decent food—most of the time not incompatible at all with a good pint. I think I had my head up my ass when I wrote this thing. Had the ass-kicking actually occurred, I would have richly deserved it.

WOODY HARRELSON: CULINARY MUSE

I meant every word of this and still do. I shake with rage at the thought of a smug, self-satisfied Woody, sitting in Thailand—with its amazingly old and diverse culinary culture, and its many rightfully proud cooks—insisting on eating only the same raw salad day after day. And the thought that Woody's peculiar worldview might spread, like some destructive virus, fills me with horror. If anything, I've become even more hyperbolic on the subject since I wrote this piece, once even referring to *Raw* as "the most evil document since *Mein Kampf*" (which might, admittedly, be a little over-the-top). Poor Charlie Trotter, who's been nothing but kind and generous to me in the past, has unfortunately born the full weight of my sense of betrayal and rage. Roxanne Klein's Larkspur eatery thankfully closed. But the pernicious spread of raw food continues, and its prodigiously farting adherents continue to multiply.

They must be stopped.

IS ANYBODY HOME?

The food writing "community" is a swamp. A petri dish of logrolling, cronyism, mendaciousness, greed, envy, collusion, corruption, and willful self-deception, in which nearly all of us are hopelessly compromised. This piece was a reaction to a momentary episode of profound disgust.

It was also my way of acknowledging the growing realization that I'd been beating up on Emeril far too long. Early on, making fun of him had been a cheap, easy laugh—a crowd-pleasing shtick. But in the years since referring to him as an "Ewok" I'd seen so much worse. And I had never really acknowledged that unlike so many of the "celebrity chefs" who'd followed, and will undoubtedly one day replace him in the country's favors, Emeril actually paid his dues. I'd long come to believe the man deserved a lot more respect than I'd been giving him, regardless what I thought of his shows. This was my way of apologizing.

BOTTOMING OUT

This was a pretty harsh, unforgiving editorial I turned in when asked by the *Los Angeles Times* to comment on Robert Downey's most recent arrest. Writing it, I was pretty damn sure that he was a goner. And I was quick—too quick as it turns out—to write him off. Another dead guy, another dead junkie. The predictable, almost inevitable, end to the same old story. Since writing this piece, a very good friend who I had similarly written off, turned my back on, and left for dead—after decades of hard drug use—has managed to turn his life around. And Downey continues to survive and prosper and do good works with considerable charm and self-awareness. I wish them both well, and apologize for thinking the worst. Sometimes it's nice to be wrong.

FOOD TERRORISTS

Things only got worse since I wrote this impassioned defense of an embattled friend. Foie gras is under fire, or soon to be illegal, in California, Chicago, and even New York. A treasured and fundamental ingredient of classical gastronomy since Roman times, it will likely disappear entirely from menus in my lifetime. A tragedy, but a predictable one. The PETA folks have been very clever in picking foie gras as a front. Though they know full well that there are worse, more widespread examples of institutionalized animal cruelty (mass-produced chicken, for instance), they likely saw this as an easy win. What politician can realistically be expected to stand up for chefs, taking the public position that they are *for* the force-feeding of cute ducks and geese so a few rich people who can afford it can sup on their distended livers? Not a vote-getter . . .

We shall surely lose this struggle in the end. I'm resigned to it—just as I'm resigned to the fact that I can no longer smoke in a bar in New York, a pub in Ireland, or a restaurant in Sicily. But in the losing, I'd sure like to see the rotten fucks who terrorized Chef Manrique's family identified, arrested, convicted, sentenced to prison for a very long time, and mistreated terribly there—learning firsthand, one would hope, about the gag reflex. It's no less than they deserve.

SLEAZE GONE BY

Oooh. I'm *so* bad. I'm *so* street . . .

A pretty glib, wildly over-romanticized look at the New York City of my misspent youth, as written for British readers. Like crack was somehow a good thing? What a twat I was when I wrote this.

Not that I don't miss the Forty-second Street grind houses and the Terminal Bar and Hawaii Kai. But feigning nostalgia for getting ripped off at knifepoint? Withdrawal symptoms? Selling my possessions on the street? Dope dealers with clubs and guns? Feral crackheads? Who was I kidding? The bullshit meter is flashing bright red.

PURE AND UNCUT LUXURY

An earnest attempt at food porn, and a pretty good one, I think, as I'm getting a hard-on rereading it. I did not exaggerate. This is exactly how good Masa was that magical evening. Whenever I want to treat myself to something very special, I take myself there and indulge. Beg, borrow, steal, stick up a liquor store— whatever it takes to get the money—but for God's sake, go! Bring plenty of extra, as you'll want additional pieces of tuna.

THE HUNGRY AMERICAN

My love affair with Vietnam continues. What I failed to mention in this piece is that on this, my second trip to the country, as soon as I arrived (with Chris and Lydia in tow), as soon as we stepped through the airport doors, saw Linh, looked out at that enchanted place we'd previously come to adore, we all burst into tears. Why Vietnam, above all other countries I've visited? Maybe it's pheromonic. Maybe every person has a special place, a place that's just right for them. Maybe it's Linh and Madame Ngoc and the friends I've made there. Or the simple good things there are to eat, everywhere you look. Or the women in their *ao dais* pedaling by on ancient bicycles. Or the smell of burning joss, jasmine, and *nuac mam*. Or that it's beautiful. Who can really describe why they fell in love?

DECODING FERRÁN ADRIÀ

This was written at and about a real turning point in my life. A number of turning points, actually. Chris, Lydia, and I were about to head into what we'd thought would be season three of *A Cook's Tour* for the Food Network. During an earlier book tour, I'd met Ferrán Adrià for the first time, and I'd managed (amazingly) to get him to consent to let us into his life and his restaurant and workshop and do a show about it. We'd scheduled a shooting period, which I rightly understood to be a once-in-a-lifetime opportunity. Then things started to go sideways . . .

The network didn't want any more foreign shows (or not nearly as many). They wanted more barbecue. Tailgate parties. Dude ranch shows. They were completely uninterested in some guy named Ferrán Adrià in Spain, no matter how good or how important or unique everybody said he was. People who talked funny, with accents, or (God forbid) in foreign languages—and expensive shows about them—did not, they insisted, "fit their business model." As the scheduled shooting date approached, negotiations dragged on. The production company, New York

Times Television, were (to say the least) unsupportive. Chris, Lydia, and I felt that this was going to be one amazing show, so in the end, we just said "Fuck it," and using entirely our own money went ahead and spent a week with Adrià, producing a stand-alone documentary we remain very proud of (it's now been shown all over the world). It was the beginning of an enduring relationship—and for better or worse, an entirely new life. We broke with NYT. We ended our relationship with the Food Network and determined that we'd wander the media hustings until we could work together again, making the shows we wanted to make, the way we wanted to make them. Thankfully, the Travel and Discovery Channels happily took us on.

This was also a time when my feelings about "molecular gastronomy" and cuisine and my craft in general underwent a tectonic shift. I'd previously been very hostile to the idea of laboratories and food science and the very notion of Ferrán Adrià. It was a deeply traumatizing moment of clarity when I realized I was enjoying what Adrià was doing. And I still have yet to figure out fully what it might mean in the grand scheme of things—and for the future of cooking. But then that's what the piece is about: the acknowledgment that there are things you don't know, an acceptance of the possibilities and pleasures of the new.

BRAZILIAN BEACH-BLANKET BINGO

My first assignment of travel/food writing, written for *Food Arts*. I'll never forget getting the call, in the middle of my first book tour, while still working at the restaurant (with extended breaks). "You want me to go . . . where? Brazil? And you'll . . . like *pay* me for it?!" I've since been back to Brazil a number of times and have come to love São Paolo more (I didn't the first time), Rio less (a friend was shot to death there shortly after I last saw him), and Salvador more than ever. Sushi Samba has gone on to become an empire of restaurants all over the country. Michael and Taka are no longer with them.

THE OLD, GOOD STUFF

I love the "old school" stuff and tend to wax sentimental about it. Michael Batterbury, the publisher of *Food Arts*, took me to Le Veau D'Or, knowing I'd love it, and over many glasses of wine, and the kind of food I've always believed to be the enduring glory of France, inspired me to write this piece about "dinosaur" classics and some of the few places you can still find them. Pierre an Tunnel closed its doors in August 2005.

DIE, DIE MUST TRY

Like I said, I've really come to love Singapore.

A CHEF'S CHRISTMAS

About as sappy, romantic, and idealistic as I could muster, this was an honest attempt to write a children's Christmas fable—but with language that children probably shouldn't read. In a departure from just about everything else I've ever written, and everything I've ever experienced, for that matter, I wanted very much to write just one story with an unambiguously happy ending.

A NOTE ON THE TYPE

The text of this book is set in Linotype Sabon, named after
the type founder, Jacques Sabon. It was designed by Jan
Tschichold and jointly developed by Linotype, Monotype, and
Stempel, in response to a need for a typeface to be available
in identical form for mechanical hot metal composition and
hand composition using foundry type.

Tschichold based his design for Sabon roman on a font engraved
by Garamond, and Sabon italic on a font by Granjon. It was first
used in 1966 and has proved an enduring modern classic.